Withdrawn from
Davidson College Library

Library of
Davidson College

POLITICS, SECURITY AND DEVELOPMENT IN SMALL STATES

Edited by

COLIN CLARKE
School of Geography, University of Oxford

and

TONY PAYNE
Department of Politics, University of Sheffield

London
ALLEN & UNWIN
Boston   Sydney   Wellington

© C. G. Clarke, A. J. Payne, and contributors, 1987
This book is copyright under the Berne Convention. No reproduction without permission. All rights reserved.

Allen & Unwin, the academic imprint of
Unwin Hyman Ltd
PO Box 18, Park Lane, Hemel Hempstead, Herts HP2 4TE, UK
40 Museum Street, London WC1A 1LU, UK
37/39 Queen Elizabeth Street, London SE1 2QB, UK

Allen & Unwin Inc.,
8 Winchester Place, Winchester, Mass. 01890, USA

Allen & Unwin (Australia) Ltd,
8 Napier Street, North Sydney, NSW 2060, Australia

Allen & Unwin (New Zealand) Ltd in association with the Port Nicholson Press Ltd,
60 Cambridge Terrace, Wellington, New Zealand

First published in 1987

British Library Cataloguing in Publication Data

Clarke, Colin G. and Payne, Tony (eds).
  Politics, security and development in small states.
1. Social history – 1970– . 2. States, small.
I. Clarke, Colin G. II. Payne, Tony, 1952– .
909.82'8   HN16
ISBN 0-04-320203-9

Library of Congress Cataloging in Publication Data

Clarke, Colin G. and Payne, Tony (eds).
  Politics, security, and development, in small states.
Bibliography: p.
Includes index.
1. States, Small – Politics and government. 2. States, Small – Economic conditions. 3. States, Small – Social conditions. 4. States, Small – National security.
I. Clarke, Colin G. II. Payne, Tony, 1952– .
JC365.P65 1987   320.1   87-1199
ISBN 0-04-320203-9 (alk. paper)

Typeset in 10 on 12 point Bembo by Computape (Pickering) Ltd
and printed in Great Britain by Billings & Sons Ltd,
London and Worcester

Contents

Introduction   *page* vii
COLIN CLARKE AND TONY PAYNE

Part A   Surveys   1

1 *Political Aspects*   3
PAUL SUTTON
    The creation of small states   4
    The political definition of small   6
    Political characteristics of size   8
    The domestic context   8
    The international context   19
    Conclusion   23

2 *Social Features*   26
DAVID LOWENTHAL
    Substantiality   26
    Durability   28
    Popular consensus   29
    Small states and non-states   30
    Features characteristic of small states   31
    Sociocultural and other traits: a holistic approach   33
    Conservatism and tradition   35
    Managing intimacy   38
    Obsessive autonomism   43
    Conclusion   45

3 *Economic Issues*   50
TONY PAYNE
    Neoclassical constraints   51
    Dependency theory   54
    Development strategy   55
    Regional integration   58
    Conclusion   61

4	*Security Dilemmas* ROBERTO ESPÍNDOLA	63
	Security threats	64
	Security resources	69
	Policy alternatives	75
	Conclusion	78

Part B **Case studies** 81

5	*Grenada* COLIN CLARKE	83
	Gairy's Grenada	85
	The People's Revolutionary Government	87
	Post-invasion Grenada	91
	Conclusion	93
	Acknowledgements	94
6	*Antigua and Barbuda* TONY THORNDIKE	96
	Dependency and smallness	96
	The achievement of independence	100
	The political process I: accumulation, 1946–67	102
	The political process II: polarization, 1967–81	104
	The political process III: internationalization, 1981–5	107
	Conclusion	110
7	*Fiji* WILLIAM M. SUTHERLAND	113
	Economic base	113
	Economic openness and indebtedness	117
	Smallness and racial factionalism	119
	Geopolitical prospects and pitfalls	120
	Conclusion	123
8	*Mauritius* MARTIN MINOGUE	125
	The economy	126

	Politics	133
	International relations	135
	Conclusion	137
9	*The Gambia*	141
	ARNOLD HUGHES	
	Economic aspects	141
	Political aspects	149
	Security aspects	152
	Conclusion	154
10	*Swaziland*	156
	ANTHONY LEMON	
	The economics of dependence	158
	The politics of choice	164
	Conclusion	167
11	*Malta*	170
	JAMES CRAIG	
	Dependent sovereignty, 1964–71	171
	Positive neutrality, 1971–84	179
	Conclusion	182
12	*Cyprus*	184
	FLOYA ANTHIAS	
	The form of the state	186
	Nationalism and ethnic conflict	188
	Post-1974: ideology, politics, and class	193
	Conclusion	198

Part C Perspectives 201

13	*An Academic Perspective*	203
	ROBIN COHEN	
	The triumph of self-determination or the weakness of empire?	203
	The collapse of ideological legitimacy	206
	The rise of rival powers	208

	Characterizing the problems of small states	209
	From nations without states to states without nations	212
14	*A Policy Perspective*	214
	NEVILLE LINTON	
	Military threats	215
	Political aspects	217
	International provision	220

Conclusion — 225
COLIN CLARKE AND TONY PAYNE

Contributors — 229

Index — 234

To the memory of James Craig

'It is the vice of a vulgar mind to be thrilled by bigness, to think that a thousand square miles are a thousand more wonderful than one square mile, and that a million square miles are almost the same as heaven'. *(E. M. Forster)*

Introduction

COLIN CLARKE AND TONY PAYNE

It is not difficult to identify the moment when the problem posed by small states within the international political system returned to the prominent position in world affairs which it currently occupies. It was October 1983 and the news had just broken that the island of Grenada in the eastern Caribbean had been invaded by armed forces of the US. The action constituted the world's first military confrontation, if that is the right word, between a small state and a superpower. Grenada was an island 340 square kilometres in size, with a mere 110 000 inhabitants, whose best known export was nutmeg; and yet the world's greatest military state had deemed it imperative to invade. The whole extraordinary episode was a vivid expression of how the political problems of small states could suddenly become global issues with potentially serious consequences for world peace and stability.

After a few days Grenada disappeared from the headlines and other issues in larger places again came to the fore. But even when the immediate crisis had subsided, it was clear that the Grenada invasion had started ripples in several parts of the international political system. United Nations experts gathered in earnest discussion of the special difficulties of small states; British parliamentarians consciously investigated the events in Grenada as an example of the way that the problems of small countries in faraway parts of the globe could unsettle international order; Caribbean politicians openly fretted about their own obvious vulnerability; and the Commonwealth set in hand a special survey of the needs of its own small states.

In fact, as an organization the Commonwealth had been among the first bodies to express disquiet at the US invasion. Its

Secretary-General, Sonny Ramphal, observed that, to his mind, the main lesson of the events in Grenada was of 'the deep passions and anxieties that are aroused when the contests of superpowers are brought within regions of small developing countries' (Commonwealth Secretariat 1983). He tried to set up a fully fledged Commonwealth security force to replace the US in Grenada but was unable to bring the scheme to fruition. However, when the biennial Commonwealth Heads of Government conference opened in New Delhi approximately a month after the invasion, the issue was placed on the agenda. By that time some of the immediate tensions aroused by the attack had subsided. What instead dominated the minds of Commonwealth leaders was the realization that over half the member states of the organization could in some way be considered small. The problem, in short, was a general one. To this end, in their so-called Goa Declaration on International Security they expressed deep concern about the vulnerability of all small states to external attack and interference in their internal affairs, and subsequently established a group of Commonwealth experts who were mandated to prepare a study of the special needs of small states in time to be presented to the next summit.

Meanwhile, interest in issues relating to the rôle of small states had been generated for much the same reasons in academic circles. We, the editors of this book, had long been specialists in the political and economic problems of the states of the Commonwealth Caribbean; indeed, we had been in Grenada only a month before the invasion, engaged in research on the development impasse which seemed to have beset all the little islands of this region, apart from Grenada. We knew, therefore, of the geopolitical sensitivity of what was going on in Grenada and, although we were shocked, we were not surprised when the US invasion eventually came. What we did not know so well, but could presume, was how many other 'Grenadas' were lurking among the many small states in the world.

It made sense to us to append to our regional study a wider analysis of politics, security, and development (for the three seemed inextricably interwoven) in small states generally. We hoped that we could address the same issues as the technical experts and politicians, and possibly even contribute something to the debate about policy, while at the same time undertaking a properly detached academic analysis. Help was obviously needed since small states existed in Europe, in Africa, and in the Pacific and Indian Oceans as well as in the Caribbean. Our own knowledge was manifestly inadequate. We resolved, therefore, to invite other regional specialists to a conference where we hoped that the combined experience of everybody present would generate a valuable exchange of information and ideas. We knew, of course, that such gatherings had been held before and that, in this sense, we were following in well trodden footsteps. Therefore our first task was to review some of the arguments and conclusions of scholars who had examined the problem of 'smallness' during the preceding two decades.

The pioneering effort in the field was undoubtedly the volume edited by Burton Benedict in 1967 entitled *Problems of smaller territories*. It emanated from a seminar on this theme promoted by the Institute of Commonwealth Studies of the University of London as early as October 1962. The seminar was clearly motivated by the fact that, due to universal opposition to colonialism since the end of World War II, many of the smaller islands and enclaves had become politically independent and many more were in the process of doing so. The problem of smallness was just beginning to make its appearance on the international scene, though the context had already been set by the 1960 UN Declaration on the Granting of Independence to Colonial Countries and Peoples, which made no attempt to discourage decolonization in very small territories. Burton and his collaborators made a determined endeavour to define smallness: notions of area, population, population density, accessibility, economic resources, market size, degree of political development – all were apparently considered at length only eventually to be rejected.

In the event, 'it proved impossible for the seminar to decide what "smallness" means with any precision'. Countries could clearly be small in one sense (Hong Kong in terms of area) and not in another (Hong Kong in terms of population). 'Whatever scales of magnitude are employed seem arbitrary and it is difficult to pick out on them where smallness begins or ends.' As a result, the participants came to accept the only sensible conclusion to this kind of debate, namely, that smallness 'is a comparative and not an absolute idea' (Wood 1967:29). The search for definitional rigour apart, the overriding theme of the discussions concerned the sort of independence which such small territories could have. How could they defend themselves? How could they survive economically? How could they administer themselves? How could they provide for their increasing populations? The evidence was not, and could not yet be, available, so many of the contributions were openly speculative in their conclusions, even if the tone was generally one of disbelief that such small places could survive on their own.

For all that, the early chapters on the political, economic, and sociological aspects of smallness did set out several of the themes which have continued to characterize the debate about small states. Examining the political dimension, Donald Wood noted that in the late 1950s it seemed that there were still certain yardsticks of statehood to determine whether a colony could ever gain full independence in its own right. In his interpretation of the rule of thumb, there had to be some political expertise, an administration more or less able to cope with the responsibilities of independence, a feeling of national unity that was capable of lasting, and a reasonable economic framework. But, as he conceded, by their nature rules of thumb are approximate and flexible: 'this particular one, which never hardened by open official expression into a dogma, proved to be particularly outmoded and loose' (Wood 1967:23).

Independence was granted to colonies which by virtue of their size or prevailing notions of economic and political maturity seemed unsuited to its demands, and others, which had already been grouped into federations for their well-being, were permitted to break away to stand on their own feet. What a rather bemused Wood referred to as 'the sound barrier of smallness' had thus been broken. 'The only certainty in a confused situation', he wrote, 'is that decolonization will continue. No one can predict the limiting instance or in what forms independence will appear' (Wood 1967:24). As to the political future of these newly independent states, it was simply too early to say.

On the economic prospects Knox found that in comparisons of small and large countries the former had a greater reliance on foreign trade, a greater concentration of their exports in a limited number of markets, and a lesser diversification in the range of commodities they exported, but was unable to take his analysis beyond the bland concluding observation that, economically, they were 'likely to suffer a number of disabilities' (Knox 1967:44). Benedict, however, was much more perceptive in setting out the sociological aspects of smallness. He observed that it was 'a commonplace in anthropological studies of small communities that economic, political, religious, and kinship systems are very often coincident or nearly so. The same individuals are brought into contact over and over again in various activities.' Relationships thus tended to be particularistic rather than universalistic, with the result that in small-scale societies 'who a man is matters very much more than what he does' (Benedict 1967:49).

Not that particularistic relationships necessarily led to harmony for, as Benedict again noted, the intense factionalism of small communities, especially in politics, was a matter of repeated comment by all kinds of observers. Indeed, telling evidence of the potential conflict inherent in rôle relationships in small societies was provided in a later chapter on legislative–executive relations by Archie Singham. In this he described in detail the infamous conflict that was waged in Grenada in the late 1950s and early 1960s between Eric Gairy, the elected chief minister operating, let us tolerantly say, in accordance with the particularistic values of local society, and the colonial Administrator, trying to sustain a constitutional order that required a commitment to some universalistic values.

Apart from this analysis, however, the other case studies in the Benedict volume made disappointing reading. They included chapters on British Honduras, Luxembourg, Polynesia, Swaziland, and Tory island, a rock of just over 130 hectares situated off the coast of Donegal to the north of Ireland. In terms of constitutional status, economic resources, and political development these represented an extremely varied collection of small territories, which unfortunately served to vitiate the possibilities of comparison. As a consequence, the conclusions of the book were weakly developed. Benedict (1967:9) asked at one point if there had been found any 'solutions' for the smaller territories, but had to conclude that 'there is no overall formula which will work', for the problems and situations they faced were too diverse.

Some small territories, he suggested, could exist as separate states because they could take advantage of the requirements of larger states for military bases or tourist havens. Others might conceivably become farms or plantations operating a labour force on a seasonal or contract basis. A few, however, might even have to be evacuated, including, interestingly, the Falkland Islands. Dismal prospects indeed! Benedict and his colleagues still believed in the old colonial guideline regarding the non-viability of states below a certain size. Accordingly, in the face of all the evidence of the failure of federations and amalgamations as modes of decolonization, the only positive advice they could offer to newly independent small states was 'to look for some form of economic integration with their neighbours' (Benedict 1967:9), preferably with prosperous partners but if necessary even with other territories as poor as themselves.

Following the publication of the Benedict volume, the subject was largely allowed to rest by British academics until in 1972 the Institute of Development Studies (IDS) of the University of Sussex organized a conference on small developing countries at the University of the West Indies in Barbados. The conference papers were subsequently edited by Percy Selwyn and published in 1975 as *Development policy in small countries*. As the title implies, this collection had a more overtly policy orientation. Planners as well as academics had been invited to Barbados in order to give the meeting a practical emphasis.

The central theme of the discussion was formulated in the following way: 'What constraints are faced by small countries on possible policies and actions merely by virtue of their size, and what is their scope for independent action?' (Selwyn 1975:7). Case studies of the general problem of smallness were eschewed in favour of papers focusing on the prospects of industrial development in peripheral small countries, problems of planning and administration, the potential for establishing autonomous monetary policy, and the difficulties of responding properly to offers of development aid. Much of the content of the book was therefore quite technical, but its general argument was succinctly brought together in Selwyn's introduction which he subtitled 'Room for manoeuvre?'.

What was immediately striking, especially in contrast to the general tenor of virtually all previous discussion about smallness, was Selwyn's observation that members of the conference did not assume that, in some way, small countries were a 'problem'. There was, he said, no assumption that there was disadvantage in smallness or, to put the point the other way, some special virtue in size. It was argued instead that the recent emergence of many small countries was 'not only part of the reaction against colonialism' – and therefore automatically to be applauded – but could also reflect 'positive values', in particular 'the desire of people to have a national unit with which they can identify, as opposed to the "anonymity of the mass society"' (Selwyn 1975:11–12).

The small country, which the Barbados conference no more succeeded in defining with precision than did its London predecessor, thus had a value in itself, regardless of viability. Indeed, anticipating those who might want to raise this old *canard*, Selwyn referred to the argument advanced in one of the chapters that any national unit which could maintain its separate existence was *ipso facto* viable. Small states existed, therefore they must be able to exist. Moreover, as Bernard Schaffer pointed out, there was no mystery to this. In the modern era there had emerged an ideology of 'extantism', which he defined as the 'support given by the international community to existing international frontiers' and which acted as the critical prop for new small states once they had been established (Schaffer 1975:26).

Nevertheless, it was still assumed that smallness would of itself impose certain constraints upon development and, as one would expect from an IDS gathering in the early 1970s, these were directly related to the question of dependence. Selwyn conceded that there had been disagreement within the conference on the matter of how overwhelming this dependence was, but suggested that the real issue was more practical than conceptual, namely, 'what cards do small countries have to play and how can they best play them?' (Selwyn 1975:13).

Disregarding the strictures of the 'trapped' school of dependency analysis, Selwyn answered his own question in positive terms. He thought that there were many recent examples of skilful political manoeuvring by small countries in what might appear to be unfavourable circumstances. As regards trade, the heavy dependence of small countries was well documented, but Singapore at least showed that it was possible to build up industrial exports on the basis of narrow home markets. When it came to monetary policy, there was much more room for action either via delinking currencies from their traditional international ties or even by localizing foreign banks. As for aid, a paper in the collection claimed to demonstrate that small countries got more aid per head and in relation to national income than larger countries. And, finally, on the matter of the relationship with dominant multinational corporations Selwyn again was not unoptimistic. It was not impossible, in his view, to effect a harmony of interest between corporate and local development needs. In sum, the volume concluded that 'there is a good deal of evidence from recent history that small countries can and do exploit these areas for manoeuvre, and that a few at least have done so with some success' (Selwyn 1975:17).

Could they do even better? The feeling of the conference was that decision-makers in small countries could indeed play their cards more effectively, since a number of reasons why they often failed to do so emerged in the discussion. Firstly, a lack of sufficient national feeling, combined with the sort of psychological dependence often identified in the Caribbean, seemed to reduce the self-confidence of decision-makers, rendering them defeated even before they started. Secondly, the quality of political leadership was crucial. Governments of poor small countries tended to be risk-avoiders, and 'frequently the least risky course of action may appear to be to do nothing' (Selwyn 1975:18). Thirdly, lack of information was a central reason for failure to exploit all possibilities of manoeuvre. Lastly, there was inertia – 'the continued use of systems, policies, attitudes, habits of work for years after they have become obsolete and irrelevant' (Selwyn 1975:19) – something to which not only small countries were susceptible but which in their case might be more serious.

Oddly, Selwyn concluded his observations in just the same way as Benedict – by making reference to regional co-operation as a potentially valuable means of adding to the development options of small states. The arguments advanced were familiar, involving the case for the sharing of specialized services, the creation of common markets, and the deployment of collective bargaining power. The history of regional integration schemes is, of course, another story which Selwyn's volume made no attempt to tell. It is, however, worth noting the way in which the idea of a regional solution appears to have dogged the debate about smallness, although, one might add, more in aspiration than achievement.

Finally, a third project to bring together a collection of essays on the theme of smallness attracted our attention, Robin Cohen's *African islands and enclaves*, published in 1983. It was not quite comparable with the previous two volumes in that only three of the chapters emanated from a smallness conference (held in September 1981 in the Canary Islands) and the focus was related to a particular continent. Yet it addressed exactly the same problem. Cohen explained in the introduction that the criteria he used in selecting the country case studies (which made up the whole of the book) from the 77 small units with populations of less than half a million people were designed to achieve a reasonable balance between enclaves and islands, between Indian and Atlantic Ocean territories, and between territories that were self-governing and those that were still integrated into metropolitan political units. There were accordingly chapters on the following territories: the Canary Islands, The Gambia, Equatorial Guinea, Cabinda, St Helena, Cape Verde, Diego Garcia, the Seychelles, the Comoros and Mauritius.

The character of Cohen's book showed how much the world of small states had moved on in a decade. With the partial exceptions of Arnold Hughes's analysis of some of the advantages smallness gave for a while to The Gambia and Raphael Kaplinsky's exposition of the prosperity at the periphery briefly enjoyed by the Seychelles in the second half of the 1970s, the dominant tone of the volume was one of gloom. The mood was given full vent in Cohen's intelligent but notably lugubrious introduction. To be fair, he did not fail to recognize the advantages that derived from possession of sovereign status: as he put it, 'states, however small, have the right to levy tariffs, customs, and import duties; to print currency; to raise taxes; to be eligible for all kinds of international grants and assistance; to operate free ports; to be a home for international bankers and investors; down to the right to print postage stamps' (Cohen 1983:11). But, in his judgement, the opportunities had been considerably outweighed by the dangers.

Cohen, unlike the editors of the two volumes previously considered, was able to reflect upon the various sorry experiences which had befallen so many small states in the preceding decade. Quite apart from the damaging impact of prolonged world recession upon some of the peoples least able to resist its depredations, there was the evidence of the invasion of small societies by criminal elements, currency speculators, and various unscrupulous international financiers. There was also the evidence of an increase in political weakness, instability, and secession, and almost daily further indications of the destructive social, economic, and environmental costs of tourism – once the panacea that was going to sustain small state economies. Well might Cohen draw attention to the marked contrast between contemporary reality and the romantic view of island societies that is still deeply embedded in Western culture.

The Cohen volume was also important in that it fully recognized the emergence of a new factor – the rediscovered strategic importance of small islands by the major world powers. They often commanded important sea lanes; they could serve as conveniently remote sites for the stationing of dangerous weapons or other security-tight installations; and they happened sometimes to possess, or by virtue of the territorial waters surrounding them control, valuable strategic resources. It was because of these strategic considerations that Cohen considered it likely that the real crisis for small states was still to come, especially as the traditional islanders' option of migration has been increasingly closed off to them in recent years. Although he may properly have called upon islanders to 'evolve autonomous solutions to the challenges that confront them', this expression of optimism needs to be weighed against the realism of his concluding sentence: 'I cannot but help express some pessimism as to their eventual capacity to resist the powerful extraneous forces I have described' (Cohen 1983:19). Reading that remark in the middle of 1985, it was hard to believe that anything had happened since it was written to give Cohen cause for second thoughts.

Clearly, the external and security dimension of the problems of small states had to be a prominent feature of this study.

Other lessons also emerged from this survey of the literature which we applied in planning our conference. We took the view that it would be wise to avoid the seemingly inconclusive debate about what was the true essence of a small state and decided as a result to impose a definition on our conference participants. The task was made easier by the fact that something of a consensus has recently emerged about taking a population of 1 million or less as the critical threshold. This criterion was used by the United Nations Institute for Training and Research in its report on small states as long ago as 1971 and was also adopted by the 1985 Commonwealth Consultative Group. We followed suit and used it as the upper limit in defining a small state. We also chose to confine the analysis to states that were politically independent and since two-thirds belong to the Commonwealth, to select countries which were members of that organization (Figure). We wanted the key question to be: How have small states coped with their smallness in the context of recent international economic and political trends? The problems that have attached to small territories which remain colonial dependencies, such as the Falkland Islands, seemed to us to reflect intrinsically different issues and were not generally regarded as within the scope of this study.

In our consideration of the previous studies, we also found that the division of the material into the general and the particular adopted by Benedict worked the most effectively. Accordingly, this book is divided into several parts. The first embraces four surveys of the general situation faced by small states, treating in turn the political, social, economic, and security dimensions of their existence. The second part consists of eight case studies showing how a sample of small states, drawn from all the major regions of the world where such states exist, has handled the realities of political independence in the last two decades or so. In addition, a third part contains two broad perspectives on the problems of small states written from contrasting academic and policy backgrounds, reflecting our awareness that the whole issue unavoidably sits at the interface between these two worlds. Finally, a brief conclusion summarizes the lessons that seem to us to emerge from the study as a whole.

The errors of organization in the book are undoubtedly ours, but such credit as accrues must be more widely acknowledged. In particular we wish to thank the Nuffield Foundation for a grant in 1983 which enabled us to collaborate on our work in the Eastern Caribbean. It was during this research that we began to re-examine some of the issues associated with Caribbean smallness, and it was in the aftermath of the subsequent invasion of Grenada that we decided to incorporate security into the analysis. We are grateful to the Nuffield Foundation for additionally supporting our request to look comparatively and systematically at the general problems of small states by funding a conference held at the School of Geography and Jesus College, Oxford, over 27–29 September 1985, on the proceedings of which this book is based.

References

Benedict, B. 1967. Sociological aspects of smallness. In *Problems of smaller territories*, B. Benedict (ed.), 45–55. London: Athlone Press.

Cohen, R. (ed.) 1983. *African islands and enclaves*. Beverley Hills, Calif.: Sage.

Commonwealth Secretariat 1983. Statement issued by the Commonwealth Secretary-General, Mr Shridath Ramphal, on developments in Grenada, 25 October.

Knox, A. D. 1967. Some economic problems of small countries. In *Problems of smaller territories*, B. Benedict (ed.), 35–44. London: Athlone Press.

Schaffer, B. 1975. The politics of dependence. In *Development policy in small countries*, P. Selwyn (ed.), 25–53. London: Croom Helm.

Selwyn, P. 1975. Introduction: room for manoeuvre? In *Development policy in small countries*, P. Selwyn (ed.), 8–24. London: Croom Helm.

Wood, D. P. J. 1967. The smaller territories: some political considerations. In *Problems of smaller territories*, B. Benedict (ed.), 23–34. London: Athlone Press.

PART A

Surveys

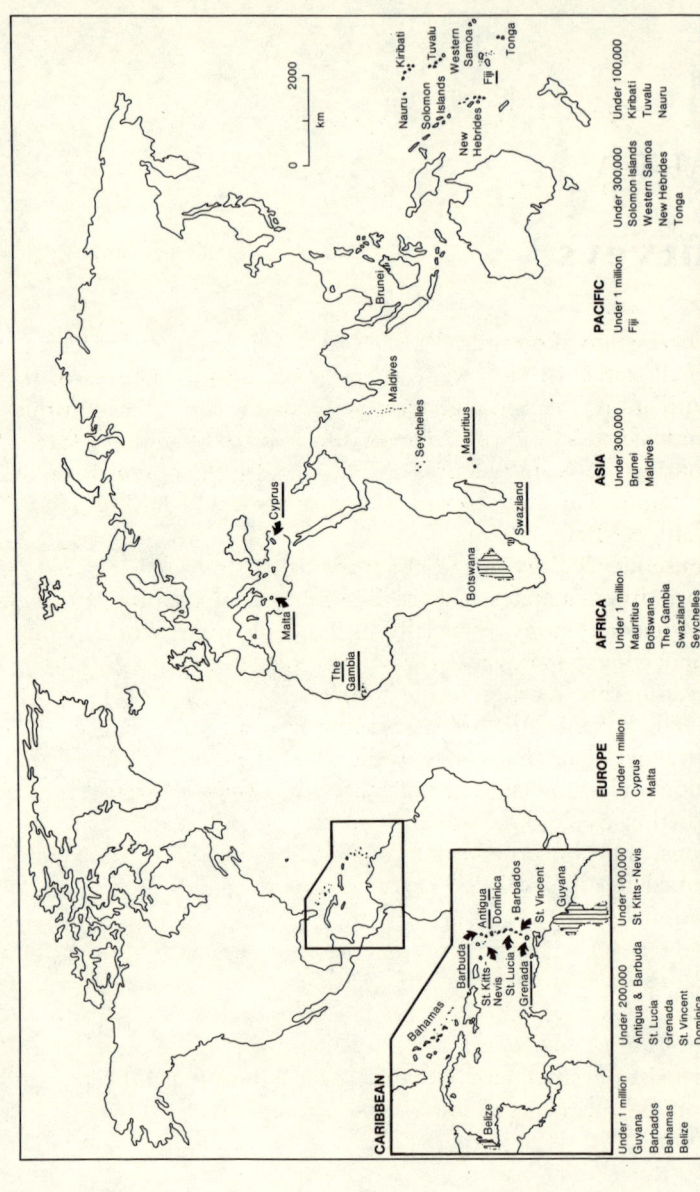

Commonwealth small states. The case studies used in this book are underlined.

1 *Political Aspects*

PAUL SUTTON

There is no shortage of studies of the international relations of small states. In fact, there is an embarrassing richness of them with more than enough variety to daunt the most committed student pursuing research on the subject (Handel 1981). By contrast, the consequences of smallness for the domestic political system of any state appear relatively neglected (UNITAR 1971; Dahl & Tufte 1973). There are few general studies of any consequence, leaving the norm to be constituted by monographs on individual states or edited collections of country studies for particular regions, especially in the developing world. Thus, if there is a gap in the literature, it is of single or co-authored works treating this question in the abstract.

The last time the political study of small states and territories attracted general attention it did so in the context of decolonization and viability. The way the argument was then presented, whether by colonial governments, nascent national administrations, or concerned international organizations, inextricably linked the internal and external domains, domestic and international politics. The study of the political aspects of small states and territories must therefore take cognizance of this as a central feature, yet at the same time recognize the failure of modern political science as a whole adequately to conceptualize the question of the 'boundary'. It is clear that the general political theorist of 'smallness' labours under a double handicap: limitation of theory and limitation of comparative studies in the abstract. In these circumstances it is evident that a necessary caution must accompany any conclusions. The observations recorded here are suggestive only of the type of political behaviour generally attributed to, or associated with, the condition of smallness, as scattered throughout the literature of political science.

The creation of small states

A study undertaken in 1970 by the United Nations Institute for Training and Research (UNITAR) identified 14 different categories of states and territories with a population of 1 million or less according to status. By far the largest number were regarded as Non-Self Governing Territories (28), followed by States Members of the United Nations (17). Other major categories identified were Overseas Territories Integrated with a Metropolitan State (10); Non-Self-Governing Territories according to UN Decision but disputed by the Administering Power (8); Protected States (7); and States in Association (6) (UNITAR 1971:Table 7).

The 1985 standard listings ordered according to the categories employed above reveal considerable changes. The largest single category is now States Members of the United Nations (35 – 12 original, 23 new entries), and there has been a proportionate major reduction in the Non-Self Governing Territories (15 – 14 original, 1 new entry). Two categories have seen considerable changes in membership, with Non-Self Governing Territories according to the UN but disputed now consisting of 3 (2 original, 1 new entry) and States in Association now numbering 2 (1 original, 1 new entry). The category of Protected States has disappeared completely, but that of Overseas Territory integrated with Metropolitan State has increased slightly to 11 (10 original, 1 new entry).

The other eight categories identified by UNITAR were, in effect, either instances of UN responsibility for dependent territories or examples of quasi-integration and devolution. In the former category 10 entities were listed, of which 12 are now relevant (8 original, 4 new entries), but in the latter category integration and devolution have counterbalanced each other, reducing the original 10 to 8 (3 original, 5 new entries).

The main conclusion to be drawn from this survey is not startling but should nevertheless be underlined. The principle of self-determination as set out in General Assembly Resolution

1514 (xv) of 14 December 1960 (Declaration on the Granting of Independence to Colonial Countries and Peoples) has been reconfirmed time and again. There is little reason to believe that in the near future it will be rendered invalid or that its application will have reached a limit. My evaluation of the recent past and current trends suggests that up to seven territories may become 'states' within the next five years – Montserrat, Aruba, New Caledonia, some part of the Trust Territory of the Pacific, Namibia, Western Sahara, Greenland – with more likely to follow where these leave off, particularly among the French overseas *départements*.

The necessary complementary conclusion to this, of course, is the continuing demise of formal colonialism. The disappearance of the category of Protected State is some additional evidence of this, but equally the general pattern of change established within the UNITAR categories points unambiguously in this direction. By the end of this century colonialism in the form known in the previous century will have all but gone. Only the rocks will remain.

None of this is to deny that states will have territory, population, and property overseas. They will, but the means to preserve their interests will be either through the well-established processes of neocolonialism or by various sovereignty arrangements, the number and variety of which could be infinite (or rather subject only to the ingenuity of man). The perspective I am offering here is that of General Assembly Resolution 1541 (xv) of 15 December 1960 on self-government through a choice of methods among which are: (1) free association with an independent state; and (2) integration with an independent state. The record of the past suggests the viability of the latter as against the former – UNITAR (1971:Table 8) lists 13 small territories which have lost international status since 1945, only one of which has sought to reaffirm it – although I believe both may be deployed.

Let us take actual as well as speculative case examples. On 6 April 1984 the people of the Cocos Islands voted by 231 to 30 for integration with Australia in a UN-observed referendum. In another dependent territory administered by Australia, Norfolk Island, it is stated that the eventual intention is to achieve full internal self-government for its peoples. At that point, presumably, some decision will have to be made about the future international status of the territory. The speculative case concerns the Caribbean. If the remaining British and French dependent territories were told that their status was no longer acceptable and they were offered the choice of independence or integration with the US, then the British territories would overwhelmingly opt for integration with the US on whatever terms were offered, whereas the French would proceed to independence. I am certain that other examples from other regions can be cited with equal plausibility. The determination in each case will be the concrete circumstances of the time.

The arguments in this section can thus be summarized quite succinctly. We can expect both the continued creation of small states and the integration of some small territories into larger units. The problem of small states is therefore likely to be with us for some time even as the issue of colonialism disappears.

The political definition of small

Having established the present and the future of small states it is important to consider briefly the question of definition. The presumption of the editors of this volume has been that 'small' is a population of 1 million or less. This is a useful and increasingly recognized definition but one which, even if less arbitrary than others, still remains open to critical comment. In respect of politics, for example, it can be asked whether it has any meaning whatsoever. The starting point is Louis XIV and his remark, 'L'Etat, c'est moi'. A decision-making 'system' (if not a political system) of one is as feasible in a state of millions as a decision-making system of thousands is feasible in a state of tens of thousands.

Take another example: that of political rôles. Some years ago Benedict (1967:45) argued that 'the criteria of size for territories are area and population, the criteria of scale for a society are the number and quality of rôle relationships'. There is no reason why a large state in area and population could not have as few formal rôles as a small state. Or to put the same point more concretely via the 'iron law of oligarchy', what basis is there for Kremlinology or power élite studies of the US?

Finally, what of political participation and class? Here it is possible to run the whole gamut from the view of the state as the 'executive committee of the bourgeoisie' to modern conceptions of legitimation which, though conceding political space to the majority in theory, note in practice that it is circumscribed by all manner of devices. How else is one to make sense of one of Dahl & Tufte's (1973:65) many conclusions in their study of small democratic states in Europe, namely that 'political participation and sense of effectiveness among citizens do not depend to any significant degree on the size of a country'?

In short, there is no basis whatsoever to believe that small size in population means a small-scale political system (however defined). To impute such a relationship is to fall into the same trap as attended the earlier discussions on the presumed viability of small states. This was to see the concept as static (the product of finite specific characteristics) when, in fact, it was, and is, highly variable. The proof of this lies not only in the way the threshold has been continually lowered in the international system to the point where it no longer has any meaning, but can also be exemplified more objectively.

In an interesting study of small tropical islands, François Doumenge has attempted to quantify the concept of viability and has then applied it to the French *départements* and territories of Martinique, Guadeloupe, New Caledonia, French Polynesia and Réunion. He finds that in 1977 New Caledonia was considerably more viable than in 1981, with the reverse true for Martinique (Doumenge 1985). It will not have escaped attention, of course, that this stands in inverse relationship to the agitation for independence in these countries. The desire for nationhood, in other words, is a political demand with its own logic and basis. Similarly, the political system itself may have its own logic and basis and be highly variable on this account. Indeed, the 'viability' (whatever that may mean) of a small state depends precisely on the flexibility of the political system in the domestic and the international context. As Selwyn (1975:13) noted, 'even physical size can in the last resort be changed by forms of political association'.

Political characteristics of size

Notwithstanding these theoretical considerations, what in practice have been the main conclusions drawn in respect of the effect of small size on political behaviour? The immediate problem is the number of units with less than 1 million population – 44 independent states and 42 dependent territories scattered over the globe. To state anything meaningful about the politics of all of them is to stretch the bounds of credibility to the limit. Accordingly, some limitation must be imposed, and in this book Commonwealth membership has been the deciding criterion, along with that of developing country status. Two features identified by Dahl & Tufte (1973:30–40) as so powerful that they overwhelm any possible effects of population size – cultural diversity and socio-economic diversity – are thus to some extent accommodated, if not wholly discounted. The category so reduced stands at 27 independent states and 19 dependent territories within which, given the concerns of the moment, I have emphasized the former as against the latter. The range of political behaviour considered therefore encompasses the international as well as domestic politics of 27 sovereign Commonwealth states.

The domestic context

It is possible to isolate five features of domestic politics often attributable or closely related to small size. These comprise institutional fidelity, governmental pervasiveness, exaggerated personalism, concerted political harmony, and pragmatic conservatism.

Institutional fidelity

According to the official history of decolonization in the British Empire, a great deal of discussion and study was focused on the problems of the smaller territories (Morgan 1980). If this was so, then one must conclude that remarkably little imagination attended the deliberations, since almost nothing in the way of innovation is evident in the processes of transition from self-government to independence. In nearly every case the smaller territories emerged into statehood through the tried and tested procedures of tutelary devolution of responsibility and the adoption or adaptation of the Westminster–Whitehall system of government and administration. In their formal aspects the smaller Commonwealth states thus appear similar, even if there is considerable variation within the basic framework.

The principal observation with regard to variation is that the Commonwealth Caribbean states express greater institutional fidelity to Britain than the rest. Of the ten states so comprehended, eight retain Queen Elizabeth II as head of state, only Dominica and Guyana having opted for republican status. This is repeated for the principal institutions of government and the methods of recruitment to office. Except for Grenada between 1979 and 1984 and to a lesser extent Guyana from 1970 onwards, all have affirmed the practice of parliamentary democracy and deployed institutions appropriate to it. For Antigua and Barbuda, the Bahamas, Barbados, Belize, Grenada, and St Lucia, this has meant the full panoply of a two-chamber legislature – a nominated upper house and an elected lower house. A single-chamber legislature, wholly elected, is to be found only in Guyana, but Dominica, St Kitts–Nevis, and St Vincent have also opted for this form, although in a way which combines an elected and a nominated element.

How may this Caribbean conservatism be explained? The reasons for it are no doubt many and varied, although I would argue that the length and depth of the colonial heritage, as expressed in contemporary political culture, hold the key. Fidelity to the Westminster system is here a reflection of the modernity of Caribbean peoples and an affirmation of a West Indian identity on the part of some of them. The Westminster system is regarded in the region as an autochthonous form of government, whatever its real origins happen to have been.

In contrast, there has been a readiness to adapt in the African, Pacific, and Indian Ocean cases. Four states have retained their own system of monarchical or chiefly representation (Brunei, Swaziland, Tonga, and Western Samoa); and single-chamber legislatures, either wholly elected (Nauru, the Solomon Islands, Tuvalu, Vanuatu) or combining an elected and nominated element, predominate (Botswana, The Gambia, the Maldives, Mauritius, the Seychelles, Kiribati, Tonga, and Western Samoa). Two broad explanations for this can be identified, again both relating to political culture. The first is to be found in the persistence of tradition and the representation of chiefs. Examples are Fiji, Tonga, Vanuatu, Western Samoa, Botswana, The Gambia, and Swaziland. The second is the vexed issue of communalism so apparent in the cases of Fiji and Mauritius where ethnic interests must be accommodated. Whether the examples cited actually 'work' is difficult to gauge, though on the whole they appear to impart a measure of stability to their respective political systems. In this sense, the various arrangements effected should be regarded as more than 'transitional' in form, although of course this does not rule out further adaptation and change in the future.

It almost goes without saying that scale *per se* appears unrelated in any meaningful way to the above (though the smallest do have unicameral legislatures). More interesting is the question of 'islandness'. The utility of this category has been explored by Dommen (1985), though without reaching firm conclusions. I wish only to draw attention to the number of states which have sought to accommodate the representation of 'out islands'. Examples are Antigua, St Kitts–Nevis, the Maldives, Mauritius, the Seychelles, Kiribati, Tuvalu, and Vanuatu. They have done so in a variety of ways, such as nomination or specification of 'out islanders' filling elective posts or provision of local assemblies or any combination of these. That they have done so, of course, raises the question of how far these countries are in themselves unitary states with all that this implies for the future. In only one case, however, that of St Kitts–Nevis, has secession been envisaged and provided for (and in that case made more likely?).

The 'semi-formal' aspects of politics associated with the Westminster–Whitehall model involve consideration of parties. Again the picture is mixed, though certain regularities are apparent. For example, in respect of parties, three patterns emerge:

(a) Single party systems: the Seychelles (and Swaziland).
(b) Multiparty systems: in descending order of number of parties, Mauritius (10), Botswana (7), the Bahamas (6),

Dominica (6), St Vincent (6), Antigua (5), Grenada (5), Guyana (5), Barbados (4), Fiji (4), Cyprus (Greek – 4), Belize (3), Malta (3), St Lucia (3), Western Samoa (3), The Gambia (2).
(c) No parties: Brunei, Kiribati, the Maldives, Nauru, Tonga, Tuvalu.

Clearly the pattern which needs to be explained is the prevalence and range of multiparty systems. Has scale anything to do with this? One explanation met frequently in the literature stresses factionalism as a consequence of the presumed salience of personality in small-sized polities. I would not dispute this, except to note that factionalism is characteristic of politics in general and that personalist parties are also a particular characteristic of large-scale Latin American political systems. In the same vein, I would argue that the frequent creation and dissolution, thus multiplicity, of political parties is not a product of scale alone, but rather of the unavailability of resources, which in turn depends upon access to office, that is patronage. Again Latin American examples come to mind. In short, size cannot be ruled out, but neither is it convincing in itself. Indeed, taking the Commonwealth sample as a basis, I would point to regional features. In the Pacific political parties are 'new' and indicative of experimentation, whereas in the Caribbean they are 'familiar' and the recognized form of political participation. Only Africa and the Indian Ocean have one party states. In short, determination of the number of political parties is more a product of ecology than of size.

Finally, I want to consider the Whitehall dimension of the Westminster model, that is the structure of central government. This has a number of facets, but the most immediate is the relevance to small states of the Whitehall pattern of single ministries dealing with specified areas within which specialism is permitted and by means of which bureaucrats advance their careers. On the surface most small new states of the Commonwealth have adopted this pattern. The number of ministries in each state for which there are data is as follows: Antigua (10), the Bahamas (13), Barbados (11), Belize (10), Dominica (8), Guyana (20), St Lucia (9), St Vincent (7), the Maldives (9), Mauritius (18), the Seychelles (9), Botswana (10), The Gambia (9), Swaziland (11), Fiji (16), Kiribati (10), the Solomon Islands (15), Tonga (9), Tuvalu (5), Vanuatu (9), and Malta (14).

My experience of the Caribbean, however, is that many of the ministries will be empty vessels and that real power of administrative decision is to be found in the office of the Prime Minister or President. On further review one finds, in fact, that only Brunei, Kiribati, Nauru, St Kitts–Nevis, the Seychelles and Tuvalu have, according to the various directories, denied themselves this potential powerhouse. In these instances one would imagine that particular circumstances apply, such as the Sultanate of Brunei. Elsewhere we must presume that what is being exhibited is either the working out of the principle of 'elective dictatorship' to be found in the Westminster–Whitehall model or the necessary product of scale. Certainly, one of the most often encountered recommendations of the public administration reports on small states has been the need for flexibility and co-ordination within an administrative centre if one can be established. Practice would here appear to follow precept to quite an extraordinary degree.

Governmental pervasiveness

A repeatedly asserted attribute of small states is governmental ubiquity. Government is said to dominate, since it seeks on the one hand to duplicate the range of services offered in the larger states, and on the other is subject to fewer constraints from countervailing sectors, pressure groups, or non-governmental institutional activity (Commonwealth Consultative Group 1985). Central government is thus often the largest employer of labour in the country and is frequently the most important agency for the articulation and aggregation of demands, as well as being crucial to their settlement.

There is a measure of truth in much of this but there is also a need for caution. A recent study by the IMF, for example, has linked central government employment to population size (the larger the population the lower the central government share). But it has also indicated that it matters considerably whether a country is developed or underdeveloped, and whether it is centrally planned or not (Heller & Tait 1983). Individual figures for small states, insofar as they are available, bear this out. The IMF study discloses the following figures for government employees per 100 population in states below 1 million: Iceland (6.42), Luxembourg (4.68), Botswana (3.04), Mauritius (5.99), Swaziland (3.35), Cyprus (3.34), Bahrain (6.39), Oman (4.36), the Bahamas (4.98), Barbados (10.7), Belize (1.94), and St Lucia (4.18) (Heller & Tait 1983:Table 21). These figures show a wide variation within themselves and are not significantly out of line with ratios for much larger states (total sample 61). With respect to the range of services offered by small states, the IMF sample was not really large enough for any firm conclusions to be reached. However, directly relevant to our concerns is the observation that notes

> those countries that have been most influenced by the British Commonwealth system of government appear to employ larger numbers of government civil servants in administration than do other countries ... Those employed in the administrative sector of government appear to be paid rather more than the average for the public service. (Heller & Tait 1983:36)

In other words, it is with the colonial heritage that these states must deal rather than size *per se*, though clearly the remedy for the cost of the public service (reputedly high in small states) lies in their own hands.

Although it is widely believed that only limited pressure-group and allied activity is to be found in small states, no easily quantifiable measure is available. It is therefore, as Dahl & Tufte (1973) noted, very much a matter of conjecture. But it is an issue which, in itself, can shed some light on the salience of other dimensions of politics to be found in small states and to that extent it can be persuasive. In smaller political systems, they reason, it is likely that there is a higher chance that conflicts among groups will be translated into personal conflicts among individuals; that conflicts among organizations will be less frequent; that processes for dealing with organized group conflict will be less institutionalized; that group conflict will be infrequent but explosive; and that such conflicts are more likely to polarize the whole community. In other words, there is little virtue in aggressive pluralist politics but much wisdom in the careful cultivation of consensus. Specific interests, when they do arise, are also likely to be *ad hoc*, personalized, and/or attached to specific group concerns. When these coincide with race or ethnicity, as they do in a number of small Commonwealth states, the need to proceed with care is, of course, given even greater urgency.

Finally, governmental pervasiveness raises the question of the impartiality of administration and justice. In small states refuge in anonymity is not possible and pressures toward partisanship are all too palpable. Hence, at least in a number of new Commonwealth small states, explicit provision has been made to elevate universal norms above particularistic values. These can take a variety of forms. Most have constitutions entrenching provisions for human rights and fundamental freedoms, and many have established public service commissions to oversee recruitment and matters relating to career advancement in such areas as the police force, civil service, and education.

With respect to law, a number have retained the final right of appeal to the Judicial Committee of the Privy Council in London, whereas in the Eastern Caribbean all except Grenada and Barbados have a common membership of the Eastern Caribbean Supreme Court. English, nearly everywhere, is the language of administration, and though customary law and practice may be permitted and protected, it is usually consigned a lower place in the general order.

Lastly, it is interesting to note that in several small states provision has been made, notwithstanding the strain which this must place on scarce resources, for the office of ombudsman. Guyana, Mauritius, and Fiji have all appointed ombudsmen, and the constitutions of Dominica, St Lucia, the Solomon Islands, and Vanuatu make mention of it. Size is clearly not the only reason for this, since nearly all these countries may be regarded as first and foremost plural societies, but it is reasonable to suppose that it was an exacerbating factor in most instances and that, accordingly, a premium was placed on impartiality.

Exaggerated personalism

The significance of personality is a theme remarked upon in nearly every monograph dealing with the politics of small states (UNITAR 1971:52–3; Dahl & Tufte 1973:87–8). Those features most often cited are:

(a) the rôle of the individual takes on greater significance;
(b) the individual, as a member of a group, is more susceptible to pressures, both internal and external;
(c) politicians exercise greater influence over administrators, frequently based more on personal than on party factors;
(d) senior administrative and political office holders have more direct contact with the man in the street, and accordingly there is less of the aloofness traditionally associated with a bureaucracy;
(e) top political leaders are more likely to communicate directly with one another and directly to oversee the actions of their lieutenants;
(f) there is less functional specialization among politicians and both they and senior administrators are likely to accumulate rôles;
(g) politics may be less than a full-time job, constituting either a means to promote other interests or an avenue of mobility into other areas in a situation of limited economic opportunities;
(h) criticism of political leaders and senior administrators may be muted, often informal, but where it does appear is likely to be personal in form and strident in tone.

What effect do these features have on politics? In general, they can be regarded as potentially positive or negative. With regard to the former, it is clear that leaders, being personally accessible, are more likely to be in direct touch with affairs and to be held directly accountable for their actions. Their real personal strengths and weaknesses are also likely to be well known and form the basis of informed judgement as to their suitability for office. On the negative side, it is abundantly evident that small societies can be vulnerable to domination or dictatorship by one or a few odious individuals. In the Commonwealth context Grenada under Gairy is an example, and it was probably this somewhat eccentric figure that Christopher Diggines, the former British High Commissioner to Grenada and Trinidad and Tobago, had in mind in writing (in 1985):

> In small societies it is relatively easier for a determined, unscrupulous individual with rather more than his share of charisma and ruthlessness to dominate all or most aspects of the country's life. He can gradually acquire business interests which give him a say – perhaps a decisive one – in virtually all major decisions affecting business and the economy, particularly in such matters as the placing of contracts, investment from abroad and import licences. Through control of one or more trade unions he can secure a decisive voice in the employment of labour, wages and working conditions. It is usually not difficult for him to control and direct press, radio and other media. Because of his effective power of veto over government appointments, he can decisively influence the direction and methods of public services, including police, public health, education and the Civil Service.

Whether positive or negative features predominate in any one country, it appears statistically to be the case that small countries retain political leaders longer in office than elsewhere. Blondel (1985) notes the average duration of ministers in the world as 3.55 years and their attrition rate as 4.13 years. Those from the Commonwealth have, in his analysis, greater security in office than others, a tendency Blondel (1980) has also noted in his parallel study of world leaders. It is therefore not simply a matter of scale. Even so, the presumption of relative longevity in office invites an association with the establishment of networks of patron–client relationships, a feature which is often regarded as prevalent in small states. Unfortunately, there is little comparative empirical work on this subject and impressions only can be recorded. However, it is clear that many of the classic features of patron–client relations – unequal exchanges on a face-to-face basis – are to be witnessed in many small states, notwithstanding the fact that the majority are neither the peasant nor the traditional societies usually associated with such behaviour.

Concerted political harmony

A recent study on the security of small states concluded:

> Although we do not advocate any specific political system, we believe that a state is likely to remain politically stable under a system where there is: first, freedom of speech and of assembly, including some means of voicing criticisms of the government, whether at public meetings, or through the media; secondly, some form of democratic process enabling the political leadership to be changed by peaceful means; thirdly, respect for human rights (including provisions for the protection of minority groups, where applicable). (Harden 1985:88)

On these criteria small states in general, and Commonwealth ones in particular, appear to do remarkably well. They tend to score positively on a political rights and civil rights index and not to figure very markedly in the long lists of states that practise political and economic discrimination on ethnic, linguistic, or religious grounds (Taylor & Jodice 1983:Vol. 1). They also enjoy regular and frequent polls and experience regular executive transfers (and a not disproportionate number of executive adjustments) (Taylor & Jodice 1983:Vol. 2). A basis for orderly and effective change is therefore evident in a number of them. The corollary to this is the relatively low incidence of civil disorder that is recorded. Small states – Cyprus excepted – have proportionately fewer protest demonstrations, political strikes, riots, armed attacks, assassinations, deaths from political violence, and irregular executive transfers than do larger states (Taylor & Jodice 1983:Vol. 2). They are, in a nutshell, apparently more tranquil and harmonious – with Barbados the leader in the field.

Why is this? No single explanation will suffice but it is the general presumption that small states enjoy a sense of community concordant with national boundaries which is denied to larger entities. There is less alienation, higher degrees of system legitimacy, and a basic consensus of values. This applies even to 'plural societies' and is attributable to the 'dominant European maritime culture' which many have acquired as a consequence of history and 'islandness' (Caldwell *et al.* 1980). Most small states are, in consequence, more homogeneous than might appear at first sight. They are also, by custom, more adaptive (though not usually innovative). Representative democratic systems have been successfully transplanted in a number of instances and are valued in themselves. Those features of size which give greater opportunity for citizens of small democracies to participate effectively in decisions and to perceive a relation between their own self-interest, the interests of others, and the public or national interest (Dahl & Tufte 1973) are accordingly strengthened. These aspects are also, at least in the Commonwealth, deliberately orchestrated by the overwhelming majority of the political élite. Political parties, national elections and parliamentary debate are the favoured forms of political participation.

Pragmatic conservatism

A policy of pragmatic conservatism is usually conceived as best serving the interests of any small state. Very few adopt radical ideologies with the result that a careful cultivation of the centre is the favoured stance. Thus of the 29 small states listed by Day & Dagenhardt (1980) as possessing active political parties, in no less than 15 cases the majority government party could be regarded as centrist in orientation (12 instances for Commonwealth states), whereas parties to the right (conservative and traditionalist) and parties to the left (socialist and Marxist) constituted the major government party in only 7 instances in each case (4 each in respect of Commonwealth states). With reference to the other 15 small states, the orientation of political parties was either not known or parties were banned or in recess. In the latter instances the orientation of the ruling élite tended towards the traditional. Overall, the majority of small states are therefore on the centre-right of the political spectrum.

For this to be related to size, however, it must not simply be a matter of political will, but must also accord with structural features conducive to such a stance. Two such features can be cited. The first is the likelihood in small political systems that, in relation to the numbers holding the majority view in a conflict, those who openly dissent are fewer (Dahl & Tufte 1973). The prospects for effective opposition are accordingly diminished, especially if that opposition is radical in content or requires a more than minimal commitment to mobilization or coalition building. The second feature relates to avoidance of decision making. Public servants in small systems lack anonymity. They are frequently unprepared to take risks or make decisions out of the routine without reference to superiors. Administration is therefore politicized, often centralized, and subject frequently to the narrow political vision of the small state politician. He or she may be prepared to act, but on larger matters, as mentioned above, may well *not* be. Avoidance of decision making may thus in itself become routine, with the result that crisis, when it looms, will be that much larger and change, when it has to be accommodated, will appear that much more threatening than would otherwise be the case (Bachrach & Baratz 1970). Small-state political systems may therefore be more prone to sudden and dramatic collapse than larger-scale political systems.

The international context

There have been numerous studies of small-state behaviour in the international system. However, the relevance of many of these for the very smallest states must be questioned since there has been a tendency to confuse small states with weak states and weak states can, of course, be very large indeed (the 19th-century Ottoman Empire, Nationalist China in the 1930s). Many of the studies fail to distinguish sufficiently between material size and systemic size. The fact is that a large state could be systemically small or, more relevantly, a small state may seek to be systemically large. Moreover, the upper limit of population size frequently cited for a small state (15–20 million) seems excessively large by the criteria so far employed in this study.

The classical literature on the international politics of small states is provided by Blair (1967), Plischke (1977a), and Reid

(1974). Characteristically, the focus of this work is on constraints which are the presumed consequence of limited resource levels. Foreign policy reflects this by being limited in range and extent. Diplomatic representation is restricted to the places where a small state believes its major external interests lie, these generally being with the immediate geographical area and with one or more of the major powers. Much diplomatic activity will be concerned with the search for development assistance, which is often the highest priority in the foreign policy arena. Finally, it is argued that there is a lack of institutionalization within foreign policy formulation which is said to allow for a high degree of personal intervention and a corresponding *ad hoc* approach to issues. Together, all are combined in a mainly passive and reactive foreign policy which sees in strong support for international law and the operations of international organizations the best safeguards for long-term security.

Many of these observations are borne out by the Commonwealth sample of small states. To begin with, the resident diplomatic missions established by them abroad are few in number and usually less than those accredited to them. The respective figures are: Mauritius 10/8; the Seychelles 1/10; Botswana 5/12; The Gambia 7/10; Swaziland 7/6; Antigua 4/–; the Bahamas 4/2; Barbados 7/6; Belize 3/5; Guyana n.a./16; St Lucia 3/2; St Vincent 2/–; Brunei 7/10; Malta 4/18; Fiji 6/12; Kiribati –/2; Nauru 1/1; the Solomon Islands n.a./4; Tonga 1/5; Tuvalu 1/n.a.; Vanuatu n.a./3; and Western Samoa 4/3. Nearly all the states maintain missions in London and a considerable proportion have representation in the US. This is reciprocated by the UK and the US, with particular use being made of embassies and High Commissions in Barbados and Fiji to serve neighbouring states. The USSR is comparatively poorly represented in small Commonwealth states, having only one embassy in the Caribbean (Guyana) and none in the South Pacific. This could reflect a lack of interest in such states, or the marginality of the Cold War in these regions, or more likely the pro-Western and conservative stance of most small states as commented on earlier.

An explanation in terms of the latter is to some extent evidenced in per capita aid figures. Small states do very well compared to larger developing countries, which suggests the existence of specific patron–client relationships (to the US, the UK, the EEC, New Zealand, Australia). Figures provided for 1980 (UNCTAD Secretariat 1985) on concessional assistance per capita from Development Assistance Committee (DAC) member countries, OPEC member countries, and multilateral agencies demonstrate this very well. They are as follows (US $): Tuvalu 700; Vanuatu 373; the Seychelles 354; Kiribati 331; Dominica 239; the Solomon Islands 184; Tonga 170; Western Samoa 164; Mauritius 153; Botswana 132; St Kitts–Nevis 119; the Maldives 108; St Vincent 101; Cyprus 92; The Gambia 91; Belize 91; Swaziland 90; Antigua 75; St Lucia 74; Barbados 58; Fiji 58; Guyana 51; Malta 46; Grenada 32; the Bahamas 9 (figure for all developing countries 15.6). Small states on this reading are, then, privileged, and with hindsight it is apparent that such levels of assistance have, in recent years, disposed of the 'viability' argument. Small-state diplomats are well aware of this, and seek not only to improve their position but, almost as importantly, to maintain it. If this requires, as they see it, low-key and conservative diplomacy, then to some degree it is perfectly understandable.

At the same time, however, small states do not have to limit themselves. Some have extensive diplomatic relations and are leading states in their own region or on the international scene. Examples that come to mind are Malta, Guyana, Grenada under Bishop, the Seychelles, Botswana, Fiji, and perhaps Vanuatu. The mix of factors prompting this activist stance may be many. For example, in the case of Fiji it appears geographical, for Malta and Botswana geopolitical, and for the others ideological factors could be cited. Personality also undoubtedly plays a part, but perhaps not as much as is generally credited. I have no doubt that as a rule executive Presidents and Prime Ministers are kept well informed of foreign affairs, but only in the very smallest do they actually exercise specific ministerial responsibility in this matter (Antigua, St Kitts–Nevis, St Lucia, St Vincent, the Seychelles, Kiribati, Nauru, Tuvalu, and Western Samoa).

Perhaps it is nearer the truth to talk of a lack of coherent procedures in the practice of international relations which itself is the product of size. Sir Colin Allen, speaking on the basis of extensive experience of the Indian Ocean and the Pacific, has noted: 'an inevitable tendency for ministers and indeed officials –

especially the inveterate travellers – to enter into commitments or make statements often irresponsibly of one kind or another, when abroad, without the blessing of the Minister let alone the Cabinet' (1980:398). Furthermore, my own experience of a state just outside our sample, Trinidad and Tobago, confirms this in every respect. But, there again, such observations are not confined to small states, and chains of command in even the largest and most centralized of countries can go awry.

Finally, there are the interests of small states in international organizations and international law. Plischke (1977b) has argued that small states exercise selectivity about joining specialized agencies and prefer affiliation to functional institutions. Data from the Commonwealth sample confirm this. Not all small states are members of the UN General Assembly (Kiribati, Nauru, Tonga, Tuvalu excepted) and several have chosen only special membership of the Commonwealth (the Maldives, Nauru, St Vincent, Tuvalu). All, however, with the exception of the Maldives, had by 1983 opted for affiliation to the appropriate UN regional economic commission, and high levels of membership are recorded for institutions such as the World Bank (Antigua, Kiribati, Malta, Nauru, St Kitts–Nevis, Tonga, Tuvalu excepted), the IMF (Belize, Kiribati, Nauru, St Kitts–Nevis, Tonga, Tuvalu excepted) and the UNCTAD (Kiribati, Nauru, St Kitts–Nevis, Tuvalu excepted).

Support for international law is in many respects an obvious policy and one with which small states in general have historically been closely associated. All I would add is that it constitutes a handy moral, if not actual, defence against intervention (*pace* Grenada), as well as having considerable real potential, especially with regard to the law of the sea. This particularly concerns the Pacific and some of the smallest states. Proportions of land to sea area are for Tuvalu 1: 34 615; Nauru 1:15 238; Cook Islands 1:7625 (and Pitcairn 1:160 000). Indeed, one of the more positive aspects emerging from the recent Commonwealth study of small states was its promotion of Part V of the Law of the Sea Convention (the establishment of Exclusive Economic Zones) as a development option to be vigorously explored by the majority of small states. As the study itself noted:

Most small states in the Commonwealth are islands. In the current era of advanced scientific and technological development, the sea has assumed a new importance as possibly the last major frontier for resource exploration. This provides a unique opportunity for many small island states to gain access to a resource base which can underpin their aspirations for self-reliant development. Conversely, their enlarged area of national jurisdiction has the effect of heightening their strategic relevance, which could project them more centrally into international resource diplomacy and power politics. (Commonwealth Consultative Group 1985:102)

Conclusion

The general conclusion to be drawn is that though the factor of size offers some insight, it yields little in the way of explanation. In respect of domestic politics it is perhaps best seen as a syndrome of interrelated characteristics or as a qualifying feature to tendencies already inherent, rather than as a cause of such features in the first place. In respect of international politics similar reasoning applies, with the added proviso that though the behaviour of small states appears distinctive in some respects, in others it is not that different from the behaviour of larger states. Equally, while small states have many interests in common, it could be argued that these are the interests of all states.

It seems clear that we are not going to develop a theory of the small state in politics equivalent to the theory of the firm in economics. Much of this has to do with the failings of the discipline of political science itself. It simply does not have the concepts to handle the task or the empirical material available to facilitate theory construction. To study the politics of small states as a comparative exercise in the abstract is difficult and perhaps impossible. To study the policies of a number of small states is possible, but perhaps meaningless other than as a very short-term exercise bounded by the specific demands of the moment. To abandon the study of the politics of small states altogether ought to be, of course, untenable.

So what is to be done? The usual plea is for more research. In this instance I believe it to be justified, although subject to the proviso that at the beginning basic data collection be placed before theoretical speculation *per se*. We have remarkably few political facts about small states available to us and even fewer at our fingertips. About dependent territories which may emerge into statehood we know practically nothing. Such omissions may be understandable, but they are surely inadvisable in an increasingly interdependent world. For within such a prospect all, even the very smallest, have their part to play. Indeed, precisely because of their size they may be called upon to contribute most to the realization of an interdependent world. Small size, no longer a constraint, becomes a virtue, and the reward for all is an infinite variety to delight and invite social inquiry.

References

Allen, Sir C. 1980. Bureaucratic organization for development in small island states. In *The island states of the Pacific and Indian Oceans: anatomy of development*, R. T. Shand (ed.), 383–403. Development Studies Centre Monograph No. 23, Australian National University, Canberra.

Bachrach, P. & M. Baratz 1970. *Power and poverty: theory and practice*. New York: Oxford University Press.

Benedict, B. 1967. Sociological aspects of smallness. In *Problems of Smaller Territories*, B. Benedict (ed.), 45–55. London: Athlone Press.

Blair, P. W. 1967. *The ministate dilemma*. New York: Carnegie Endowment for International Peace.

Blondel, J. 1980. *World leaders: heads of government in the postwar period*. London: Sage.

Blondel, J. 1985. *Government ministers in the contemporary world*. London: Sage.

Caldwell, J. C., G. E. Harrison & P. Quiggin, 1980. The demography of micro-states. *World Development* **8**, 953–67.

Commonwealth Consultative Group 1985. *Vulnerability: small states in the global society*. London: Commonwealth Secretariat.

Dahl, R. A. & E. R. Tufte 1973. *Size and democracy*. Stanford, Calif.: Stanford University Press.

Day, A. J. & H. W. Dagenhardt (eds) 1980. *Political parties of the world*. London: Longman.

Diggines, C. E. 1985. The problems of small states. *The Round Table* **295**, 191–205.

Dommen, E. (ed.) 1985. *States, micro-states and islands*. London: Croom Helm.

Doumenge, F. 1985. The viability of small intertropical islands. In *States, micro-states and islands*, E. C. Dommen and P. L Hein (eds.), 70–118. London: Croom Helm.

Handel, M. 1981. *Weak states in the international system*. London: Frank Cass.

Harden, S. (ed). 1985. *Small is dangerous: micro-states in a macro world*. London: Frances Pinter.

Heller, P. & A. Tait 1983. *Government employment and pay: some international comparisons*. Occasional Paper 24, IMF, Washington.

Morgan, D. J. 1980. *Guidance towards self-government in British colonies, 1941–1971*. London: Macmillan.

Plischke, E. 1977a. *Microstates in world affairs: policy problems and options*. Washington, DC: American Enterprise Institute for Public Research.

Plischke, E. 1977(b). United Nations and the problem of state proliferation. *Optima* **27**, 61–80.

Reid, G. L. 1974. *The impact of very small size on the international behaviour of microstates*. Beverley Hills, Calif.: Sage Professional Papers, International Studies Series.

Selwyn, P. 1975. Introduction: room for manoeuvre? In *Development Policy in Small Countries*, P. Selwyn (ed.), 8–24. London: Croom Helm.

Taylor, C. L. & D. Jodice. 1983. *World Handbook of Political and Social Indicators*, 3rd edn, Vol. 1. New Haven, Conn.: Yale University Press.

Taylor, C. L. & D. Jodice. 1983. *World Handbook of Political and Social Indicators*, 3rd edn, Vol. 2. New Haven, Conn.: Yale University Press.

UNCTAD Secretariat 1985. Examination of the particular needs and problems of island developing countries. In *States, Microstates and Islands*, E. Dommen (ed.), 119–51. London: Croom Helm.

UNITAR (United Nations Institute for Training and Research) 1971. *Small states and territories: status and problems*. New York: Arno Press.

2 Social Features

David Lowenthal

What should a state be? A few specific characteristics embody the common image. To the public mind, a state connotes a realm of substantial area and population, durable over time, reflecting and responding to corporate concerns consensually articulated by its inhabitants. I do not mean to suggest that all or most states live up to these criteria, only that it is generally felt that they *ought* to. Even large states often fall far short of 'statehood' so conceived: dissent between governed and governing may result in upheaval or tyranny; invasion or expansion may conjoin peoples of incompatible cultures or conflicting aims; massive social flux may submerge the continuity and content of national identity. States that lack or contravene these criteria seem defective or aberrant, misnomers for some other kind of entity – an empire, a colony, or a dependency deficient in qualities of nationhood. In short, the common image of the state combines sovereignty with nationality: the paradigmatic state is a nation–state (Seton-Watson 1977, Gellner 1983).

Small states meet these criteria of substantiality and durability very poorly indeed, and that of consensuality only with significant reservations. I examine each in turn.

Substantiality

Small states fail the test of substantiality almost by definition. How far smallness depends on area or gross national product or population, whether it begins below 5 million or 1 million or some other figure, depends on variables whose weight shifts with context and over time. This chapter deals mainly with entities below 1 million, but even most of those up to 5 million conflict with today's received image of the state as a substantial entity.

I say 'today's' because this image of the state is one only recently held. Up to the mid-19th century, the normal if not normative state was a 'small' entity – small not only in our terms but to people of former times, who contrasted 'states' with great imperial realms such as the Hapsburg or Holy Roman empires. The ancient Greek and the Renaissance city–state remained the European ideal, and as late as 1850 Germany alone contained more than three hundred sovereign principalities. Approximating to Aristotle's ideal state – one where each of the 5040 inhabitants could see the whole of it at once and recognize all the others – such tiny entities were the rule, larger nation–states like England and France the exception. India and Africa, too, were congeries of small states (Hein 1985, Pitt 1985).

Not until the late 19th century, as Europe's older nation–states increased in size and power and Germany and Italy also achieved unification, did the small state cease to be the norm. Then even their continued existence was resented as an obstacle to the larger nationhood felt to embody the soul of a people and to enable them to realize their full potential. Because small states flew in the face of such geopolitical laws, centrist theorists like Treitschke and Ratzel advocated their extermination as an act of historical necessity. So swiftly and thoroughly did nation–states gobble up smaller entities that in 1904 Joseph Chamberlain could reasonably conclude that 'the day of small nations has long passed away. The day of Empires has come' (Amstrup 1976, Diggines 1985).

A few small states survived these engorgements; a few more came into being, mainly Balkan and Baltic great-power pawns in the wake of Versailles. Not until after World War II, however, did small states again emerge as numerous players on the world stage. By the end of the 1960s, mainly as a consequence of decolonization, there were as many small sovereignties as larger entities. Imperial devolution continues to hive off more small states, but the end of that process is now in sight; the total number of para-sovereign entities along with wholly independent small states has already declined from a 1970 peak of almost 100 to about 85 (Harden 1985).

In short, within this generation the small state has made a

comeback unimaginable at the turn of the century. These states play an international rôle, in the United Nations and elsewhere, of consequence far beyond their size. Indeed, they symbolize the new principle of self-determination that now exemplifies the anti-imperialist ethos – the view that every people, however few or impotent, have the right to enjoy and express their corporate identity through their own chosen institutions. As Bernard Levin (1977:14) put it, we 'mark with reverence the feeling of a people that they *are* a people, however absurd their claims on the definition may seem to others'.

Yet the new prominence of small states and the celebration of the principles that sustain their existence have made no substantial dent in the public image of what a state ought to be. Save for the quixotic followers of Schumacher (1974) and Kohr (1973, 1977), the state in the eyes of most people remains paradigmatically large. Even those alarmed by the unwieldy might of the superpowers perceive the normative state as one large enough to generate substantial economic and political self-sufficiency and to sustain a serious national purpose. Much smaller states are apt to be perceived as political gestures, sometimes worthy, sometimes farcical, kept afloat mainly by international charity or local chicanery.

Durability

From the history just recounted it is clear that most small states fit the criterion of durability no better than that of substantiality. Most are barely a human generation old, many still younger. Only the few residual European buffers and enclaves vaunt an origin preceding the nation–state epoch. Certain other small states are quite venerable as social units, to be sure, but their sovereign status is much more recent. (One exception is Barbados, more self-governing in the 17th and 18th centuries than many para-sovereign entities today.) The postwar demise of such states as Estonia, Latvia, and Lithuania strengthens the general impression that small states are frequently at risk, their sovereignty of limited duration. And the very newness of most present-day small states contributes to the common view of their evanescent and insubstantial character. We readily assume that they are apt to submerge as speedily as they have emerged.

Popular consensus

The sanction of a common culture and common purpose endorsed the growth of the 19th-century nation–state. Consensuality remains the essential justification of most of them today, notwithstanding recent emphasis on disaffected ethnic and regional minorities (Isaacs 1975). The *raison d'être* of the modern nation–state is that its citizens share its symbolic identity and participate in its functioning – paying taxes, obeying its laws, serving in its armed forces, being socialized in its schools – through allegiance rather than coercion. (I am conscious how ludicrous this generalization seems when applied, say, to South Africa, or Indonesia, or Chile, and I do not mean to imply that the pacification of dissidents in such states is a proof of popular acquiescence.) In Gellner's (1983) terms, the nation–state embodies the transition from oligarchic despotism over a voiceless majority to a more or less democratically realized consensus among a largely homogeneous and literate population.

How nearly small states approach this ideal is hard to estimate. Smallness, isolation, and their need, as dwarfs in a world of giants, to assert their identities induce their inhabitants to link their personal identities closely with that of the state itself. In this they conform with the criteria enunciated by most Utopian theorists since Aristotle (Hein 1985). And small states are less likely than large ones to suffer ethnic or religious cleavage – although when such divisions surface, as in Cyprus or Sri Lanka, they may be more crippling. On the other hand their recent emergence from the crucible of imperial rule means that many if not most small states endure the usual Third World deprivations (Harden 1985, Diggines 1985). Intense class divisions and highly visible extremes of wealth and poverty, privilege and squalor, power and impotence, make consensus and democracy in many small states more pious principles than practical realities.

These negative conclusions should be qualified in two respects, however. Firstly, the very smallness of small states gives their inhabitants an influence *vis-à-vis* their leaders denied to most in larger entities. Rulers known personally even to the poorest are unlikely to seek, let alone to succeed, to ignore or exclude any group from consideration. And the leaders themselves are apt to retain and promote an ingrained sense of communality and equity, even egalitarianism. Secondly, the propensity of people in small states to emigrate while continuing to play a rôle in their home societies both amplifies and complicates local consensuality.

Small states and non-states

Small states thus strikingly diverge from those qualities most often associated with statehood. Moreover, no sharp boundaries distinguish small states from small entities that are not states. Processes comparable to those that today engender new small states not infrequently bring about their demise as autonomous units. By contrast, most large states seldom hover between being and nothingness; whatever their problems, they have amazing staying powers. Amin's excesses have ruined but not removed Uganda; ethnic rivalries and tribal hostilities led to prolonged civil war but left Nigeria intact; bankruptcy would not terminate Mexico's sovereign status; even the savaged states of Central America seem apt to endure as national units.

No such assurance augurs the persistence of smaller states. In many ways, small states have less in common with larger autonomous units than with non-sovereign entities of similar size, such as the French overseas *départements*, the Atlantic island dependencies of Portugal, the Pacific Trust territories. Some of these are in fact on the verge of statehood, and a few have recently reverted from it. Like most small states, these self-governing dependencies are mainly Third World territories of European conquest, indigenous decimation, foreign settlement, and creolized culture. A proper purview of small-state characteristics must therefore take these non-sovereign entities into consideration as well.

Features characteristic of small states

Beyond their disconformity with images of modern statehood, and their liability to evanesce, what qualities characterize small states? Few scholars have essayed anything beyond unsupported listings of traits. In voicing the need for a typology of small states, Pitt (1985) expressly comments on the absence of any existing framework. The few comparative studies made during the 1930s had no impact on later research, and generalizing has since become even more difficult, the confusion greater every passing decade; it seems that whatever is said of some small states can be disproved by reference to others (Amstrup 1976). Their very smallness makes them hard to comprehend collectively. Because small states are usually geographically remote from one another, have had quite different histories, and are institutionally as well as culturally diverse, it is hard to find, let alone validate, adequate comparable data on them.

Insularity

One geopolitical feature of small states nevertheless seems to me incontrovertible: insularity. Other analysts deny that islandness is a criterion. Being surrounded by water strikes Dommen (1980) as less consequential than smallness *per se*. Conceding that transport problems, biological endemism, and certain 'cultural factors' sharply differentiate islands from other micro-states, Selwyn (1980) none the less feels that to equate them with islands would be an 'illegitimate extension of biological categories to social relationships'.

Yet insularity is very much their common lot. Most small states and the overwhelming majority of quasi-autonomous entities are islands, parts of islands, or groups of islands. Only 20 of the 79 small territories in Harden's (1985) listing are not islands. And of these at least 7 are island-like – continental enclaves cut off from other states by physical barriers as formidable, if not more so, than the waters that maroon islands. The Guianas, the Arabian Gulf states, and Western Sahara lie islanded in their own continents by tropical rain forest or barren desert.

Other distinctive features markedly differentiate the 14

remaining small territories from the island majority. There are the destitute and impotent client states of Botswana, Swaziland, and Namibia, whose quasi-sovereignty serves South African convenience. There are the European relics, Luxembourg, Liechtenstein, and Andorra, along with the special-purpose states of San Marino, Monaco, and the Vatican City, set apart by their fiscal and social status within the European community. There are the coastal and peninsular residues of empire, Ceuta and Melilla, Gibraltar, the Panama Canal Zone; these are scarcely distinguishable from islands like Hong Kong and Macao, and like them destined for early absorption within contiguous mainland states. Finally there are the African states of Djibouti, Guinea-Bissau, Equatorial Guinea, Gabon, and The Gambia, their existence clouded by embroilment with larger neighbours; and Belize is likewise troubled by Guatemalan incursion. I particularize these anomalies to show that most of them are exceptions only in a superficial sense; they actually fortify rather than violate the near-universal insularity of small states. The circumstances of all but a tiny handful are genuinely insular.

To equate small-stateness with insularity would still be wrong, for the formula is highly asymmetrical: although the majority of small states are islands, the majority even of inhabited islands are not small states and unlikely ever to become such. Yet the histories and circumstances of these latter islands are also revealing, for they share important sociocultural characteristics with insular small states.

Insularity itself is not an easy condition to define. Islands exhibit a host of significant differences: there are large and small, oceanic and offshore, archipelagic clusters and isolates; some are homogeneous, others divided by sovereignty, ethnicity, language, or culture. This whole range of differences shows up in islands that are small states.

Third World Status?

These exceptions highlight one feature of small states intimately linked with their insularity: most of them are emphatically of the Third World. In Diggines' (1985) summary statement, they share problems of poverty, malnutrition, indebtedness, and political instability with other Third World states. The paradigmatic small state of our time is thus an insular entity of quite recent sovereignty and of Third World socio-economic rank.

Yet if small states can justifiably be lumped with persistent Third World difficulties and deprivations, they are in certain ways quite uncharacteristic of that realm. Few small states are to be found among the world's poorest countries. Most of them enjoy levels of living substantially above those of larger Third World states. Although they account for half of the world's sovereign entities, small states included only 7 of the least developed countries in 1982, in a UN calculation based on gross domestic product, the manufacturing proportion thereof, and adult literacy. And small states numbered only 8 out of 28 additional low-income countries, based on World Bank calculations of gross national product (*Geofile* 1982). In sum, small states account for half the global total but only one-fourth of the least prosperous moiety.

Small states are thus unlike other Third World countries in vital respects. In view of their miniscule size, they might be expected to register extremes of destitution elsewhere averaged out. But the opposite proves to be the case. The concomitants of dire, persistent poverty that afflict sizeable, often landlocked, countries such as Afghanistan, Bangladesh, Ethiopia, Malawi, Nepal, Niger, Sudan, and Uganda are not to be found in most small states.

Sociocultural and other traits: a holistic approach

The social and cultural features of small states are being treated separately from the economic and political issues that concern other chapters in this volume. To do this is difficult, for political and economic behaviour are subsumed within social structures, and along with environmental circumstances both ensue from and shape social and cultural traits. Not only are all these aspects of small-state life inseparable, they are *seen* to be so by the inhabitants. One effect of smallness is to dissolve the academic boundaries between such categories. Economic, political, religious, kinship, and other systems in small states tend not merely to overlap but to coincide; people expect every social act to have economic and political consequences, and vice versa (Benedict 1967).

The task of abstracting sociocultural characteristics is made more difficult by the paucity of attention they have generally received. Smallness has generated a substantial sociological and anthropological literature, but one that deals for the most part with relationships at a more microscopic scale than that of most small states. Research has focused on small groups within larger societies, village communities, and small-scale societies rather than small political entities (Benedict 1967, Pitt 1985, Doumenge 1985). I have alluded to complaints that small-state studies tend to be non-cumulative. But at least there is no shortage of work on such topics as tourism, monoculture, diseconomies of scale, governmental costs and benefits, or small-state international relations. On the social dimensions of small-state life nothing comprehensive has been written. Anthropological studies of particular entities abound, but few of these are readily generalizable. These topical disparities can be demonstrated from Comitas's (1977) comprehensive Caribbean bibliography, in which political and economic affairs (Chs 37–42, 57–63) cover 600 pages and social and cultural characteristics (Chs 19–26) less than 200 pages.

The topheavy emphasis on political and economic affairs also skews the terms of the debate between those who denigrate and those who extol small states. Critics base their attacks overwhelmingly on economic and political criteria. Some early analysts had seen them as useful alternatives to absolutist, centralized nation–states. But political precariousness and economic unviability – the lack of clout that led Churchill to term pre-Bismarckian German states 'pumpernickel principalities' – made small states anathema to 19th-century theorists (Schumacher 1974, Amstrup 1976). Economic and political disabilities dominate various lists of the disadvantages endured by small states, notably by insular ones. Small-state protagonists like President Gayoom of the Maldives, who told Commonwealth leaders in 1984 that it was not 'good enough for the small states . . . to be just well defended bastions of poverty', view economic development as 'the front line of battle' (Harden 1985:8).

By contrast, those who consider smallness a virtue often emphasize social and play down economic considerations. Hence Schumacher's (1974:68) assertion that 'people can be themselves only in small comprehensible groups', Selwyn's (1975) claim that people want national units small enough to identify with (as against mass anonymity), McRobie's (1981) and Max-Neff's (1982) emphasis on the human scale, self-reliance, non-violence, and Pitts (1985) stressing of harmony with nature. The virtues of smallness in Diggines' (1985) list are solely social.

Three clusters of sociocultural traits tend to feature small states: conservatism and adherence to tradition; the careful management of enforced intimacy; and a pervasive concern with autonomy. None of these traits is exclusive to residents of small states, but they are manifested more prominently there than elsewhere. And they are especially salient where smallness coincides with insularity. As concomitants of insularity, these traits also feature life in non-autonomous islands.

Conservatism and tradition

Those who live in small states cling tenaciously to familiar patterns of life. Their settled conservatism stems from a caution born of long experience with resources whose exploitation is severely limited by scale, by isolation, and by physical and economic hazards beyond their own control. These constraints incline residents toward the maintenance of continuity, the practice of conservation, and the hedging of bets by taking on multiple occupations.

Just as smallness cramps resource exploitation, so does it put many goods and services beyond local reach. Small states cannot afford amenities elsewhere taken for granted. Paved roads, electric power, piped water, and telephones may require equipment, capital outlay, or minimum levels of consumption that exceed local capacities. These diseconomies of scale are not static: advances in global technology progressively worsen the plight of small states. It is not enough for them to maintain a stable population, for social viability demands ever larger numbers of consumers. In large states big schools replace smaller ones, health facilities centralize to accommodate sophisticated medical equipment and facilities and services concentrate in bigger and bigger centres. Smallness deprives small states not only of new advances but even of previously customary services which technology has now made obsolete (Lowenthal 1976).

Small states are as fragile socially as ecologically and for similar reasons (MacArthur & Wilson 1967, Lack 1976, Lowenthal 1985). Smallness makes them excessively vulnerable to demographic change. Large states can undergo substantial population fluctuations without serious damage to resource management or institutional structures. But their small initial base and their precarious population–resource balance magnifies the impact of such changes in small states. A sudden or sustained increase stemming from mortality reduction or an influx of outsiders severely strains and may exhaust the state's limited resources. A sudden or sustained reduction owing to lower natality, epidemic disease, or increased rates of emigration has dire effects on productivity, resource maintenance, and social structure (Doumenge 1985). Where local enterprises and services are already marginal, even small imbalances can endanger the fabric: the departure of just a few workers, school children, or medical personnel may close a factory, a school, a cottage hospital, and erode the entire social structure.

Montserrat, which lost one-third of its inhabitants to Britain between 1957 and 1962, illustrates these social effects of sudden depletion. Had the loss been evenly distributed the damage would have been serious enough, but selective emigration made it far worse. Ninety-five per cent of the island's secondary school graduates left within a few years. The departure of trained personnel and potential leaders crippled government, business, and social services. In just one year, the Post Office and Treasury lost 70% of their employees. 'Temporary' promotions barely filled the places they vacated; junior clerks became inspectors, typists from one department became supervisors in another, and incompetents were coddled lest they too should leave (Lowenthal & Comitas 1962, Lowenthal 1972, Philpott 1973).

Mass departure, especially of the able-bodied young, not only cripples agriculture and leaves arable lands idle, it leaves behind a residual population that is less innovative and more dependent, unable to cope even with normal environmental vicissitudes or to sustain traditional social networks.

Well aware of the fragility of their economic and social fabric, small-state inhabitants are conscious that any major change comes at the risk of catastrophic loss. Hence they often view innovation with profound mistrust and deal conservatively with most decisions they must take. Realizing that potential improvement may ultimately entail an unacceptable shift in resource exploitation or in the scale of local enterprise, they usually opt to conserve what they have rather than venture new development. 'Progress' may upset the delicate equilibrium of services and goods that is the lynchpin of community interdependency; short-term gains may spell ruin in the longer run.

The virtues of stability induce small entities to bolster traditional ways even at pecuniary sacrifice. Thus Orcadians rejected uranium exploration lest success leave their traditional farming and fishing economy in a shambles (Wilson 1979). Jersey protects its traditional agricultural sector not because farming is economically profitable (it yields only 6% of Jersey's gross domestic product and employs only 10% of its work-force) but because it is important to maintain the rural fabric for visual and social reasons. Because the farming community is the vital core of their way of life, Jerseyans restrict development and curtail their economic appetite in order to protect that community (Jersey Island Development Commission 1983).

Andorra similarly adheres to traditional land use. Tourism, expatriate retirement homes, and duty-free shopping facilities have transformed this small state's economy since World War II; foreign-owned enterprises now dominate the capital. But Andorrans continue to raise one of their staple commodities, low-grade tobacco, which is harvested as usual but now sold off to foreign entrepreneurs, who are required to purchase amounts proportional to their trade; the entire crop is then dumped and burned. Andorra thus keeps up a traditional landscape and way of life as an attraction for visitors, a source of employment for inhabitants, and a form of insurance against the vicissitudes of international commerce.

Ecological caution similarly pervades life for the 1500 inhabitants of Barbuda in the West Indies. On this dry, infertile island,

Barbudans holding and working the land in common have combined extensive grazing and swidden agriculture with fishing, lobstering, and charcoal burning in a self-sustaining fashion. Periodic attempts by outside authorities to develop the island more intensively have foundered owing to environmental constraints and local opposition; meanwhile, Barbudans secure their continued livelihood and resource base through the diversity and conservation-oriented quality of their enterprises. Communal ownership and shifting cultivation condemned by 'experts' as backward and wasteful are in fact well adapted to the local environment, husbanding an ecology which permanent cultivation would severely impair (Lowenthal & Clarke 1979).

In short, small-state conservatism encourages resource diversification in place of monoculture, keeps open many possible occupational options against the failure of some, inhibits specialization in favour of all-round competence, maintains economic and social resources in long-term balance, and celebrates the virtues of stability and tradition.

Managing intimacy

A second consequence of smallness in states is that their inhabitants must get along with one another. Most of them grow up within an interdependent network where each person figures many times over; as in Gluckman's 'multiplex' societies, nearly every social relationship serves many interests. Relationships in small states seldom concentrate on a single act or specific function but tend instead to be functionally diffuse and to last for a long time, though their specific content changes over the course of the life span (Benedict 1967).

Small-state social connections interlock in the fashion Demos (1982:311–12) describes for 17th-century New Englanders:

> Imagine the bricklayer who rebuilds your house is also the constable who brings you a summons to court, an occupant of the next bench in the meetinghouse, the owner of a share adjacent to one of yours in the 'upland' meadow, a fellow-member of the local . . . militia, an occasional companion at the

local 'ordinary', a creditor (for services performed for you the previous summer but not yet paid for), a potential customer for wool from the sheep which you have begun to raise, the father of a child who is currently a bond-servant in your house, a colleague on a town committee to repair and improve the public roadways... And so on. Do the two of you enjoy your shared experiences? Not necessarily. Do you know each other well? Most assuredly.

Life in most small states still exhibits such multiple and enduring relationships. Because small-state geography continues to impose particularistic patterns of social life no longer common in the wider world, visitors to small states often gain an impression of stepping back in time.

The small size of the social field, together with ingrained awareness of ecological and social fragility, fosters what I term 'managed intimacy'. Small-state inhabitants learn to get along, like it or not, with folk they will know in myriad contexts over their whole lives. To enable the social mechanism to function without undue stress, they minimize or mitigate overt conflict. They become expert at muting hostility, deferring their own views, containing disagreement, avoiding dispute, in the interest of stability and compromise. In a large state it is easy to take issue with an antagonist you need seldom if ever come across again; to differ with someone in a small state where the two of you share a long mutual history and expect to go on being involved in countless ways is quite another matter. Not simply the small size of the state but the complexity and durability of most relationships fosters sophisticated modes of accommodation.

I am not suggesting that small states are all sweet harmony. To the contrary, bitter and prolonged factionalism occurs and can have devastating effects (Benedict 1967). But partly because factional differences are seen to be potentially so damaging, inhabitants of small states often take pains to conceal or mute the hostilities they may feel. In discussion, they seldom express opinions dogmatically and are reluctant to voice divergent views. Assertiveness is proscribed: public meetings may open with prolonged periods of agonizing silence because no one wants to be the first to speak (Cohen 1982a,b,c).

Three peripheral effects of managing smallness deserve further mention: familism, intergroup tensions and emigrant rôles.

Familism

Bonds of family underpin small-state intimacies. Families generate most other linkages; family loyalties suffuse small-state economic, social, and political enterprise. Those in positions of consequence and authority in small states with still smaller élites are bound to be interrelated. Large-state outsiders consider nepotism morally wrong; to use a position of power or authority to benefit one's relatives seems iniquitous (Benedict 1967). But where everyone is related personal involvement in public affairs is inevitable and nepotism unavoidable. Small-state citizens accept kinship relations as the warp and woof of public affairs and family favouritism as a fact of life. Theirs is a realistic perspective on how human beings normally conduct their affairs.

Intergroup tensions

I suggested above that small states tend to mute intergroup tensions, much as they do personal hostilities, because they can otherwise become serious impediments to harmony and dangerous harbingers of a divisive future. Two opposing ethnic groups of equivalent size or power especially aggravate such tensions, as Cyprus, Guyana, and Sri Lanka variously illustrate. Perhaps the most cogent case is Fiji, where indigenous Fijians still hold 85% of the land and after six generations still consider Indians non-Fijians. Numerically almost equal, Fijians and Indians confront each other in an island state whose resources are strictly limited and zealously protected. The constraints of smallness exacerbate communal rivalries, for everyone knows there is only so much – land, jobs, money, power – to be shared.

What is remarkable about Fiji is how both sides normally gloss over these tensions. As an Indian Fijian remarked at an international conference recently (Prasad 1986):

> We have never had an outbreak of the type of communal strife that rocks many other plural societies. We live in peace and

harmony ... and we expect to remain that way. While other multi-cultural nations must contend with ... violence, tension, suspicion, and hatred, Fiji moves ahead in an orderly and harmonious fashion.... Resentment is never strong enough to destroy the bonds of understanding, affection and tolerance that unite us as a nation.... We may complain about each other in private ... but that does not stand in the way of friendship, tolerance and understanding.... The good engulfs the bad.

And how does this happen? Well, 'Fiji society is conservative. We don't really like extremists. They make us suspicious and uncomfortable.' In short, as his Fijian co-discussant remarked, 'In a small country there is no room to differ.' It is not surprising that one of the few local academics willing to speak out frankly about communal tensions recently left the University of the South Pacific to go to Hawaii. Ethnic tensions can be contained by personal familiarity, by a recognized need for co-operation, and by mutual fears of conflagration and outside intervention. But meanwhile no one must rock the boat.

Emigrant rôles

The rôle of small-state emigrants is a third special consequence of smallness. Emigration is a ubiquitous aspect of modern life, but in many small states, as in small islands generally, it has long been a persistent feature. The strength and durability of their emigrant ties distinguishes small states from other cradles of emigration. Those who leave are seldom lost to their homelands but extend their boundaries, helping to bolster small-state economies, strengthen their autonomy, and resist unwanted change. The sudden loss of many able-bodied may strain a state's stability, but remittances cushion the departure, and migration and return often become an established routine, working away a normal part of the life cycle. Few small-state emigrants stay away for good; many remain citizens. The effective number of Anguillans or Barbudans or Caymanians is more than double the resident population at any given time. Thus many small states survive as social entities when their apparent numbers seem to doom them.

Periodic return of the absent ensures continuity and community participation.

Emigrant communities are highly supportive in various ways. Cook Islanders in New Zealand and Papuans in Australia show that networks of obligation with homelands can persist for generations (Graves *et al.* 1983, Rumbiak 1985). Diaspora Guamanians in California and West Indians in Toronto retain or replicate so much of their homeland culture they replenish rather than diminish it (Underwood 1985, Marshall 1985). Indeed, emigrants whose education and economic success foster self-awareness often assert their national identity more strongly in exile than at home (Lowenthal 1985).

Frequent movement back and forth makes it easier for returning migrants to fit in again at home. When many of its citizens have experienced life abroad, a small state is less apt to be polarized between those who have kept the faith at home and those who have sought wider horizons. Emigrants now tend to see the homeland less as a place in need of development than as a haven from the metropolitan hurly-burly. While success abroad reinforces a sense of personal achievement, return reinforces local conservative and conservationist tendencies. Like tourists, returning emigrants are sometimes lured back by displays of traditionalism that may belie residents' own preferences for modern convenience. But even newly invented relics and contrived solidarity with ancient ways may in time become respectable features of small-state 'traditional' life. Emigrants contribute more than remittances and rallying points, however; they often return home to reshape society with their investments, their metropolitan contacts and concepts, and their cosmopolitan energy and dynamism (Doumenge 1985, Richardson 1985).

Yet the small-state propensity to hive off actively involved migrant communities leaves the boundaries of the state itself in doubt. With a network of Barbadian social and economic enterprises extending from Bridgetown to Brooklyn and from London to Toronto, is it realistic to think of Barbados purely as a small Caribbean island state? Barbados is that, to be sure, but it is also those Barbadians spread throughout the Caribbean and beyond. And from Anguilla to Ascension, Guam to Guyana, São

Tomé to Suriname, most small states exhibit comparable overseas networks (Pitt 1985).

Obsessive autonomism

People in small states zealously guard their statehood. Yet statehood costs them dear. Small-state governments are both meddlesome and burdensome. In general, a government's share of total enterprise varies inversely with state size. Any state requires an irreducible minimum of infrastructure, and the smaller the state the larger its government looms in its economy and society. The need to mount services that private entrepreneurs cannot afford further aggrandizes the government's sphere. Maintaining autonomy, both substantive and symbolic, likewise demands a palpable government presence. Small-scale governments are characteristically topheavy.

The omnipresent government, moreover, feels omnipotent. Its aggrandized rôles make it a party to every significant enterprise. As it controls access to most skills and funding, no one can move far up any ladder of enterprise without bumping into government. A small-state government can thus veto any undertaking that clashes with its own overweening prerogatives. Every entrepreneur must play ball with its leaders. This closes off many potentially attractive avenues of innovation (Benedict 1967).

The weight of government in small states exacts other costs too. One stems from the political personalism noted above in connection with nepotism. But there are graver problems than favouritism. Inhabitants of small states have virtually no recourse to impartial authority. Neither the civil service nor the judiciary can escape influence, if not coercion, exerted by political leaders. These costs were spelled out in graphic detail by W. Arthur Lewis (1965), in explaining why West Indian micro-states would be disastrous alternatives to a federation. His arguments remain germane, though it is less clear today how large a state ought to be to avoid such disabilities.

Yet however costly or coercive their governments, most inhabitants of small states prefer these liabilities to those they would probably suffer should they lose their sovereignty. Even clustered among supportive neighbours, small states sense the pervasive pressure of nearby larger states and great powers. These outsiders not only interfere in times of crisis; they impinge on the day-to-day livelihood and well-being of small states, circumscribing their autonomy in countless ways.

Small-state self-rule is thus not just empty chauvinism; it expresses a cohesion needed to bolster autonomy against the incursions of larger states, the pressures of global development, and the perils of piracy. To this end, small states inculcate attachments to anything national, everything that distinguishes them from other states, their people from other people. As Doumenge (1985:102) notes for islanders, they 'are never happier than when asserting they are completely different from their neighbours'. Hence their ritual emphasis on endemic parliamentary and other institutions and their exaggerated claims to cultural unanimity. Linguistic nationalism in Iceland and Ireland, the Faroes and Luxembourg, serves alike to exclude non-nationals and to buttress the sense of belonging among those who are nationals.

Little wonder that small states sometimes seem paranoid about external subversion. Keeping outsiders from owning local land and other resources is a *sine qua non* of continued local control; local control alone makes statehood viable. Barbuda's prolonged efforts to keep in force an old ordinance affirming communal ownership of all local land by Barbudans alone exemplifies the point (Lowenthal & Clarke 1980, 1981).

Thus small states safeguard whatever autonomy they have and strive to enlarge it. The bloated infrastructures of Nauru and Barbados, Sark and Man, are the envy of devolutionists in Brittany and Cornwall. Self-government is expensive, and the smaller the government the higher the per capita cost. But a measure of sovereignty yields manifold benefits. A state that rules itself can prime its own pump. Even an inefficient or venal government creates employment, generates business, and disperses funds (Lowenthal 1962, 1976, 1984, Lowenthal & Clarke 1980). It can promote fund-raising schemes – stamps, coins, casinos, tax havens – seldom available to dependencies. Sovereignty also yields access to international aid agencies. When

Grenada opted for sovereign status in 1972, Eric Gairy, the island's then leader, was asked how Grenada would be able to afford it. 'Grenada will not support independence', he answered. 'Independence will support Grenada' (V. Lewis 1974, Lowenthal 1984). (At least it enriched Gairy.)

Autonomy also buffers states against imperial parsimony. Larger states are often mean and grudging in doling out aid to outlying appendages, especially when diseconomies of scale make services there more costly. By contrast, a self-governing state can decide its own priorities, allocating funds for some services outsiders might think unnecessary, but forgoing other expenditures.

Most important, autonomous citizens can freely express and enjoy their autonomy, however self-inflated this self-image may appear to others. Self-government enables entities to arouse public protest, campaign against great power iniquities, mobilize against takeover or abandonment. No wonder that Anguilla's 5000 and Barbuda's 1500 inhabitants sought sovereign status (Clarke 1971, Westlake 1972); that Orkney and Shetland warned Scottish devolutionists the islands might go their own way, taking North Sea oil with them (*Orcadian* 1975); and that Nantucket and Martha's Vineyard threatened to secede from Massachusetts unless the Bay State agreed to a federal bill to protect their environments from development (Schumacher 1977). Indeed, the use of para-sovereign status to screen out entrepreneurial intrusion is itself an innovative development coveted by regional separatists the world over.

Conclusion

My listing of small-state sociocultural characteristics is by no means comprehensive. But it seems to me to highlight features on balance more advantageous than otherwise, worthy of note and perhaps even of emulation in a world increasingly given over to superpowers and multinational agencies, one too large and remote from private concerns for most citizens to feel that they belong, let alone play any real political rôle.

Small states generally get a bad press. Apart from their own problematic viability, they are arraigned as foci of global instability, touchpoints or power vacuums liable to ignite global tensions. Grenada is often so cited, even in this volume. However, great-power animosities generally come to a boil over global issues or larger states – Afghanistan, Cuba, Nicaragua. Small states lack sufficient infrastructure or room for manoeuvre to make them truly useful international pawns. Nor are small states much to be feared as loci of global lawlessness. Small states produce drugs in negligible quantities, and seldom harbour régimes censured for torture or other savage violations of human rights.

Small states have positive as well as negative virtues. Their existence enhances human diversity. Their sovereignty fosters the continuance of cultures of myriad kinds. Their devotion to their own survival, narrowly chauvinist though it may sometimes seem, nurtures attachments to particular and uniquely precious lands and landscapes. No one would wish to preserve a small state as a museum piece in the modern world against its inhabitants' own wishes. But by the same token, no one ought to seek to deprive them of that status against their will.

References

Amstrup, N. 1976. The perennial problem of small states: a survey of research efforts. *Cooperation and Conflict* **11**, 163–82.

Benedict, B. 1967. Sociological aspects of smallness. In *Problems of Smaller Territories*, B. Benedict (ed.) 45–55. London: Athlone Press.

Clarke, C. G. 1971. Political fragmentation in the Caribbean: the case of Anguilla. *Canadian Geogr.* **6**, 130–9.

Cohen, A. P. 1982a. A sense of time, a sense of place: the meaning of close social association in Whalsay, Shetland. In *Belonging: identity and social organisation in Britain*, A. P. Cohen (ed.), 21–49. Manchester: Manchester University Press.

Cohen, A. P. 1982b. Belonging: the experience of culture. In *Belonging: identity and social organisation in Britain*, A. P. Cohen (ed.), 1–17. Manchester: Manchester University Press.

Cohen, A. P. 1982c. Blockade: a case study of local consciousness in an extra-local event. In *Belonging: identity and social organisation in Britain*, A. P. Cohen (ed.), 292–321. Manchester: Manchester University Press.

Cohen, A. P. 1982. *Belonging: identity and social organisation in British rural cultures*. Manchester: Manchester University Press.

Comitas, L. 1977. *The complete Caribbeana 1900–1975: a bibliographic guide to the scholarly literature* (4 vols). Millwood, NY: Kraus-Thomson.

Demos, J. P. 1982. *Entertaining Satan: witchcraft and the culture of early New England*. New York: Oxford University Press.

Diggines, C. E. 1985. The problems of small states. *Round Table* **74**, 191–205.

Dommen, E. C. 1980. Some distinguishing characteristics of island states. In *Islands*, E. C. Dommen (ed.), 931–43. Oxford: Pergamon Press.

Doumenge, F. 1985. The viability of small intertropical islands. In *States, microstates and islands*, E. C. Dommen & P. L. Hein (eds), 70–118. London: Croom Helm.

Gellner, E. 1983. *Nations and nationalism*. Oxford: Basil Blackwell.

Geofile. 1982. The 31 least developed countries. No. 1.

Graves, T. D., N. B. Graves, V. N. Semu & I. Ah Sam. 1983. The price of ethnic identity: maintaining kin ties among Pacific islands immigrants to New Zealand. In *Symposium on mobility, identity, and policy in the Island Pacific*. Pacific Science Congress 15, Dunedin, New Zealand, Section C, unpublished.

Harden, S. (ed.) 1985. *Small is dangerous: micro states in a macro world*. London: Frances Pinter.

Hein, P. L. 1985. The study of microstates. In *States, microstates and islands*, E. C. Dommen and P. L. Hein, (eds), 16–29. London: Croom Helm.

Isaacs, H. R. 1975. *Idols of the tribe: group identity and political change*. New York: Harper & Row.

Jersey Island Development Commission 1983. *Island plan I: survey and issues*. States of Jersey.

Kohr, L. 1973. *Development without aid*. Swansea: Christopher Davies.

Kohr, L. 1977. *The overdeveloped nations*. Swansea: Christopher Davies.

Lack, D. 1976. *Island biology*. Oxford: Basil Blackwell.

Levin, B. 1977. A nation for all that, even if it is just a dot on the map. *The Times* 23 February, 14.

Lewis, V. 1974. Commentary. In *Independence for Grenada – myth or reality?* 53–5. St Augustine, Trinidad: Institute of International Relations.

Lewis, W. A. 1965. *The agony of the eight*. Bridgetown, Barbados: Advocate.

Lowenthal, D. 1962. Levels of West Indian government. *Social and Economic Studies* **11**, 363–91.

Lowenthal, D. 1976. The return of the non-native: new life for depopulated areas. In *Population at Microscale*, L. A. Kosinski & J. W. Webb (eds), 143–8. Palmerston North: New Zealand Geographical Society.

Lowenthal, D. 1972. *West Indian societies*. London: Oxford University Press.

Lowenthal, D. 1984. An island is a world: the problem of Caribbean insularity. In *Perspectives on Caribbean regional identity*, E. M. Thomas-

Hope (ed.), 109–21. Liverpool University Centre for Latin American Studies, no. 11.

Lowenthal, D. 1985. Mobility and identity in the island Pacific: a critique. In *Mobility and identity in the island Pacific (Pacific Viewpoint*: 26, 1), M. Chapman (ed.), 316–26. Wellington: Victoria University.

Lowenthal, D. & C. G. Clarke 1979. Common lands, common aims: the distinctive Barbudan community. In *Peasants, plantations and rural communities in the Caribbean*, M. Cross & A. Marks (eds), 142–59. Leiden; Royal Institute of Linguistics and Anthropology.

Lowenthal, D. & C. G. Clarke 1980. Island orphans: Barbuda and the rest. *Journal of Commonwealth and Comparative Politics* 18, 293–307.

Lowenthal, D. & C. G. Clarke 1981. Barbuda alone. *Geographical Magazine* 53, 465–70.

Lowenthal, D. & L. Comitas 1962. Emigration and depopulation: some neglected aspects of population geography. *Geogr. Rev.* 52, 195–210.

MacArthur, R. H. & E. O. Wilson 1967. *The theory of island biogeography*. Princeton: Princeton University Press.

McRobie, C. A. 1981. *Small is possible*. London: Cape.

Marshall, D. 1985. Mobility, identity, and policy in the Eastern Caribbean. In *Mobility and identity in the island Pacific*, M. Chapman (ed.), 265–79. Wellington: Victoria University.

Max-Neef, N. 1982. *From the outside looking in*. Uppsala: Dag Hammarskjöld Foundation.

Orcadian 1975. 29 May, 1.

Philpott, S. B. 1973. *West Indian migration: the Montserrat case*. London: Athlone Press.

Pitt, D. 1985. Anthropological and sociological theories and microstates. In *States, microstates and islands*, E. C. Dommen & P. L. Hein (eds), 30–9. London: Croom Helm.

Prasad, S. 1986. Ethnic relations in island development: the Fiji experience. In *Islands '86 Conference*, Victoria, BC, unpublished.

Richardson, B. C. 1985. *Panama money in Barbados, 1900–1920*. Knoxville: University of Tennessee Press.

Rumbiak, M. 1985. Nimboran migration to Jayapura, Irian Jaya. In *Mobility and identity in the island Pacific*, M. Chapman (ed.), 206–20. Wellington: Victoria University.

Schumacher, E. F. 1974. *Small is beautiful*. London: Sphere Books.

Schumacher, E. 1977. Islanders off Massachusetts get tough about secession. *International Herald Tribune* 11 April, 3.

Selwyn, P. 1975. Introduction: room for manoeuvre? In *Development policy in small countries*, P. Selwyn (ed.), 8–24. London: Croom Helm.

Selwyn, P. 1980. Smallness and islandness. In *Islands*, E. C. Dommen (ed.), Oxford: Pergamon.

Seton-Watson, H. 1977. *Nations and states: an enquiry into the origins of nations and the politics of nationalism*. Boulder, Colo.: Westview Press.

Underwood, R. A. 1985. Excursions into inauthenticity: the Chamorros of Guam, In *Mobility and identity in the island Pacific*, M. Chapman (ed.), 160–84. Wellington: Victoria University.

Westlake, D. E. 1972. *Under an English heaven.* New York: Simon & Shuster.

Wilson, B. 1979. Orkney sinks uranium plan. *Observer* 30 December.

3 Economic issues

Tony Payne

The study of the economics of small states may be said to have begun at the 1957 conference of the International Economic Association (IEA), which was devoted to a consideration of the 'economic consequences of the size of nations'. Indeed, introducing a subsequent collection of the papers presented at the conference, Robinson was able to report that 'many of us had a feeling of incredulity when we failed to discover a volume of antecedent literature such as the subject seemed to have deserved' (Robinson 1960: xiii). No such remark could be made today, for since that time there is no doubt that a prolific literature has emerged on the subject.

Yet one can still legitimately feel a sense of disappointment on reading much of what has been written about the economic implications of smallness. The main problem has been that the analysis has never been grounded in a common economic definition of small size. As a result, it slips and slides over the general area of smallness in a loose and unsatisfactory fashion. Even when population is taken as the agreed basis, the variations of view offered are enormous. Kuznets (1960), for example, took a 10 million population as the category, Demas (1965) narrowed it to 5 million, but Chenery & Taylor (1968) pushed it up again to a figure of 15 million. At the other extreme Kohr (1977) has suggested that the 'economic optimum social size' requires only an adult membership of perhaps 1000 or a full membership of 4000 to 5000 inhabitants.

In addition to these confusions, there is the further analytical difficulty that small states include those with developed and developing economies, the problems of which are patently not the same. All too often in the literature on the economics of smallness this has not been sufficiently appreciated. For example, the two case studies of small economies presented at the 1957 IEA conference were those of Belgium and Switzerland. No detailed attention was drawn to what might be thought to be the special characteristics of small developing economies.

The meaning of all this for the particular purposes of this study (which defines a small state as one with a population of under a million, most of which also fall into the 'developing' category) is that much of the literature on the economics of small size is tangential at best and irrelevant at worst. It was thus not invalid for the Commonwealth Secretary-General, in addressing a conference on the policy choices facing small Commonwealth economies, held in 1981, to observe that 'relatively little economic research has been done on the problems of small economies' and further to complain that 'there is also lack of adequate statistical information and sustained empirical work on the past development experience' (Jalan 1982: Preface). Nevertheless, we have to build upon what has been learnt about the economies of this type of state and it is to the exegesis of this body of knowledge that the chapter now turns.

Neoclassical constraints

The major thrust of the early work that was undertaken was devoted to identifying the main economic characteristics which small states had in common. They were typically viewed as constraints upon development and nearly always examined within a neoclassical framework. In the Benedict volume, for example, Knox engaged in precisely this kind of exercise (Knox 1967). He concluded that, broadly speaking, small states had small home markets and were likely to have at their disposal less diverse resources than might be found in larger states. This tallied with the high degree of specialization found in small states. As he put it, 'they generally concentrate what resources they have on a comparatively limited range of products and satisfy their other requirements through international trade' (Knox 1967:35). Small states were therefore likely to be more heavily dependent on foreign trade than large states. Associated with this was a concentration in both the sources of their imports and the destinations of their exports, as well as in the range of commodities typically exported.

Other writers have built upon these observations to the extent that something of a classic syndrome of constraints and disabilities has emerged. The best summary of these arguments has been provided by Ward (1975), who set out the problem in traditional supply and demand terms. Among the fundamental supply problems he listed were:

(a) *Land.* Not only is land restricted in area, but often the inherent physical properties of the land as well as its variety of resources are limited. In addition, in so far as many small developing countries are tropical islands and desirable for tourist and residential expatriate development, there may be problems of controlling real estate speculation and land price rises.

(b) *Labour.* There is likely to be a narrower spread of labour skills in a small state, as well as comparatively less effective manpower capability, even though the proportion of people in the labour force may be the same as in a larger developing country. The country will probably also be more affected by inbalances in its demographic structure, especially of an age, sex, or racial nature.

(c) *Capital.* In a small developing country a large proportion of the available capital will probably be owned and controlled by foreign organizations. The government also has to rely heavily on outside grants and loans of one sort or another. In general, therefore, the borrower is small in relation to both actual and potential lenders and investors.

(d) *Entrepreneurship.* Independent local businessmen in small countries tend to be few in number, to lack organizational skills and to face many obstacles in their local economic environment, such as the difficulty of securing freehold tenure for industrial activities.

Among the demand constraints mentioned by Ward, two were given prominence:

(a) *The domestic market.* The basic problem of the limited size and narrowness of the domestic market is often further complicated by demographic characteristics which increase the diversification of the pattern of demand and lead to even greater fragmentation of an already small market. The maximum, let alone optimum, technically efficient scale of plant that can be introduced in such small economies thus renders some productive activities completely uneconomical unless a substantial export potential is also available.

(b) *External markets.* As a result of these limitations the rate of growth of the economy in a small state tends to be primarily a function of the rate of growth of exports of goods and services. In turn, as previously noted, exports are typically highly concentrated on one or two products, whereas imports are very diverse. The small-state economy is thus dependent on foreign trade but lacks the capacity to exert any influence over the international market either in respect of price or quotas.

Ward's analysis has been described at some length, not only because of its intrinsic usefulness and summary value but also because he derives from it a classification of small developing countries. A fourfold typology was proposed, of which the Type IV country is of particular relevance to this study. It is small in population size and cultivable land area, has a low GNP per capita but a high share of trade in GNP, and relies primarily on export markets for its economic development (Ward 1975:132). Within this category in turn, two variants were specified: island economies, which face problems of relative isolation, costly transport and difficult access to larger markets but can at least readily assess customs duties and indirect taxation in general; and landlocked territories, which potentially have access to a much wider range of neighbouring markets without incurring excessive transport costs but cannot so easily estimate indirect tax revenues in preparing development plans. Ward's formulation is apposite because it is Type IV countries with which we shall subsequently be dealing.

Dependency theory

It should be noted that, even in the work of neoclassical economists concerned with size, the fact that small-state economies had necessarily to exist within a wider international economic system was not ignored. The reliance of such economies on foreign trade was commented upon by just about everybody, but it was not elevated into the centrepiece of analysis. That had to await the advent of dependency theory. The clash of the two perspectives was revealed very clearly in a seminal book review of Demas's text, *The economics of development in small countries* (Demas 1965). Demas had argued, in broadly conventional terms, that a small domestic market imposed sharp limits on the process of import-substitution industrialization and thus removed the option of balanced growth, incorporating a roughly equal mixture of export stimulation and import substitution, a goal which he believed could only really be attained by large continental countries.

Yet, in his review of this argument, another Caribbean economist, Best, criticized Demas for his almost exclusive emphasis on 'natural' variables, such as size, as opposed to 'societal', and therefore 'manipulable', policy variables (Best 1971:29). In this view, Demas failed to demonstrate 'that smallness necessarily places economies at a disadvantage in the exploitation of their own "endowment" of resources' and often seemed to imply that 'the significant feature of the development of what he classifies as transformed and wealthy nations was the fact that they began as economies with large populations and favourable resource endowments' (Best 1971:29). Might it not have been, Best asked, 'that the crucial factor was their ability to discover and exploit whatever resources they had?' If, as Best believed and implied, the answer was in the affirmative, then it followed that 'there may be a path of innovation which may lead to the fullest transformation of a small economy' and that, from an analytic point of view, 'the bulk of the potential for explaining economic growth – even in small countries – has still to come from more systematic examination of the instruments that control rather than of the "natural" variables themselves' (Best 1971:29). In short, should not economists place emphasis as much upon the organization of small economies as on their size *per se*?

Neither in his review, nor indeed subsequently, did Best spell out the path of transformation that was, in his opinion, available to small economies, but he did at least succeed in introducing an entirely new note into the debate about the economics of smallness. That note was indicative of the dependency thinking which came to dominate the study of the Third World in the 1970s. In this vision, underdevelopment was seen no longer as a passive condition in which states found themselves at birth but rather as a phenomenon brought about by their dependence upon, and peripheral location within, the international economy as a whole. The economies of small states were, generally speaking, more dependent and peripheral than most and so it became commonplace to talk and write of small, dependent economies.

This was satisfactory enough as long as it was understood to mean that such economies were both small and dependent, but it became misleading as soon as it was assumed, as often it was, that they were dependent because they were small. The thrust of dependency analysis was to identify a series of factors (the rôle of foreign investment, the position of certain comprador classes, a tradition of monoculture, the intermediary function of the state) capable of explaining underdevelopment and economic weakness quite apart from the fact of small size. Small economies could thus be developed, just as much as large economies could be underdeveloped. With this distinction clear, dependency theory can be seen to have added something of value to the analysis of the economic constraints facing small states.

Development strategy

The other half of the debate about the economics of smallness has been focused on the solution rather than the problem. The argument has related to strategy and the question of what small states can actually do to overcome or ameliorate their particular economic problems. To start with a negative point, it has usually been accepted in the literature that the option of autarky, for all its many attractions to those of a romantic disposition, is simply not realistic. Countries that chose to withdraw from the international economic system would have to meet their food and energy needs from local resources, and these two items constitute the major imports of nearly all small countries. To become self-sufficient in food would in most cases require their inhabitants to relearn the agricultural skills of growing food for local consumption after centuries of plantation agriculture with its different techniques; to become self-sufficient in energy might be literally impossible for many countries. In other words, it would only be by accepting primitive standards of development for all the people that autarky could be made in any way practicable, and these days there are very few, if any, states or islands remote enough for such a strategy to be politically sustainable. Even in the Pacific, perhaps the one remaining part of the world in which such ideas do not immediately appear absurd, the pace of absorption into the world economic and political system is quickening all the time.

The converse of this rejection of self-sufficiency has often been a firm assertion of the need for small states to achieve closer and more effective integration with the international economy. Yet it would not be automatically right to believe that the more extensive the trade linkages, the greater the capital flows, the better is the prospect of development for small states. Dommen & Hein (1985:180) note the conventional critique of this argument, even if they do not sympathize with it:

> One of the main problems which small islands may face, in implementing their trade policy and entering into some of the most dynamic sectors available, is that their policies may appear unfashionable, if not downright unpopular, in international 'development circles'. A number of islands are already accused of encouraging smuggling or harbouring dubious operators. Any mention of tourism, overseas entrepreneurs, migration, work on foreign ships, i.e. crews of convenience, export processing zones, tax havens, offshore banking, strategic bases, concentration on specialized exotic products, flags of convenience, etc. goes against the mainstream of the prescriptions of self-reliant, grass-root development apologists.

Fashion and popularity are not, however, the key issues. What is revealed by the observation is the need to introduce some consideration of political ideology into the discussion of development strategy for small states.

Small states do have choices to make about how to organize their economies. These will be limited, but they embrace a wider set of possibilities than that of complete acquiescence in a dependence upon international capitalism. That needs to be remembered, for too often the debate has been conducted wholly within capitalist norms, as if manifestly nothing else is even conceivable. At the other extreme, of course, it is very much a moot point whether 'socialism in one (small) country' is possible. In fact, very little attention has been given to the idea. Just about the only economist to have tackled the question directly is Thomas. In *Dependence and transformation*, published in 1974, he explicitly attempted to construct a socialist development path for small developing economies. The basic idea advanced was that a strategy which hinged on 'planning resource use and consumption in order to attain previously established material goals' (Thomas 1974:124) could lead small states from a position of neocolonial dependence to becoming meaningful examples of socialist interdependence within the world economy.

As he put it, the strategy of effecting a convergence between domestic output and domestic demand patterns was 'not simply constrained by the requirement of satisfying local needs in an autarkic sense, but allows for engagement in export activity where such exports are an extension of domestic demand needs'. 'Trade is then', he continued, 'as it were a "super-engine" of growth. This follows because the necessary and basic internal productive conditions will have been established to ensure that participation in a capitalist-dominated international economy does not result in a global division of labour which works against the local community' (Thomas 1974:134). The thinking underlying Thomas's 'iron law' of transformation is thus clear enough and, in theory, is applicable to all small developing states, no matter how tiny. Yet it is only fair to point out that the notion of smallness with which he was working was considerably larger than that of states with a population of under 1 million. The details of his analysis were focused upon countries the size of

Cuba and Tanzania, which have populations of 10 million and 18 million respectively. The achievement of a convergence between output and demand in such states as Antigua or The Gambia might conceivably bring into being socialist economies, but it is not obvious that they would at the same time be particularly prosperous or developed.

As for positions between the ideological parameters of capitalism and socialism, there has been even less consideration. For example, the general implications of small size for a 'mixed economy' model of development still remain largely unexplored, despite the fact that many small states today seek to implement such a model. Yet it is likely that limitations in the available numbers of both entrepreneurs and planners will alter the nature of the policies that can be followed. Indeed, the whole interface between the private and public sectors in the economic management of small states may well be affected by the constraints of size. Even the possibility of salvation via aid is attenuated if the capacity of the state to absorb and utilize external assistance is inadequate. These, and many other aspects of what might be called a broadly social democratic approach to the development of small states, have been ignored by economists to the detriment of our general understanding.

Regional integration

Substantially more time has been given to the exposition of techniques of regional integration as means to alleviating the dilemma of smallness. The literature here is extensive, but it is still all too naive about ideology. The point is that as a strategy of development regional integration is not value-free: it must inevitably take a view of what economic development means, and views, of course, have varied with both time and perspective. As a result, the link between regional integration and the kind of economic solution it offers to small states has become confused, and it is in need of some untangling if it is to be helpful (Payne 1983).

The origins of the theory are conventionally traced to the publication in 1950 of a book by Viner entitled *The customs union issue* (Viner 1950). In this form customs union theory purported to analyse the circumstances under which the removal of customs barriers between countries would lead to advantageous or disadvantageous static shifts in the pattern of production, consumption, and trade within the union as a whole. The so-called 'production effects' could be either trade-creating or trade-diverting. Trade creation occurred if a union caused a member to replace its own high-cost production of particular commodities with imports from other members of the union which had lower costs. On the other hand, trade diversion was said to occur when the effect of the union was to cause members to switch their purchases from low-cost sources external to the union to high-cost sources within the union. The union would not, in these terms, have been beneficial because it would have caused a shift of resources into less efficient uses and thus brought about a deterioration in specialization on a world scale.

Analysed in this way, customs unions could be said to have certain static welfare benefits for developed industrialized economies, but they seemed to have little to offer the small states of the developing world. The removal of trading barriers between such countries would not have a great redistributive effect on the pattern of production within the union (replacing high-cost domestic production by low-cost supplies from partner countries) because the level of industrialization throughout the developing world was almost always too low. Moreover, external trade was huge compared with domestic trade, so in most cases one would have had to anticipate an excessive trade-diverting effect and, therefore, a net loss in terms of the efficiency with which resources would be utilized within the area covered by the union. Hence neoclassical customs union theory tended to conclude that regional integration between underdeveloped countries would be irrelevant at best and harmful at worst.

Yet it was out of the inadequacies of conventional customs union theory that there emerged in the mid-1960s a more dynamic theory of regional integration of direct relevance to developing economies. No one name is associated with this development, which was prompted by the difficulties which postwar attempts at import-substitution industrialization were beginning to encounter in several of the smaller Third World countries. From this perspective the gain brought about by regional economic integration was the wider market it created and the chance of capturing economies of scale and external economies thereby offered to small developing countries otherwise constrained by their size. These ideas had an impact on governments and regional integration groupings, such as the Central American Common Market and the Caribbean Free Trade Association, which sprang up in several different parts of the developing world.

In turn, though, they generated their own critique. Far from bringing about a greater degree of economic independence for small developing states, it was argued that regional integration served to entrench such countries more firmly than ever in a structurally subordinate position within the world economy. It did so, the suggestion ran, precisely by making them more attractive as locations of inward capital investment from multinational sources. Alternative theories of regional integration based on the deliberate promotion of joint production enterprises between constituent states were advanced by these critics (Brewster & Thomas 1969), but they were rarely adopted with conviction by governments. The general result was to damage confidence in the whole concept of regional integration.

At present the notion is still propounded by economists writing about the problems of small states, but one feels that they often do not know what they really mean by it. The idea has become trite or, to put the point another way, it is no longer grounded in a particular theory of development. Sometimes, for example, it is used to refer to a loose kind of collective self-reliance between small developing states. But even this is not without its confusion. As Hoogvelt has pointed out, collective self-reliance is itself 'an ideology uneasily balanced upon contradictory principles: greater interdependence between rich and poor worlds, and independence from the rich world; better links with the rich world, and de-linking from it' (Hoogvelt 1982:86). We are thus brought back again as much to politics as economics.

Conclusion

What, then, emerges from this examination of the economic literature on small states? Few economic advantages are seen to attach to smallness. The best that can be said, it seems, is that small countries are likely to enjoy greater cohesiveness in the face of the many social changes which economic development inevitably entails (Knox 1967). And even that seems a rather dubious claim. Generally speaking, though, the emphasis has been upon an elaboration of the special problems of smallness and the attempt at national and regional levels to overcome these difficulties. The debate has ranged quite widely, but it has been excessively woolly in its substance and has consistently been beset by a failure to grasp the varying ideological permutations within which economics can be discussed. This suggests that what is needed, as we proceed, is not so much the further refinement of an economics of smallness, but the emergence of a genuine political economy of small size, a body of analysis that is more closely in touch with the realities of the world in which small states have to exist and survive.

References

Best, L. 1971. Size and survival. In *Readings in the political economy of the Caribbean*, N. Girvan & O. Jefferson (eds), 29–34. Kingston: Institute of Social and Economic Research, University of the West Indies.

Brewster, H. & C. Y. Thomas 1969. Aspects of the theory of economic integration. *Journal of Common Market Studies* **8**, 110–32.

Chenery, H. B. & L. Taylor 1968. Development patterns: among countries and over time. *Review of Economics and Statistics* **50**, 391–416.

Demas, W. G. 1965. *The economics of development in small economies with special reference to the Caribbean*. Montreal: McGill University Press.

Dommen, E. C. & P. L. Hein 1985. Foreign trade in goods and services: the dominant activity of small island economies. In *States, microstates and islands*, E. C. Dommen & P. L. Hein (eds), 152–84. London: Croom Helm.

Hoogvelt, A. 1982. *The third world in global development*. London: Macmillan.

Jalan, B. (ed.) 1982. *Problems and policies in small economies*. London: Croom Helm.

Knox, A. D. 1967. Some economic problems of small countries. In

Problems of smaller territories, B. Benedict (ed.), 35–44. London: Athlone Press.

Kohr, L. 1977. *The overdeveloped nations*. Swansea: Christopher Davies.

Kuznets, S. 1960. Economic growth of small nations. In *The economic consequences of the size of nations*, E. A. G. Robinson (ed.), 14–32. London: Macmillan.

Payne, A. J. 1983. Regional integration and development: the evolution of theory. *Huddersfield Papers in Politics* **7**, 1–16.

Robinson, E. A. G. (ed.) 1960. *The economic consequences of the size of nations*. London: Macmillan.

Thomas, C. Y. 1974. *Dependence and transformation: the economics of the transition to socialism*. New York: Monthly Review Press.

Viner, J. 1950. *The customs union issue*. Studies in the administration of international law and organization, 10. London.

Ward, M. 1975. Dependent development – problems of economic planning in small developing countries. In *Development policy in small countries*, P. Selwyn (ed.), 115–33. London: Croom Helm.

4 Security dilemmas

Roberto Espíndola

The accelerated development of military technology in Europe during the 1940s and the more sophisticated use of economic variables in strategic thinking during the 1950s and 1960s focused the interest of analysts on 'national security', or the 'security' of the modern nation–state. Their debates reflected several traditional assumptions: threats to the state were assumed to be external, to originate from another state, and to relate to fairly conventional forms of military action. Wolfers (1962) linked security to 'the ability of a nation to deter an attack or to defeat it'. Lipman (1943) pointed out that the protection of 'core values' was the final purpose of security, but still identified war as the main threat to a state.

Studies based on these assumptions have concentrated on assessments of war capability by using quantitative indicators such as size of armed forces, weaponry, military budgets, and gross national product (GNP). They constitute a useful contribution to the understanding of traditional armed conflicts between contemporary states, but they have failed to account for security problems of a less formal nature, such as subversion, political control of the armed forces, and destabilization by means of economic action or the use of small bands of irregular forces. In particular, they neglect the security problems faced by small states, for whom the risk of war with another state is extremely remote as compared with the threat presented by bands of mercenaries or insurgents, drug smugglers, or even economic conglomerates.

Those analyses which have attempted to quantify the security problem of small states have tended to be too formalistic. Quester, for example, has been credited with having proposed a formula based upon a ratio of controllers to controlled of 1 : 2000 (Alford 1984): a neat solution seemingly, and one used by Quester (1983) to suggest 'the need for a garrison of some 50 for Grenada', an island with a population of approximately 100 000 people. Quester was, however, referring exclusively to police control of a civilian population. He did not include the armed forces or the national guard and territorial troops which could reinforce the police in case of a major disorder. The ratios obtained, hence, bear no relation to the overall security needs of a small state or to the foreign forces potentially required to control its population.

To a very considerable degree, therefore, the field has been left to Maniruzzaman, who tried to go beyond these quantitative issues by looking at the actual problems faced by small states. He made the valuable point in this context that security consists of the protection and preservation of the minimum core values of any nation: political independence and territorial integrity (Maniruzzaman 1982). That is a more comprehensive definition than previous ones, but it still does not cover the threat presented to small states by armed groups from within. Such actions would radically alter the political process in a small state, but would not necessarily affect either its political independence *vis à vis* other states or its territorial integrity. Something obviously needs to be added to his terms of reference. In an attempt to formulate a definition of security more appropriate to the world of small states, I suggest that it be understood as the ability of a state to avoid or overcome any violent threat to its territorial integrity, politico-economic independence or institutional arrangements. On the basis of that formulation, this chapter now addresses itself to the security dilemmas of those weak small states with less developed economies and small populations, which are unable financially and politically to afford security forces large enough to protect them.

Security threats

Small states face two overarching security threats at present: escalating East–West tension and an increase in the use of military force in the resolution of conflicts. Having contained the development of each other's spheres of influence in Europe and having reached a dangerous stalemate in nuclear deterrence, the two superpowers have translated their conflict into a zero-sum game played out at every corner of the Third World (Cassen 1985). They are no longer interested only in those countries with strategic value because of their geographical position or natural resources. Low-cost operations to destabilize a country or effect a change in its affiliation to a superpower are now undertaken, even if the country in question is of little real strategic value. The object is to make the other superpower blink, force it to stretch its political and military resources away from the main theatres of conflict, and acquire additional bargaining pawns.

Coupled with the extension of superpower confrontation, the end of the 1970s brought about an intensification in the use of military force in international relations, with the consequent weakening of belief in the possibility of peaceful resolution of conflicts. The end of the Vietnam War appeared to have demonstrated the futility and high cost of military solutions, but reliance on alternative means was short-lived, as has been shown in the South Atlantic, the Sahara, Chad, Afghanistan, the Arab Gulf, Lebanon, Ethiopia, Kampuchea, Southern Africa, Grenada, Central America, and the Seychelles. Military manoeuvres, particularly naval exercises, have come to symbolize the presence of the superpowers throughout the Third World.

The security problems presented by East–West conflict affect every aspect of the life of a small Third World state, although they do not often reach the point of overt military intervention. A key aspect of these problems relates to the dependent nature of small states' economies. Economic dependence can be argued to be the root cause of most of the security problems under discussion. Small states need external aid to develop their infrastructure; markets in which to sell their commodity production; and foreign investment to introduce a measure of industrialization to their economy. Some even require financial assistance to balance the budgets, and most need help in securing oil supplies. The solution to these problems is in the hands of the developed industrial nations, but their assistance is not free; it requires the allegiance of the small state which, accordingly, becomes a client of one of the two blocs. This relationship of dependence typically leads to an escalating external debt and gives a great degree of influence over the decisions of the small state to the hands controlling the flow of credit and access to markets.

There are other specific security threats affecting small states in the Third World. Regional powers, often acting on behalf of, or as proxies for, a superpower, can develop expansionist foreign policies towards small states, seeking to take them into their area of political and economic influence or even advancing claims over their territory. This is particularly marked in the case of industrializing, more developed regional powers, which endeavour to capture in the periphery markets denied to them at the centre of the world economy. Most regional powers confine their actions to their surrounding area (Mexico, Turkey, Nigeria, Venezuela, Brazil, Indonesia), but there are some, such as Cuba, Israel, Libya, Argentina, the Koreas, and Taiwan, which project their influence well beyond their regional context. Their attempts to influence small states do not replace similar attempts by a patron superpower; normally they complement each other. An obvious example of this is the present conflict in Central America, where the confrontation not only involves the US and USSR but also Cuba, Israel, Mexico, Venezuela, Argentina, and France. Even countries often considered as proxies of the superpowers, such as Cuba and Israel, develop policies towards small states which, though not conflicting with those of their patrons, try also to advance their own economic and political interests.

Regional groups and organizations such as the Association of Southeast Asian Nations (ASEAN), the Organization of African Unity (OAU), the Organization of American States (OAS), the Caribbean Community (CARICOM), and the Organization of Eastern Caribbean States (OECS), can also present security threats to small states by attempting to impose on them particular alignments, standards of international behaviour, or forms of internal political organization. In recent years several small states have clashed with their regional organizations, accused of being out of step with the region's superpower allegiance, of conducting their internal affairs through faulty political processes, or of having built up their armed forces to the point of constituting a threat to the security of other states in the region. Sanctions which regional organizations have applied range from political and commercial isolation to support for, or organization of, military intervention. A useful rule of thumb is that the smaller the membership of a regional group, the greater the potential security risk for a small state. Within a small subregional system any attempt by a member state to develop its economy by adopting an unconventional path inevitably affects the economic interests of other members. In the Eastern Caribbean, for instance, Barbados has resented efforts by Grenada and St Vincent to develop their economies by becoming independent tourist destinations and thus eliminating the need for visitors to stop over in Barbados. It would be hard to argue that Barbados's recent willingness to engage in military action relating to these two neighbours was completely unrelated to its perception of its economic interests.

Small states are particularly vulnerable to subversion, especially when local activists have external support. Supplies of funds or weapons, even on a small scale, could enable a group – whether of messianic extremists or political dissidents – to overpower a tiny, ill-trained and ill-armed police force, which is all most small states can afford as security. Even if an attempt at subversion does not meet with outright success, an occasional outburst of terrorism suffices to wreck a small state's economy, scaring away tourists and foreign firms.

Equally, small states – and in particular small islands – are vulnerable to attacks by exogenous irregular forces, whether they are exiles, mercenaries, or mere adventurers. Mainland states have the advantage of having better control of their borders than small islands, since they are more capable of making neighbouring countries responsible for irregular attacks originating in their territory. A small island can easily be taken over by a well armed, company-sized group of trained guerrillas or mercenaries if all they have to face is a police force lacking the motivation, training, and weaponry required to oppose an infantry landing. A police force normally geared to fight petty crime, control traffic, and keep an eye on tourists and sailors on shore leave would not be able to oppose such a takeover. Nor in peaceful times would it be able to prevent the use of the island and its territorial waters for traffic in drugs, or illegal fishing by foreign vessels within the island's Exclusive Economic Zone (EEZ). Drug traffickers are sufficiently accomplished to outrun the police forces of most small states.

If funds from multilateral or bilateral aid programmes are provided for the formation of local security forces strong enough to protect the small state's borders, control its EEZ, and prevent subversion, new security risks replace old ones. Strong defence forces could lead to a military hegemony within a small state where the political system has not developed cultural and institutional counterweights to such forces. The participation of the local security force in training programmes abroad or under foreign instructors, coupled to its participation in regional security arrangements of the 'fire brigade' type, can create among security personnel allegiances either to international alignments or to specific forms of government. New foreign policies or changes in government structure or personnel, no matter how legitimate, can then meet with opposition from the security forces. That veto would then lead political groups to consider the need for armed action to bring about political change. A similar result can be expected when the security forces become excessively associated with the ruling party and are used to repress legitimate opposition activity, or when the security forces themselves install a military régime. These observations may sound pessimistic, but they reflect a major contradiction in the security requirements of small states.

The military presence of a foreign power in the territory of a small state, as in the case of foreign bases or lesser military facilities associated with a port of call, will have a deterrent effect on potential aggressors. British bases in Cyprus played an important rôle in at least preventing a total Turkish takeover in 1974; equally it could be argued that the British garrison in Belize has prevented a Guatemalan invasion. Foreign bases can also boost the host economy, to the point that in recent years several governments in the Commonwealth Caribbean have competed for the privilege of hosting a US facility. However, a foreign base commits the small state and can reduce not only its independence on the international stage but also at home, as the foreign power may try to forestall political change judged to be hostile.

Finally, foreign economic conglomerates can present a threat to the security of small states. Multinational corporations (MNCs) with budgets several times those of most Third World countries have at their disposal an international organization providing them with economic and political intelligence outside the reach of the meagre diplomatic service of a small state. Financial power and information enable a MNC to manipulate a small state to an extent which the international community may not allow in the case of a foreign power. Small states used as tax havens or as convenient sites for money laundering are particularly vulnerable.

Security resources

As important as the analysis of potential threats is the consideration of the resources on which security depends and the extent to which these are available to a small state. Scarce human and economic resources, geographical position, and political structure are some of the factors which affect the security of a small country. From this 'internal' perspective, the security resources of a small state can be grouped into those relating to diplomacy and intelligence, those concerning arms and the security forces, and those deriving from the geographical situation of a country and its political structures.

Diplomacy and intelligence

Diplomats are considered essential for those countries trying to exercise influence beyond their borders, whether they are a regional power trying to capture new markets, advance their economic interests, or bring a smaller state under their influence, or a world power competing on the global stage. In such cases, the size and professionalism of a country's diplomatic service often provides a measure of the weight a state carries within the international system, indicating the level of human and economic resources it is able and willing to commit in search of international influence. The closure of missions abroad or a reduction of diplomatic personnel is a clear indication of a shift in a country's international priorities or a decline in its international standing. In recent years, a reduction in the number of Dutch and British embassies in the Third World has shown a change in the priorities of these former colonial powers, as much as the closure of some embassies of the Dominican Republic in Europe has indicated a lack of resources and international pretension on the part of that country.

For small states, however, diplomatic contacts are a matter of survival. Diplomatic missions abroad are essential to seek the support of larger countries and international organizations, as well as to prevent, through diplomatic contacts and negotiations, risks of conflict with other states. There is, therefore, no proportionality between the size of a small state and its need to maintain a basic number of diplomatic representatives. If weak, a small state with a population of 10 000 will need to keep as many diplomats abroad as a similarly weak country with a population ten times larger. However, of the 15 small states for which data are readily available (Maniruzzaman 1982:72–5), less than half have four diplomatic missions abroad. Although reliable information on the numbers of each country's diplomats is impossible to ascertain, the typical diplomatic mission is one with no more than three diplomats, the ambassador, high commissioner or *chargé d'affaires* acting in a non-resident capacity for other capitals, often covering a wide region. Even that is a heavy burden for the resources of many small states. As a result, most have opted to maintain bilateral relations with other countries through their delegate to the UN, who also normally acts as ambassador to the US, although that too has proven too great a burden for some small countries as is shown by the number of New York lawyers who represent newly born states at the UN.

Scarcity of skilled personnel is a problem affecting not only the diplomatic representation of a small state but also its ability to gather intelligence and generally obtain, collate, and analyse information related to its interests. Small commodity-producing states find themselves at a particular disadvantage in this respect; larger states, especially those having an interest as consumers in the production of a specific commodity, can have diplomatic missions in the capitals of small states, use satellite surveillance to monitor commodity production, keep an eye on other markets, and transmit that information by modern means to centres where it is analysed by skilled personnel. Small states do not have the human and economic resources to mirror such levels of intelligence gathering and are thus often not forewarned about a market change, a security threat represented by a mercenary invasion, or the likely use of its territory or territorial waters for criminal purposes.

Collective arrangements, such as the joint diplomatic representation of several Eastern Caribbean countries in London, can help overcome these problems. Organizations of commodity producers can also provide economic intelligence and larger countries – former colonial metropoles or regional powers – can assist small states by providing information about security threats. In the case of island states, the regional organization of coastguard activity and surveillance of territorial waters can be advantageous. Yet it must be remembered that information gathered by all these means is outside the small state's control. Even if the intelligence relates exclusively to external security threats, conflicts of interest between the states involved may arise or attempts may be made to use the intelligence to influence the political makeup or choice of government in one of the smaller participants. Co-operative schemes can thus help alleviate the worse aspects of smallness in terms of diplomatic representation and intelligence gathering, but the interests of the state will ultimately have to be defended by a government lacking the resources to conduct those tasks though still remaining a sovereign state.

Armed forces

Once again, the key factor is the economic and human resources available, and the main distinction to be drawn is between those few wealthy states which, despite their smallness, have sufficient resources to provide for their defence and the majority, which are unable to afford more than a basic police force. The size and composition of security forces in small countries varies enormously, reflecting not only the resources available but also the perception of particular needs and threats (Maniruzzaman 1982:80). A country like Brunei has the economic resources to afford large and well armed forces, but human resource constraints have forced it to rely on the additional support of a British contingent of Gurkhas. In other cases, substantial external support is explained by the strategic or political importance of the small country for the protecting power. Thus France keeps a garrison in Djibouti, Britain does the same in Belize and Cyprus, Cuban and Angolan troops constitute a large proportion of the security forces of São Tomé and the US supplies a defence force for Iceland. Finally, there are instances where a foreign power assumes complete responsibility for the security of a small state; such is the case of the Senegambia federation where Senegal looks after the federation's security, having incorporated the Gambian gendarmerie into its own forces. New Zealand is also responsible for the defence of Western Samoa, and France and Spain take annual turns in providing the 32 policemen who constitute the only security forces of Andorra.

The size of the security forces, by itself, is not a good indicator of the level of security achieved by a small country. In fact, the report prepared by the Commonwealth Consultative Group (1985) argues convincingly that large forces may even be counter-productive in internal security terms. A sizeable full-time force may easily destabilize a small state, becoming the most organized political force and yet having little to do in peacetime. Even when such a force is proportionately large, it would still have little chance of successfully opposing a determined invasion by a medium-size power, as demonstrated by the 1974 Turkish invasion of Cyprus. The question of proportionality is, in fact, quite interesting. Only in three known cases is the ratio of security forces to population lower than 1:100. Two of them – Brunei and Iceland – reach that through the presence of foreign forces; the third, Guyana, is a unique case where there has been until recently a permanent threat of a Venezuelan invasion and where the security forces have been instrumental in keeping the ruling party in office (Baber & Jeffrey 1986).

The armament available to the security forces of small states also varies, but in most cases their arms do not go beyond light weapons and their skills are those resulting from basic infantry and coastguard training. With an eye to the future, Quester (1983) proposed the development of anti-ship and anti-aircraft guided missiles as a technological solution to small states' problems, albeit recognizing that even such defences would never protect a small country from clandestine operation and that, in most cases, the lack of a hinterland would reduce the effectiveness of a missile-based defence system. The cost of an effective missile system and the skills required to operate and maintain it are, however, beyond the resources of almost all small states, a point also relevant to the suggestion made by Norton (1984) for an Eastern Caribbean defence force based upon troop-carrying helicopters and coastguard vessels. A study commissioned by the David Davies Memorial Institute includes an analysis of the purchasing costs for some basic air and sea surveillance crafts (Harden 1985) and makes it obvious that even they are outside the reach of most small states. Although aircraft, patrol boats, and armaments could be obtained through international assistance or from friendly powers, even the maintenance costs would be an excessive burden for the smallest countries.

Some insular states are consequently showing a tendency to concentrate their security forces on coastguard duties, giving first priority to the control of their EEZ and the prevention of drug traffic and smuggling. Such forces would be insufficient to repel an invading military force, but would deter small bands of mercenaries or insurgents and act as a trip wire if the state was faced by a larger force. A good example is provided by the Bahamas, where the defence force now consists exclusively of coastguard units. A similar solution has been advocated by some of the proponents of the Eastern Caribbean regional security system, notably Barbados and St Vincent.

Another option has been the development of special units within the police forces of small states; these units are given additional military training and weaponry. Similarly, some states have developed paramilitary forces, whether as part-time or reserve military units or as armed militia. There are obvious risks in the development of paramilitary forces as they may become a party political tool. Guyana has been criticized in this connection, yet was praised recently in the Consultative Group's report commissioned by the Commonwealth Secretariat (1985:40–2) for the way in which a 'many-layered system' combining a defence force with national service, paramilitary, and police units has been used to increase political stability, with each unit providing a check on the others.

Political and geographic factors

The resources already outlined are necessary tools for the security of a small state, but they are not sufficient by themselves to achieve such security when a country is facing an invasion from a powerful neighbour and is weakened by internal schism or political instability, as was the case in the 1974 Cyprus crisis and the US invasion of Grenada in 1983. In both instances foreign invasions were provoked by a coup against a government considered to be legitimate; they succeeded in achieving their objectives thanks to the political instability caused by the coup and the lack of popular support for Nikos Sampson in Cyprus (Worsley & Kitromilides 1979, Bunge 1980) and the Bernard Coard group in Grenada (Payne, *et al.* 1984, Thorndike 1985).

The case of Grenada is particularly relevant, because it could be argued that the government of Maurice Bishop, the late Prime Minister, fearing precisely such an invasion, had managed to develop practically all the resources I have suggested. Under Bishop, Grenada had created a large diplomatic service, at least by the standards of a small island state, establishing missions not only in London and New York but also in Moscow, Brussels, Havana, and other neighbouring capitals. This diplomatic service was staffed by highly motivated young intellectuals, and the evidence available indicates that it was efficient in gathering economic and political information (Thorndike 1985). Bishop had also developed a well trained and well armed defence force, supported by a large militia. None of those elements sufficed, however, to protect Grenada from the US invasion. In fact, after some of its troops killed Bishop, the army put up little resistance to the invasion and the militia disbanded. Both had become instruments of factional disputes and lost the population's support.

What the Grenada episode surely reveals is that political stability, derived in most cases from the legitimacy of the political system, is an essential security resource. The existence of channels for popular participation in decision-making processes and for political minorities to express their grievances, and the population's consequent support for existing political structures, are certainly as important – perhaps even more important – for the security of a small state than the size, training, and weaponry of its actual defence forces. A political minority finding all channels for political participation closed or non-existent is likely to consider armed subversion the only means to achieve change.

Finally, geopolitical factors, including the geographical position of a country, are elements which will affect a state's security. Small states make ideal candidates for a regional or global power to use as the means to project its influence, secure transport lanes, or prevent a hostile power from acquiring outposts. This is particularly true of insular states, but the cases of Luxembourg, Djibouti, and The Gambia show that continental enclaves can have similar importance.

During the 1970s Western strategists used to argue that modern ballistic delivery systems had made obsolete the establishment of bases abroad; the two superpowers could destroy each other several times over from the sea, from the air, and from their own territories, without any need to control sea routes or project their power in faraway islands. But the intensification of East–West clashes by conventional means throughout the world has led to a resurgence in the establishment of foreign bases in the Third World, a phenomenon also encouraged by new Soviet strategies of naval deployment. Now both the US and USSR try to acquire ports of call for their fleets and bases or military facilities from which to deploy their conventional forces or those of their allies. The rôle played by Ascension and St Helena in the South Atlantic conflict and by the Gulf islands in the Iran–Iraq war show too that islands remain important in non-global confrontations.

Policy alternatives

There are three alternative courses of action open to small Third World states in order to ensure their security.

Neutrality and non-alignment

Neutrality and non-alignment are undoubtedly two separate concepts, although both imply the use of diplomacy to obtain security guarantees from the international community, and it could be argued that one complements the other. A neutral country can put itself at risk by becoming militantly aligned with one of the superpowers, or it can seek strength in getting close to other neutral states. In fact, a neutral and non-aligned bloc is now appearing in Europe, including Finland, Sweden, Austria, Switzerland, Yugoslavia, and Malta. But neutrality alone is difficult to achieve in present world politics. Of the three countries recognized as neutral in Europe, one – Austria – had neutrality imposed on it by the occupying powers after World War II. The other two – Switzerland and Sweden – have been respected as neutral because their declaration of neutrality was backed by the considerable military power at their disposal and because it suited their neighbours' interests, freeing the flanks of one of them from any potential threat. But these cases have nothing in common with the problems facing small Third World states.

Neutrality needs not only to be declared, it must be enforced. Neither a small state nor international organizations such as the UN or the Commonwealth have the means to enforce such neutrality, even if the political will existed in the latter cases. Non-alignment is even less of a security guarantee, especially as the Non-Aligned Movement has become a broad international forum incorporating any country which is not a member of NATO or the Warsaw Pact, but nevertheless including the main champions of the US and Soviet causes in the Third World. This does not mean that a geographically isolated small state cannot find some security in a neutral and non-aligned policy, provided that policy is endorsed by both superpowers or by their regional representatives. That is unlikely in the present climate of East–West tension, with both superpowers trying to project their influence in every area of the world, but it is not inconceivable. The report published by the Commonwealth Secretariat suggests that neutrality could be strengthened by the UN Security Council recognizing such status. It is a novel and useful suggestion, which would, in effect, make the small state a 'ward of the Council' and act as a deterrent against aggression (Harden 1985).

Regional security arrangements

As already indicated, the smaller a regional group or pact, the greater the security risk it poses for its smaller member states. Conversely, a regional group with a large membership poses little threat to its smaller members and could, in fact, guarantee their security if its membership were a pluralistic one, where East–West interests cancel each other out (Brown 1986). Such an organization could supply the funding and training facilities required to provide small states with a professional, well trained and equipped, highly mobile police force capable of handling any security problem short of an invasion or an attack by irregular forces. Faced with one of the latter eventualities the police force would act as a trip wire, giving the regional organization time to send relief troops at the request of the government of the country under attack.

Although not a regional organization, the Commonwealth could provide such a security guarantee to its smaller members. It has a pluralistic membership and could muster the necessary resources if the political will was there as suggested in its own recent report. CARICOM also has a pluralistic membership and could obtain the resources required. CARICOM teams could replace US and British instructors in training security forces in the smaller island states of the Commonwealth Caribbean, resources could be sought from multilateral sources and a security desk at the CARICOM Secretariat could co-ordinate training, equipment and relief assistance to police forces. However, it is unlikely that this will happen in the near future in view of CARICOM's difficulties in sorting out even trade disputes between its members. It is unlikely that the OAS, the OAU or ASEAN could fulfil such a rôle in their present form, because of their size, structure, and commitments. The OAS and ASEAN are still far from pluralistic organizations, and the many interests present in the OAU's large membership can neutralize its action.

Finlandization

This is the most obvious solution for states of particular strategic importance to a superpower. It consists in relying for security on the protection of a superpower and its regional associates. Security forces trained, equipped, and perhaps even paid with assistance from the superpower would be able to cope with most threats, except exogenous ones. In case of an attack by forces with outside support, local security units would be joined by those from neighbouring states to keep them at bay until they could be reinforced by the superpower.

This solution seriously constrains the political and economic choices open to the state, leaving it with a limited sovereignty; hence its label. Political activity antagonistic to the superpower becomes a threat to the security of the small state, likely to be repressed as such. Foreign policy choices also become restricted. Once these arrangements are established, any attempt to alter them would be a threat to the superpower's security interests; any small-state government attempting such changes could be easily destabilized or overthrown.

Conclusion

In practice, small states are likely to adopt policies close to one of the above alternatives or indeed a combination of them, depending on their assessment of their security objectives and the resources at their disposal. But, in the final analysis, their security will depend on the political will of other, larger states expressed through assistance, alliances, or the action of regional and international organizations. In a world characterized by East–West conflict, such will is unlikely to exist, and small states are likely to remain pawns in superpower games. Only concerted international action can prevent that conflict from spreading and thereby provide a more secure environment for all members of the international community.

References

Alford, J. 1984. Security dilemmas of small states. *The World Today* **40**, 363–9.
Baber, C. & H. B. Jeffrey, 1986. *Guyana: politics, economics and society*. London: Frances Pinter.
Brown, L. H. 1986. Regional collaboration in resolving third-world conflicts. *Survival* **28**, 208–20.
Bunge, F. M. (ed.) 1980. *Cyprus: a country study*. Washington, DC: US Government Printing Office.
Cassen, R. (ed.) 1985. *Soviet interests in the Third World*. London: Sage.
Commonwealth Consultative Group 1985. *Vulnerability: small states in the global society*. London: Commonwealth Secretariat.
Harden, S. (ed.) 1985. *Small is dangerous: micro states in a macro world*. London: Frances Pinter.
Lipman, W. 1943. *US foreign policy*. Boston, Mass.: Little, Brown.
Maniruzzaman, T. 1982. *The security of small states in the Third World*. Canberra: Australian National University.
Norton, G. 1984. Defending the Eastern Caribbean. *The World Today* **40**, 254–60.
Payne, A., P. Sutton & T. Thorndike. 1984. *Grenada: revolution and invasion*. London: Croom Helm.
Quester, G. H. 1983. Trouble in the islands: defending the micro-states. *International Security* **8**, 160–75.
Thorndike, T. 1985. *Grenada: politics, economics and society*. London: Frances Pinter.
Wolfers, A. 1962. *Discord and collaboration*. Baltimore, Md.: Johns Hopkins University Press.
Worsley, P. & P. Kitromilides (eds) 1979. *Small states in the modern world*. Nicosia: New Cyprus Association.

PART B

Case studies

5 Grenada

COLIN CLARKE

A particularly striking political change in recent years has been the erosion of the criteria thought essential to self-government. After World War II Britain's Colonial Office considered it 'clearly impossible in the modern world for the present separate [West Indian] communities, small and isolated as most of them are, to achieve and maintain full self-government on their own' (Great Britain 1947). For this reason many West Indians welcomed the federation established under British aegis in 1958; only such an association, they believed, could win them self-government. Even 25 years ago, few expected Jamaica and Trinidad to gain independence on their own, let alone tiny Grenada.

Not until 1960, when Premier Norman Manley was told that Jamaica could gain independence within the Commonwealth, did political leaders anywhere in the English-speaking Caribbean envisage separate nationhood. As Coard put it, 'with Jamaica's lead Trinidad soon followed. It was not so much a case of Trinidad's "size" being seen as having increased, as Trinidad's perception that the world's concept of the size required of an independent nation had altered' (Coard 1974:70). By 1962 there were nine sovereign states with populations smaller than Trinidad's 825 000: now 44 countries have fewer than 1 million inhabitants.

Jamaica's 1961 referendum broke up the West Indies Federation: Jamaica and Trinidad became independent in 1962 and Guyana and Barbados in 1966. Thereafter no theoretical justification remained to deny self-government to any Caribbean territory. Most colonies evolved into Associated States, each internally autonomous but dependent on Britain for overseas representation and defence (Clarke 1976). Full independence then beckoned as a panacea. Egged on by the UN Decolonization Commission, colonial territories, however small or poor, found it desirable to throw off imperial bonds: each new national creation caused other small units to ask 'Why not us?' As a Grenadian minister of the early 1970s noted, territorial size was irrelevant to the attainment of nationhood; he echoed a UN resolution in commenting that 'inadequacy of political, economical, social or educational preparedness should never serve as a pretext for delaying independence' (quoted in Jacobs 1974:30).

By 1983 all six of the Caribbean Associated States created after the break up of the West Indies Federation were independent, with Grenada taking the lead in 1974. Island leaders anticipated that merely declaring independence would win them international aid; indeed Eric Gairy, who took Grenada out of colonialism and associated statehood, is alleged to have stated: 'Grenada will not support Independence, Independence will support Grenada' (quoted in V. Lewis 1974:54).

Why should islands like Grenada want independence on their own? Caribbean parochialism has been fostered by geographical isolation – especially insularity – and colonial dependence. Above all, parochialism is based on suspicion, even fear of neighbours as competitors, rivals, or agents of sedition. In the 1950s and 1960s this was principally 'a fear on the part of the wealthiest islands of having to carry their weaker associates' (Ramphal 1960). This fear triggered both the collapse of the Federation itself and the rump 'federation' of smaller units in 1966; even Trinidad's offer to take its small neighbours into unitary statehood was withdrawn once Grenada responded positively to it. So associated statehood and independence were seized upon by Grenada and the rest not as *the* solution to decolonization but only after federation had ceased to be possible and because political advancement promised more local control and better opportunities for development.

Even before associated statehood was devised, W. Arthur Lewis (1965:16) had spelled out the dangers of autonomy for minuscule West Indian states:

> In a small island of 50,000 to 100,000 people, dominated by a single political party, it is very difficult to prevent political

abuse. Everybody depends on the government for something, however small, so most are reluctant to offend it. The civil servants live in fear; the police avoid unpleasantness; the trade unions are tied to the party; the newspapers depend on government advertisements; and so on. In cases where they are also corrupt, and playing with public funds, the situation becomes intolerable.

Lewis undoubtedly had Grenada in mind. In 1962 Grenada's constitution had been suspended by the British-appointed administrator who judged Chief Minister Gairy to have 'violated the principles of honest government' (Singham 1967:144).

Grenada, then, is an apt case of a small sovereign Caribbean state, though it must be added that its recent history makes it an extreme example. It was the first Caribbean island with fewer than 100 000 inhabitants to become independent, and since then it has experienced three contrasted régimes: Eric Gairy's dictatorship, 1974–9; the People's Revolutionary Government (PRG), 1979–83; and the New National Party régime elected in late 1984 after more than a year's interim government. How has each régime managed the social, political, and economic problems associated with Grenada's small size?

Gairy's Grenada

When Gairy led Grenada into independence in 1974 it had a population of 95 000 on its 340 square kilometres; the natural increase was 0.7% per annum, outmigration to the UK having drained off many thousands of Grenadians in the 1960s; and the gross domestic product (GDP) per capita was a mere US $200. Between a quarter and a third of all employees worked on plantations: most were labourers; and the majority of self-employed workers were peasants, though rural people moved between own-account and paid work. Sugar was grown largely for distilling into rum; cocoa, nutmegs, and bananas accounted for 90% of exports (Brizan 1984). Grenada was singularly powerless to influence the terms of trade with its major partner, the UK, because of its size and the nature of its produce.

Despite its small size, Grenada was socially complex and expressed a Creole stratification of plural cultures. At the top of this social pyramid there was a small Europeanized élite of ranked whites and browns, separated by a sharp social and cultural divide from the black masses of slave origin (Smith 1965). Smith has termed Grenada a plural society, a principal feature of which is social domination by an élite cultural minority whose values conflict with those of the cultural majority. Yet Grenada's independence from Britain had been strongly opposed both by the brown business community in the capital, St George's, and by the radical New Jewel Movement (NJM), headed by Maurice Bishop (EPICA Task Force 1982). For each group feared Gairy's capricious and malevolent treatment once the ties of associated statehood were severed and Grenada became responsible for defence and foreign affairs. In fact, Gairy's policy after independence did not change in any marked way: his intention remained to exploit and oppress at home and to conform to US and UK expectations in his foreign policy.

The small size of the state was not a great geopolitical disadvantage to Gairy's Grenada. Gairy was more interested in voicing his concern about UFOs at the UN and in forming a link with Pinochet's Chile than in pursuing a radical foreign policy. However bizarre, Gairy's international connections gave no concern to the US or UK.

True to his judgement that independence would support Grenada, Gairy accepted rather than confronted the *status quo*. Even before independence, his 1950s labour militancy had given way to manipulation of 'the crowd'; to attempts to get himself accepted by the social élite; and to enticement of US investment via retirement homes and the St George's University Medical School. But after 1974 Gairy set out more ruthlessly than ever to feather his own nest economically. Pocketing much of the US $10 million golden handshake from the UK, he terrorized local businessmen with his 'mongoose gang' and thereby extracted a personal share from plantations, hotels, and businesses (Jacobs & Jacobs 1983, O'Shaughnessy 1984, Thorndike 1985).

Government malpractice and mismanagement were so widespread in Grenada that per capita income dropped by 3% per annum in real terms during the 1970s, and by 1979, 50% of the labour force was unemployed and the health and educational systems were in disarray (Ambursley 1983). How then did Gairy survive? By fear, by rigging elections, by suborning the police and defence force, and by his personal style of leadership which since the early 1950s had bound the older generation of the rural masses to 'Uncle', and via him to the Grenada Mental and Manual Workers' Union and its affiliated Grenada United Labour Party (GULP) (Singham 1968, Payne, *et al.* 1984).

Years before, W. Arthur Lewis had envisioned this type of situation, arguing that 'the only safeguard ... is federation. If the government in island C misbehaves, it will be criticised openly by the citizens of island E. The federal government must be responsible for law and order, and for redress of financial and other abuse'. (W. Arthur Lewis 1965, 16–17) There is an argument against federation, however, and it is that local autonomy ensures against external tyranny; if there is a tyrant, at least it will be a problem of the inhabitants' own making whose resolution lies in their own hands. Grenadians staged an almost bloodless coup in 1979 to get rid of Gairy; they could hardly have overcome an equivalent oppressor under, for example, Trinidad's suzerainty.

The People's Revolutionary Government

Smallness was an immediate problem for the PRG, which ousted Gairy largely because the inadequate forces loyal to Bishop left the régime open to Gairy-inspired mercenary attack. In trying to resolve that potential problem by aligning itself with Cuba, the PRG increased US and UK hostility. And even in the Commonwealth Caribbean the PRG isolated itself from its Commonwealth neighbours by withdrawing its offer to hold elections. In each of these international situations, smallness spelled geopolitical vulnerability (Mandle 1985).

Small size was more crucial for the PRG than for Gairy because whereas Gairy had been content to leave Grenada unchanged, the revolution had an active policy on almost every social and economic front, based on the non-capitalist path to development and ultimately the Marxist transition to socialism (Gonsalves

1981; Sandford & Vigilante 1984). Admittedly contracts with Geest, the banana traders, were met, and tourists – 30–40 thousand per annum, mostly from the US and the Caribbean – were encouraged, but dependency *was* diversified by seeking new markets for cocoa, nutmeg, and mace in Eastern Europe (Thorndike 1985). Coard, the Minister of Finance, imposed strict fiscal control over a fairly successful mixed economy, with the peasant sector and the import houses remaining in private hands and accounting for about 80% and state enterprise largely confined to areas where Gairy had made illegal acquisitions (20%). By the early 1980s the economy was growing at 3% per annum, the national income per person was in the middle range for the Windward and Leeward Islands, and unemployment was below 20% (Ambursley 1983).

Central to the PRG's development strategy was the construction of a new international airport at Point Salines, south of St George's and close to the island's finest beach at Grand Anse. This airport, a replacement for the obsolete installation at Pearls on the opposite coast, was an essential link in a programme of diversification by tourism, a strategy which was hardly revolutionary and merely endorsed the conclusion of the Tripartite Commission of US, UK, and Canadian businessmen which visited the Caribbean in 1966. What was innovative about the PRG's 'new tourism' was its small scale, socially unobtrusive nature, and the impact it was intended to have on the rural economy by stimulating demand for peasant produce.

The airport became a symbol of the PRG's resolve to remove an impediment to rapid economic development, and Coard argued in Brussels that it was to Grenada what railroads had been to the US (Thorndike 1985:126). But the US viewed the airport as a military base that Grenada could and would offer to its Cuban and Soviet allies. Despite enormous help from Cuba in men and materials and loans of smaller value from the European Community, Libya, and Iraq, the cost of construction so escalated that it began to distort government expenditure in the year prior to the PRG's collapse (Thorndike 1985). Although it was shown that the Point Salines runway was shorter than those in several adjacent islands, and Plessey, the British subcontractor, confirmed that the installation was not for military use, the US persisted in treating the development as a provocation.

In addition to the issue of the airport, the grounds for continuous US pressure on the PRG were its Marxism, its unconstitutional takeover, press censorship, lack of elections, holding of detainees, and its pro-Cuban and pro-Soviet foreign policy. The pressure on tiny Grenada took many forms. The US mounted a military exercise called 'Amber and the Amberines' (read Grenada and the Grenadines) off Puerto Rico in 1981; explicitly omitted Grenada from the 'benefits' of the Caribbean Basin Initiative in 1982; distanced Bishop when he attempted a *rapprochement* in June 1983; and finally invaded Grenada in October 1983 during turmoil following the assassination of Bishop (Searle n.d.).

If the PRG was swept away because it was such a small, ideologically high-profile and geopolitically vulnerable target in the heart of America's backyard (and one must remember that the collapse of the PRG conveniently coincided with the US need to compensate quickly for its humiliation in the Lebanon), what part did small size play in the social and political policies of the PRG and in the tensions that pitted revolutionary against revolutionary in the prelude to invasion?

The PRG concluded that Grenada's social structure, consisting of a comprador bourgeoisie and peasant and proletarian masses, was not ripe for socialism (Jacobs & Jacobs 1983). A vanguard party, despite its in-built bourgeois tendencies, had to take power and hold it in trust for the masses while they were educated for socialism. Grenadian folk reaction to the PRG was quite otherwise. Delighted that the repressive Gairy had been ousted, the folk devoted themselves to the magnetic personality of Maurice Bishop, much as their parents had previously to Gairy.

The very smallness of Grenada was well suited to the innovations in government which the PRG favoured. Representative democracy, modelled on Whitehall, was rejected for ideological reasons, and because of Gairy's gerrymandering, in favour of participatory democracy (Hodge & Searle n.d.). Well documented attempts were made in the early 1980s to stimulate parish-pump politics by discussing the national budget at community level, though subsequent assessments have emphasized that ideas generally spread from the top down (Mandle 1985, Thorndike 1985).

Social projects in which the small size of Grenada played a positive rôle involved education, where a mass literacy campaign was successfully carried out in 1980–1 and an innovative in-service teacher-training scheme was started up in 1980, and health, where mobile teams covered the rural areas, concentrating on preventive medicine, especially health education, nutrition and family planning (Thorndike 1985).

Notwithstanding the smallness of Grenada, the PRG's desire to change everything at once was beyond its capacity. Admittedly, the senior ranks of the civil service were strengthened by high-calibre appointments of Caribbean radicals, and an enormous amount of specialist work was carried out by sympathizers with the revolution from overseas. But the mass organizations, the militia, National Women's Organization, National Students' Council, National Youth Organization, Productive Farmers' Union, and the Young Pioneers, through which the masses were to be led to socialism, were on the government's own admission inert, and the Central Committee of the NJM lacked the will and energy to put them on a sound footing (State Department and Department of Defense 1984).

Those involved in PRG decision making were pitifully few. When the PRG collapsed in 1983, the NJM had only 350 members, less than 1% of the Grenadian population, and only 72 were full party members (Thorndike 1985). Even more disadvantageous than the small size of the NJM was the isolation – more ideological than social or geographical – of its Central Committee from the masses. Although its pro-Coard faction condemned Bishop for his 'right opportunism' and weak leadership and prescribed 'a Leninist level of organization and discipline', together with joint leadership by Bishop and Coard, it never seems to have appreciated the importance of Bishop's popular appeal (State Department and Department of Defense 1984). Moreover, the Central Committee was so obsessed with these ideological considerations that it neglected numerous economic problems that required urgent attention: a liquidity crisis; declining agricultural output; and overspending on the airport to ensure its completion by March 1984, the fifth anniversary of the revolution (Thorndike 1985).

At the personal level too, smallness failed to provide the expected social cement. Although Bishop and Coard had been to secondary school together, lived next door to one another in St George's, and had been colleagues in the NJM for a decade, their association did not prevent Coard's unpublicized resignation from the Central Committee in 1982, rivalry over the leadership, the death of Bishop, or the collapse of the PRG (Castro 1983a, b). But in such a small society rivalry between two such dominant figures is difficult to contain.

Post-invasion Grenada

Widespread revulsion in Grenada at the assassination of Bishop and his closest associates ensured a welcome for the invasion forces. Popular support for liberation, coupled to the smallness of Grenada, has enabled the US to take almost complete control of the state, economically, strategically, and politically.

Within a month of the landings, the White House had appointed a task force of advisers to report on medium- and long-term strategies for restoring the economy, and by Christmas 1983 US $15 million had been spent on road resurfacing in the damaged sections between St George's and the international airport. So total was the rupture between Grenada and the Soviet bloc that during 1984–5 two-thirds of the entire Grenadian budget was provided by Western sources, the greater part by the US alone (*Caribbean Insight* 1984a).

US economic priorities have not differed greatly from those of the PRG, however. Export agriculture remains the backbone of the economy and is the largest employer, though tourism is the sector with the greatest potential, employing 2000 persons directly and indirectly and contributing 40% of the GNP. A major problem for the US and the Interim administration it installed was to switch the direction of trade for certain commodities while stabilizing export levels: in 1984 a US firm was persuaded to buy more than 1 million pounds weight of nutmegs, thereby replacing a deal with the USSR (*Caribbean Insight* 1984b).

While expelling non-Grenadian activists and denigrating the socialist philosophy of the PRG, the US has had to continue funding a range of social projects identified by the NJM in the fields of education, health, water supply, electricity provision, and road construction. Nevertheless, there has been a good deal of disruption in the nationalized industries and in education, and unemployment has risen to almost 30%.

A major priority for the US has been the opening of Point Salines Airport, which it had previously criticized as a military installation. US $21 million was earmarked to complete the project, in 1984, and the runway was formally inaugurated in October of that year, to commemorate the first anniversary of the invasion. Private US funds have been harnessed to government subventions, and substantial sums are being invested in new hotel accommodation in an attempt to underpin the viability of the airport and the economy generally.

Commonwealth objection to the incorporation of Grenada into the US orbit – a view not shared by the majority of Caribbean Commonwealth states – was expressed in a short-lived attempt to replace the Caribbean Peace-keeping Force (essentially US troops) with a Commonwealth detachment. Gradual reduction in the US presence in 1984–5, coupled to British training of the Grenada police, has stabilized the situation without weakening US control, and this control has been most obvious in the manoeuvrings surrounding Grenada's return to democracy.

Central to US policy has been the imprisonment, and political neutering, of the left-wing faction of the PRG which was in opposition to Bishop. The perpetual prevarications associated with the murder trial suggest that the permanent removal of the Coard faction from the political scene has been the objective of the US, the interim government, and the Grenadian government, elected on a newly compiled roll in December 1984.

The US, fearing that Gairy's GULP would take advantage of the dismemberment of the NJM and win, proceeded during 1984 to engineer an alliance between the main opposition groups – the Grenada National Party, the National Democratic Party, and the Grenada Democratic Movement. This amalgam, known as the

New National Party, headed by veteran politician, Herbert Blaize, polled 59% of the vote and won 14 out of the 15 seats, whereas GULP (with Gairy on the sidelines) polled 36% of the vote and took 1 seat. The Maurice Bishop Patriotic Movement, reviled by left and right, achieved only 5% of the vote and all its candidates lost their deposits. Almost 85% of Grenadians registered to vote did so.

The US presence, though increasingly concealed, is all-pervasive. In addition to the areas of politics, ideology, and political economy, it is to be found in the training of government officials, penetration of the trade unions, expansion of the St George's University Medical School, and in the island-wide emphasis on capitalist endeavour.

Conclusion

Theoretically, the significance of small size is difficult to specify, though the advantages and disadvantages can be characterized generally as balanced between having strong social bonds and lacking economic viability. Yet the simple pattern of plusses and minuses, in reality, may be disrupted by many factors – for example social complexity, ideological differences, personal rivalry, and the quality of economic management.

The PRG was mindful of the economic constraints imposed by small size, but allowed its ideological preoccupations to isolate it from the masses whose cause it claimed to represent. Yet the very smallness of the society did enable 3–4 thousand people (out of 15 000 gathered in central St George's) to congregate swiftly and free Bishop from house arrest, thereby setting in motion the denouement of assassination, internal collapse, and foreign invasion.

The PRG also neglected the geopolitical implications of small size coupled to ideological differences: it was deceiving rhetoric for Bishop to declare 'We are not in anybody's backyard' (Bishop n.d.). Grenada shows that small states must conform to the ideology of the superpowers in whose sphere of influence they are located; or at least they must keep a low profile if they do not. Grenada's anti-US stance, its location in the Caribbean close to the US, its military weakness – the People's Revolutionary Army had only 1800 soldiers – and the unwillingness of Cuba and the USSR to protect it, spelled disaster.

By contrast with the PRG, the New National Party elected in 1984 is a creature of the US. Like Gairy's régime in the past, it will not create geopolitical problems in the Caribbean. On the other hand, it is unable to confront and can only embrace Grenada's problems of dependence and social inequality, rooted as they are in smallness.

Acknowledgements

I am grateful to Tony Payne for allowing me to draw on materials from our research visit to Grenada and other territories in the South-East Caribbean in 1983, funded by the Nuffield Foundation, and to David Lowenthal for permission to use parts of our joint article (Lowenthal & Clarke 1980).

References

Ambursley, F. 1983. Grenada: The New Jewel revolution. In *Crisis in the Caribbean*. F. Ambursley & R. Cohen (eds), 191–222. London: Heinemann.
Bishop, M. n.d. *Selected speeches 1979–81*. La Habana: Casa de Las Americas.
Brizan, G. 1984. *Grenada: island of conflict*. London: Zed Books.
Caribbean Insight 1984a. No. 11.
Caribbean Insight 1984b. No. 2.
Castro, F. 1983a. *A pyrrhic military victory and a profound moral defeat*. La Habana: Editorial Política.
Castro, F. 1983b. *La invasión a Grenada*. Mexico: Editorial Katun.
Clarke, C. G. 1976. Insularity and identity in the Caribbean. *Geography* **61**, 8–16.
Coard, B. 1974. The meaning of political independence in the Commonwealth Caribbean. In *Independence for Grenada – myth or reality?* 69–78. St Augustine, Trinidad: Institute of International Relations.
EPICA Task Force 1982. *Grenada: the peaceful revolution*. Washington, DC: EPICA Task Force.
Great Britain 1947. *Report on closer association of the British West Indian Colonies*. London: HMSO.

Gonsalves, R. E. 1981. *The non-capitalist path of development: Africa and the Caribbean*. London: Caribbean Publishers.
Hodge, M. & C. Searle, n.d.. '*Is freedom we making*': the new democracy in Grenada. Grenada Government Information Service.
Jacobs, R. 1974. The move toward Grenadian independence. In *Independence for Grenada – myth or reality?* 21–33. St Augustine, Trinidad: Institute of International Relations.
Jacobs, W. R. & I. Jacobs 1983. *Grenada: el camino hacia la revolucion*. Mexico: Editorial Katun.
Lewis, W. A. 1965. *The agony of the eight*. Bridgetown, Barbados: Advocate.
Lewis, V. 1974. Commentary. In *Independence for Grenada – myth or reality?* 53–5. St Augustine, Trinidad: Institute of International Relations.
Lowenthal, D. & C. G. Clarke 1980. Island Orphans: Barbuda and the rest. *Journal of Commonwealth and Comparative Politics* **18**, 293–307.
Mandle, J. R. 1985. *Big revolution, small country: the rise and fall of the Grenada revolution*. Lanham, Md.: The North–South Publishing Company.
O'Shaughnessy, H. 1984. *Grenada: revolution, invasion and aftermath*. London: Sphere Books.
Payne, A., P. Sutton, & T. Thorndike 1984. *Grenada: revolution and invasion*. London: Croom Helm.
Ramphal, S. S. 1960. Federation in the West Indies. *Caribbean Quarterly* **6**, 21–9.
Sandford, G. & R. Vigilante 1984. *Grenada: the untold story*. New York and London: Madison Books.
Searle, C. n.d. *Grenada: the struggle against destabilization*. London: Writers and Readers Publishing Cooperative.
Singham, A. W. 1967. Legislative–executive relations in smaller territories. In *Problems of smaller territories*, B. Benedict (ed.), 134–48. London: Athlone Press.
Singham, A. W. 1968. *The hero and the crowd in a colonial polity*. New Haven and London: Yale University Press.
Smith, M. G. 1965. *Stratification in Grenada*. Berkeley and Los Angeles: University of California Press.
State Department and Department of Defense 1984. *Grenada documents: an overview and selection*. Washington, DC: State Department and Department of Defense.
Thorndike, T. 1985. *Grenada: politics, economics and society*. London: Frances Pinter.

6 *Antigua and Barbuda*

Tony Thorndike

By all accepted criteria, Antigua and Barbuda is a typical small state. It has a population of 79 000 (Barbuda: 1500), an area of 440 square kilometres (Barbuda: 160 square kilometres), and a virtual monocultural economy with tourism contributing over 40% of gross domestic product (GDP) and up to 60% of employment, direct and indirect. Far less clear, however, is the rôle of size as a variable in the political, economic, and social development of this twin-island polity. Clearly, it cannot be ignored but excessive determinism is fanciful and misleading.

It would be more accurate to suggest that, in the context of Antigua and Barbuda, smallness has helped shape the *processes* of political and social interaction and has reduced the political and economic options available. But it has not been the critical factor shaping political and social *structures* and the *direction* of economic development. Put another way, smallness illuminates the political, economic, and social dynamic but has not determined it. Size, then, coexists with other variables. In Antigua and Barbuda's case, they are the important historical heritages of slavery and more than three centuries of British colonialism, the limitations of natural resources, and geopolitical location. Collectively, they have created a pervasive milieu of psychological dependency which contains and informs the social and political process as a whole.

Dependency and smallness

The first of these variables, the experience of slavery and colonialism, ensured a thorough implantation of Eurocentric values, specifically political and cultural, in lieu of those lost in the horrors of the Middle Passage. From this, a form of psychological dependency developed: not only had the customs, values, and institutions of the metropole to be faithfully copied but also, like the slave-master of old, the metropole was expected to succour and fulfil the high materialist expectations associated with the life-style of the adopted culture. In this respect, Antigua and Barbuda is no different from its fellow West Indian territories, the New World's new states, as they have been called. They are all in the New World but not fully part of it; of the Third World but mentally constituents of the First.

Yet, in depth and extent, psychological dependency is perhaps most marked in this twin-island state. The strong US presence in Antigua is clearly a major factor: this dates from the establishment of the large US Air Force base at Coolidge Field as part of the 1940 Anglo-American destroyers-for-bases deal, and was later reinforced by the development of the tourist industry in which US visitors presently constitute over half of the total. Such a presence has helped to widen the gulf between expectations and the ability to realize them. As a local paper bewailed, 'We live in a bicycle society with Cadillac tastes' (*Workers Voice* 1978).

The entry of the US and the implantation of US values was facilitated by the lack of national identity felt or expressed by the majority of Antiguans. Although slave revolts, together with exploits of individual heroism in the struggle against oppression, have produced a rich folk-history, only fragments of it have been recorded. The national Antiguan archives have traditionally received scant regard and when they, and the national library, fell victim to earthquake damage in 1970, nothing was done to restore them. By contrast, the deep concern felt by the Barbudans when the extensive records of the Codrington family, who had owned the island and its people for nearly two centuries, were auctioned to private buyers was both widespread and loudly expressed (*Guardian* 1980).

Although there are Antiguans who feel a genuine sense of loss of their national heritage, they are clearly outnumbered by those who identify with the US and its values. The identification is immediately apparent to the visitor; the US dollar, for example, is used far more extensively than the local East Caribbean (EC) currency. Wages rose fast following the signing of the 1940 Treaty, far outstripping those of neighbouring islands, and labour had to be imported to help reap the sugar crop in place of Antiguans anxious to work for the Americans (Colonial Report 1956). After the end of the war and with the rundown of the base, both economic and psychological depression set in. 'The atmosphere is consistently depressing,' reported one commentator in the mid-1950s, 'physically sombre and silent, socially morose and lethargic' (Lowenthal 1955:71). No wonder, then, that tourism was so readily accepted as a panacea.

Although this degree of psychological dependency is special to Antigua, a more familiar associated legacy of colonialism, and something which is continually being reinforced, is that of economic dependency. Admittedly, smallness has restricted possibilities of product diversification in Antigua, notwithstanding the market opportunities available through the Caribbean Community (CARICOM). A lack of economy of scale, high factor and transportation costs, shortages of adequately trained managers, and scarcity of risk capital are problems typical of small economies. But, using McIntyre's (1966) invaluable formulation, this structural dependency is fatally reinforced in Antigua and Barbuda's case by functional dependency. The wilful neglect of food production, which dates from the days of slavery, has persisted despite some encouragement by the government in the early 1980s. The failure to diversify and to develop locally owned capital investment is another manifestation of the problem. As with the West Indies generally, Antigua's bourgeoisie are more merchants than entrepreneurs, a characteristic accentuated by the restriction of smallness on the profitability of industry.

Although it is totally unrealistic even to suggest that the shift from sugar to tourism was ill conceived – after all, Antigua has few resources other than attractive beaches and a magnificent airport facility, which was fully converted to civilian use by December 1960 – the dominance of such a largely foreign-owned and seasonal industry put the economy more at the mercy of international financial whim than ever before. Encouraged by colonial exhortation that tourism was the means to development (Ministry of Overseas Development 1967), suitable land was purchased by the island government. Visitor arrivals jumped from 5270 in 1953 to 35 101 in 1962, reflecting the reopening of Nelson's Dockyard as a prime attraction and the extension of the Coolidge runway to take the first Pan-Am jet. Progress continued and there were 65 369 stopover arrivals in 1970 and 99 536 in 1979. A decline was recorded in 1974–6, reflecting depressed economic conditions in North America, but recovery was swift after 1982. In 1984, 129 099 visitors arrived and 1985 saw a further 13.5% increase.

The apparent health of the tourist industry is, however, misleading. Firstly, it disguises an underlying trend towards shorter stopovers, particularly characteristic of the North American market. Secondly, although it was estimated that US $67 million was earned from the industry in 1983, 60% (or 40% of total foreign exchange income) was spent on imported food and beverages. Another 15% was lost through other imports, profit remission, management fees and licences, and expatriate salaries (Eastern Caribbean Central Bank 1985). Notwithstanding this, the industry's success has reduced the need to obtain IMF aid.

In 1984 Prime Minister Vere Bird ordered recourse to commercial borrowing to help pay the interest due on Antigua's debt (near to US $100 million at the close of the year), rather than submit to IMF demands for a 40% cut in the bloated public sector (IMF 1983). The World Bank (1984), however, warned that Antigua and Barbuda's credit-worthiness was at stake and, in his March 1985 Budget Address, Finance Minister John St Luce repeated a pledge made in the two previous years to embark upon a 'structural adjustment programme' (Government of Antigua 1985). But, as before, no details were spelt out. What stands out is Antigua's consistent failure to develop alternative agriculture and, above all, to forge linkages between the existing agricultural sector and the hotel industry with its voracious demand for food. This is an indictment of policy. The trade gap in 1984 was US $99.7 million (Eastern Caribbean Central Bank 1985), despite a half-hearted attempt to impose import curbs, and little improvement is expected. It may be that Antigua and Barbuda can be considered technically bankrupt.

As for the remaining variables which make up the framework

of dependency, the geopolitical factor is critical. The continuation of the United States' military presence, albeit much curtailed, long after the departure of US servicemen from the other colonies listed in the 1940 Treaty, bears clear witness to Antigua's pivotal position in Washington's strategic design in the Eastern Caribbean. In practical terms, the annual rental income for the base, US $4.2 million since 1977, is useful to Antigua considering the unexpired span of the 99-year lease, but its military worth to the United States is witnessed by the fact that in October 1985 agreement was reached on its use by the US as a centre for training regional security forces, particularly in coastguard protection and drug traffic control.

However, to both parties its symbolic value is perhaps just as important. Not only is it also used to train paramilitary forces newly established in the Eastern Caribbean following the invasion of Grenada, but it also joins the substantial Voice of America facility and the relatively large US Embassy to institutionalize the Antigua–US alliance. There are critics of this alliance who reach to the highest levels of the ruling Antigua Labour Party (ALP), but the reality is that it both underpins the continued prosperity of Antigua and Barbuda and permeates the entire political process of the twin-island state. In summary, then, dependency in its various manifestations may have been the central influence upon the development of Antigua and Barbuda, but that does not eliminate the rôle of smallness, which has played its part in a number of significant ways.

The achievement of independence

For example, smallness was undoubtedly an influential factor in the constitutional progress of Antigua and Barbuda to independence, a goal which the two islands finally achieved in November 1981 after several false starts. The first was the collapse of the West Indies Federation in 1962 on the very day it was due to assume independence; thereafter Vere Bird, Antigua's leader, helped undermine the subsequent proposals for an Eastern Caribbean Federation (Bahadoorsingh 1969). Antigua was enjoying a tourist construction boom and Bird was in no mood to fund poorer members of the would-be federation. As the colonial power, Britain was anxious to chart a constitutional course which recognized the need for political advancement for the smaller jetsam of the federal experiment and yet respected the perception of a 'threshold of viability'. This articulated fears that independence could not be sustained by such small political entities.

In reality, although Britain, Antigua, and the other fellow remnants of the Federation agreed that independence was not a viable option, their rationales were different. Whereas Britain feared the emergence upon the world stage of politically irresponsible mendicant states, the island governments saw independence as too costly and as running the risk of a reduction in British aid (Thorndike 1980). Accordingly, Britain offered a modified and less liberal version of the associated statehood agreement pioneered in 1965 by the Cook Islands. At a constitutional conference in 1966, it was accepted by Antigua, together with Dominica, Grenada, St Kitts–Nevis–Anguilla, St Lucia, and St Vincent. The arrangements were formalized by the 1967 West Indies Act and Antigua assumed statehood on 27 February 1967. The new status, in essence, gave full 'internal independence', British reserve powers being limited to defence and foreign affairs. In fact, these matters were handled in consultation with Antigua, to which much executive authority was delegated.

The new arrangements were not a success. Britain's responsibilities were not matched by power; in particular, there was an extraordinary difficulty in isolating internal from external affairs, given the high exposure of Antigua and its fellow associates to international influences. The legal imbroglio in 1969 following the tragi-comedy of Anguilla's secession from St Kitts and Nevis brought the point home forcefully, and other subsequent difficulties reinforced dissatisfaction with the scheme. By 1972, the experience of the relationship convinced Britain that, should the associates ask for independence, it would not stand in their way. The status was voluntary and unilaterally terminable by Britain, although for the associate to do so would involve a referendum and a legislative vote, each requiring a two-thirds majority.

In common with all the other associated states, commencing with Grenada in 1973, Antigua requested in late 1975 that Britain use its discretionary powers. This was later cancelled but the request was repeated in August 1980. After a constitutional conference in the following December, the draft constitution was finally approved by Westminster in July 1981. The collapse of the initial negotiations was due to the re-election in February 1976 of the conservative ALP on a 'no-independence' ticket, thus aborting the independence negotiations begun by Premier George Walter of the Progressive Labour Movement administration. The drawn-out nature of the 1980-1 negotiations with Britain stemmed directly from the opposition and the particular demands of the Barbudan community (Simon 1980). Fearful of another Anguillan fiasco, Britain quietly and successfully pressured the ALP to make constitutional, financial, and other concessions to the islanders of the former ward (Lowenthal & Clarke 1980).

Ironically, the overriding reason for the eventual successful pursuit of independence was that its non-possession closed the doors to many sources of international economic assistance. In particular, it prevented the full representation of Antigua's aid interests within the European Community, following British membership in 1973, and full participation in the process of political co-operation within CARICOM. Independence, in other words, was not sought for its own sake and intrinsic value, but rather as a means of more effectively managing the economic inheritance of dependency. It did not break the psychological hold of the past.

The political process I: accumulation, 1946-67

Modern Antiguan politics date from the decision in 1946 of the Antiguan Trades and Labour Union (ATLU) to contest the elections for the two elective seats allocated to Antigua in the then Leeward Islands Legislative Council. Winning them, its political committee renamed itself the Antigua Labour Party. The party and union remained virtually indistinguishable for the next 20 years, there being dual leadership and no differentiation of organizational rôles. When first constituted, the ATLU was strongly influenced by the British Trades Union Congress and the democratic socialism of the British Labour Party (Nicholson 1976). Over time, however, it moved towards a more conservative labourism, defined by a commitment to the improvement of the working classes within existing society (Henry 1983).

No socialist reorganization was envisaged, but strong anti-planter and anti-upper class sentiments were expressed, especially during strikes. Anticolonialism was comparatively mild, never reaching revolutionary dimensions, except when the government was perceived to be siding with the hated planters, as was the case in disturbances in 1948-50. These apart, Antiguan politics followed a largely well trodden path characteristic of most modern colonies in the Caribbean, heavily conditioned as they were by imperial values. As Lindsay (1981:6) put it, 'Everywhere and at all times, the emergence and persistence of imperialist domination has been inextricably linked to the operationalization of techniques which successfully encourage individuals and groups to accept ideas and orientations about themselves and their societies which bear little or no truthful relationships to the concrete or real world situations in which they live.'

These 'techniques' were largely unconsciously assumed by the ATLU/ALP leadership. There was no great desire to supplant British governance, only to influence it as and when the interests of the working classes demanded. Formal political power remained unchallenged in Government House and the union worked closely with the administration in allocating labour not only in the public sector but also in the privately owned plantations, a development which seemed quite normal to the colonial authority (Colonial Report 1963). When constitutional advancement came, it was more as a result of decisions taken on the scale and pace of decolonization within the Empire generally than of local pressures. For all that, the ATLU/ALP was not slow to take advantage. Holding all the seats, ministerial authority was assumed in 1956; and an elective majority in the Antigua Legislative Council was conceded in 1961 under a new constitution.

Antigua's political development was thus characterized by ATLU/ALP dominance. The smallness of the polity undoubtedly aided the process of political accumulation and leadership entrenchment. The limited size of the population, let alone the electorate, all living in villages within sight of each other, encouraged the development of widespread social networks which favoured and sustained charismatic political personalities, epitomized best of all, of course, by Vere Bird. In such an atmosphere, clientelism and patronage were critical tools in the process of political accumulation, but the corollary was the need to eliminate competition arising through factionalism, itself equally personality-based.

Admittedly, factionalism is a common feature of underdevelopment as competitive networks emerge in the battle for spoils and scarce resources. In Antigua's case, the risk deepened because of the structural problem of union–party dominance and unity which permitted little opportunity for opposition to be institutionally expressed. This dominance was facilitated by the fact of smallness as gradually early leaders of ATLU like Douglas Roberts and Reginald Stevens were forced out by the Bird faction (Richards 1964). Bird nominees quickly filled their positions. More and more, union–party congresses became rubber stamps and a benign authoritarianism settled upon Antigua and Barbuda.

The political process II: polarization, 1967–81

But smallness could equally help to create the opposite to dominance. When eventually a credible issue-based challenge emerged to this authoritarianism, popular loyalties were split asunder. The size factor intensified the divide as Antiguan was pitted against Antiguan, household against household, resulting in an extraordinary degree of polarization. The underlying cause was the union–party fusion upon which was based the Bird faction's power. This may have been useful when colonial labour ordinances had to be challenged, but as decolonization progressed and the ALP assumed more political power, union activists felt themselves increasingly and, eventually, intolerably contained. By the late 1960s the party side of the fusion was dominant. Bird was both Premier and ATLU President, his ministers the union's executive officers. As it had shifted rightwards, the leadership had also presided over a distinctive pattern of state–class relations as more of the economy was brought under its control. Matters came to a head in early 1967 with opposition crystallizing around the union's general secretary, George Walter.

The issue was the nationalization of the sugar industry, an act undertaken by the government to ensure its continuance in the face of prolonged drought and low prices (Campbell & Edwards 1965). Walter called a stike in April 1967 to back up wage demands for its employees. Dismissed by an enraged Bird, Walter and his supporters formed the rival Antigua Workers Union (AWU) in July. Membership grew rapidly, picking up the dockworkers and many public sector employees, all of whom harboured grudges against Bird. Walter moved quickly to consolidate the AWU's position by creating a political arm, the Progressive Labour Movement (PLM).

The PLM's base was widened as it worked closely with other emergent opposition groups. One was Rowan Henry's small Antigua Progressive Movement (APM), which had been forged by professional interests, outraged at Bird's enactment of a Public Order Act aimed against non-parliamentary opposition. Another was the Antigua and Barbuda Democratic Movement (ABDM), led by Robert Hall, a white planter. This had been formed as long ago as 1947, fired by Hall's intense personal dislike of Bird. The PLM left wing was made up of an identifiable group of middle-class intellectuals clustered around the teachers' union leader, Tim Hector.

Early success was recorded with the calling of a general strike in February 1968 and victory in four by-elections, but unity was short-lived. Although the PLM was more democratic in its internal organization than the ALP, it soon followed the pattern established by its rival. Each faction within the party jostled for position and a fierce struggle ensued. Gradually the AWU faction and Walter emerged supreme and the bulk of the APM group departed, eventually fading away a few years later after Henry's death. Walter then challenged the left faction by insisting upon centralized party control and thus prompting Hector and his colleagues to leave to form their own black power organization. Neither purge weakened the PLM's advance as the ALP's chickens came home to roost. In February 1971 the PLM won a bitterly fought election, the 'broom election', so called because of the processions of brooms organized by the PLM to symbolize the sweeping away of the ALP. The ploy certainly worked as even Vere Bird lost his seat in a low poll.

The PLM administration, however, rapidly fell into the pattern established by the ALP. Clientelism, patronage, and victimization became the order of the day. Further democratization, the original *raison d'être* of the PLM, was abandoned in favour of a cynical exploitation of state power, using all the power accumulated under a loosely state capitalist development policy. The party machine, with the AWU in tow, forced the ATLU out of state-owned utilities and the public sector generally and, in response to ALP and ATLU attacks in the media, a highly repressive newspaper ordinance was passed. Violence flared between rival groups of union members, and the civil service was disrupted by dismissals and selective promotions: corruption became a cancer. Nothing escaped the bitter competition, not even carnival.

Needless to say, there was a price to pay. The economy went into sharp decline under the cumulative impact of the 1973 oil crisis, Antigua's increasingly poor image overseas, strikes and violence. Visitor arrivals fell and in 1974 the government was forced to suspend all interest payments on government debt. This was not surprising: the 1974 budget showed that debt servicing swallowed up 40% of recurrent expenditure (Government of Antigua 1974). To help retrieve the situation, victimization was eased and Walter announced that independence would be sought. In what was hoped to be a political diversion, financial reasons were cited. Yet the move only led to partisan division sinking to new depths, the ALP insisting that Antigua's economy was not ready for such a move and claiming that independence under Walter would lead to financial ruin. Opposition also came from the Barbudan secessionists who feared, with justification, that their unique land tenure system would be sold to foreign entrepreneurs and their neglected economy allowed to deteriorate further.

The February 1976 election swept the PLM from power, the ALP winning 11 of the 17 seats, with 6 for the PLM and 1 for an Independent, Barbudan member Eric Burton. The turnout was an extraordinary 95%. The new government lost no time: legal action alleging corruption was brought against several PLM ministers, including Walter, and, after a lull, job victimization recommenced. Independence negotiations ceased but it was not this issue that was critical in the election; more important was the last-minute pledge by the ALP to abolish income tax. The persecutions and clientelist policies pursued by the restored ALP leadership further weakened the opposition. But Bird and his colleagues were careful not to be so authoritarian as before.

These tactics led to an increase in the ALP government's majority in the April 1980 election. Walter had been successfully cleared on appeal but was released from custody too late to join the contest. During his imprisonment, his former associate Robert Hall strengthened his position within the party. Reassuming leadership of the AWU, Walter was unable to regain his former party prominence and, in order to isolate Walter further, Hall and the PLM expelled the AWU faction, which promptly transformed itself into the United People's Movement (UPM). The opposition had thus been successfully divided and Bird and the ALP were able to change tack and lead the country to independence, the only resistance coming from the so-called Barbuda People's Movement, which favoured secession and, failing that, reversion to colonial status.

The political process III: internationalization, 1981–5

Until independence in November 1981, the rôle of smallness had been most manifest in influencing the *style* of government in Antigua. Both Britain and the US noted with approval the observance of Westminster constitutional norms, but neither chose to comment upon the mismatch between a small and less developed polity and an adversarial system developed over centuries for a much larger and more sophisticated environment, with 'apolitical' civil servants and the concept of a 'loyal' opposition. However, a new economic and political situation was slowly unfolding in the 1970s which had to be addressed once independence was achieved: that of the internationalization of Antigua and Barbuda.

Mass tourism was one factor, the other was the state's gradual incorporation into the Pax Americana. Independence meant the opportunity to replace aid from a parsimonious Britain, anxious to wash its hands of its West Indian possessions, by the more bountiful provision of the US. The psychological dependency induced by colonialism thereafter took on a new hue as the Antigua–US alliance gradually consolidated. In other words, whereas smallness in the 1960s was largely internal in its sociopolitical impact, in the 1980s it helped condition foreign policy by limiting the capacity of the entrenched leadership to consider alternative geopolitical options.

It was the radical Antigua Caribbean Liberation Movement (ACLM), formed by Hector and others after their departure from the PLM in the mid-1970s, that was to challenge this orientation. Whereas the vaguely left-of-centre Walter tried to argue that his UPM rump was 'progressive', in reality UPM policies were little different from those of the ALP and the by now very weak PLM. By contrast, the ACLM *was* different. Its major weapon was its newspaper, *Outlet*. The most widely read on the island, it relentlessly exposed neglect and corruption. It castigated the ALP's willingness to bow to foreign interests in the tourist industry, alleged Mafia penetration of loosely regulated casinos and banks and criticized its pro-US foreign policy. This orientation, it pointed out, even extended to having a US Air Force band to lead carnivals.

As evidence emerged in support of the ACLM's claims, such as the illegal sale of passports to non-Antiguans and maladministration of foreign loans, its propaganda began to reach a wider audience regionally and hemispherically. Predictably, *Outlet* was denounced as 'communist' by the US Embassy (*Caribbean Contact* 1982). Its crowning success came with the exposure of the activities of the Space Research Corporation. A Canadian company, it used Antigua in 1979–80 as a base from which to 'launder' arms shipments to South Africa. The Birds (by this time three members of the family were in the Cabinet) strenuously denied accusations variously made by Joshua Nkomo, the African National Congress, and Hector. But when faced with proof by a BBC TV documentary, the amazing naivety of the government was exposed. The Space Research Corporation was expelled immediately prior to the 1980 poll.

Once the dust of that shameful episode had settled, criticisms were made afresh and the government reacted by raids on the *Outlet* printing press and lawsuits, all of which had little effect upon *Outlet*'s popularity. Nevertheless, the ACLM decided not to contest the April 1984 election. The ALP won 16 seats, the Barbuda seat being retained by Eric Burton who, although Independent, supported the ALP in the House of Assembly with the PLM and UPM being almost wiped out. In a virtually issueless election, what was most marked was the apathy of the electorate (Thorndike 1985).

The extent of the dominance of the ALP after 1984, and 77-year-old Vere Bird's continued leadership, paradoxically sowed seeds of dissent both inside and outside the party. In particular, there was a widespread apprehension, articulated *sotto voce* on more than one occasion by US officials (*Caribbean Contact* 1985), that a major financial or other scandal, such as that of the Space Research Corporation, could lead to a political crisis in the absence of a parliamentary opposition. Others were apprehensive over the government's persecution of Hector and the ACLM, particularly after the US invasion of Grenada in October 1983, a move strongly supported by Antigua and Barbuda.

Equally important was the emergence of doubts within the government about the full extent of Vere Bird's pro-US policy. As this was associated with Deputy Prime Minister Lester Bird, the widely accepted heir-apparent to his father's throne, it was misleadingly seen as a ploy in the succession stakes. In fact, Lester Bird's reservations on this matter are distinctly muted, as well they might be given that the alliance with the US is popular and seen as the key to continued prosperity. Prime Minister Vere Bird was in the vanguard of those island leaders welcoming US involvement in regional security through its encouragement of the October 1982 Memorandum of Understanding, a mutual defence pact signed by the various states of the Eastern Caribbean. As already indicated, Antigua supported and contributed police to the Caribbean Peacekeeping Force, installed in Grenada after the revolutionary military government had been toppled, and Vere Bird was in the forefront of those in the region supporting the training by US forces of Special Service Units, in effect paramilitary branches of police forces ready to be deployed against 'subversives' of all types. In short, for Vere Bird, suggestions of fawning to US interests are laughed off in face of geopolitical and economic reality.

However, Lester Bird's criticisms of the US have struck some chords because US largesse in the post-Grenada era has not been so generous as first hoped. His comments have also addressed fundamental problems, specifically that Washington's priorities are not necessarily those of small, less developed islands. During a visit to China in June 1985, he alluded to 'external powers' who sought 'to impose economic and political solutions with little regard for the agenda of development set by the area itself' (Bird 1985). Earlier in 1984, he had remarked that the importance accorded to the private sector by the Reagan administration, within the provisions of the Caribbean Basin Initiative, was 'naive' and failed to recognize the critical need for government-financed infrastructural development. It was, he said, important for the US to show 'beyond doubt' that communism was 'not an alternative' (*Caribbean Insight* 1984). He has also made clear his reservations about the widespread deployment of US military advisors in the region. What should be added, however, is that at present all that this constitutes is words. Antigua and Barbuda has as yet made no attempt to carve out for itself, as a small state, any increased room for manoeuvre within the framework of contemporary US control of the Caribbean.

Conclusion

It is reasonable to suggest by way of conclusion that the element of smallness in area and demographic terms greatly facilitated the development in Antigua of an all-embracing party dominance, whether ALP or PLM, and that the nature of the society made personality politics all the more likely. But it is a different matter, and much more contentious, to argue that smallness made such a process inevitable. There is also no doubt that small size has attracted gangster and other undesirable elements who see small islands as admirable bases for their operations. They seem able to buy the occasional politician whose 'street wisdom' is somewhat lacking: the Space Research Corporation episode provides ample evidence of that.

Smallness can also induce a sense of insecurity which dictates the need for a protector; but it need not create such a depth of psychological dependency that not only the autonomy of the state but sovereignty itself is challenged. Yet, ultimately, size is but one variable among others. The danger lies – and this is the moral of the story of Antigua and Barbuda – in government and business leaders perceiving there to be no alternative to the choice of development and foreign policy options that historically have been made. Admittedly, these options are limited – but limited as much in mental as in physical terms. To embrace willingly this straightjacket, as Antigua has done, is a poor portent for small states.

References

Bahadoorsingh, K. 1969. The East Caribbean federation attempt. In *Regionalism and the Commonwealth Caribbean*, R. Preiswerk (ed.), 157–69. St Augustine, Trinidad: Institute of International Relations.

Bird, L. 1985. Mimeo, 3.

Campbell, L. G. & D. Edwards 1965. *Agriculture and Antigua's economy: possibilities and problems of adjustment*. Agricultural Series 1. Cave Hill, Barbados: Institute of Social and Economic Research.

Caribbean Contact 1982. **10**(5), 16.

Caribbean Contact 1985. **13**(3), 2.

Caribbean Insight 1984. **7**(3), 3.

Colonial Report 1956. *Leeward Islands, 1953 and 1954*. London: HMSO.

Colonial Report 1963. *Antigua, 1959 and 1960*. London: HMSO.

Eastern Caribbean Central Bank 1985. *Annual report 1984*. St Kitts: Eastern Caribbean Central Bank.

Government of Antigua 1974. *Budget speech*. Mimeo.

Government of Antigua 1985. *Budget address*. Mimeo.

Guardian (London) 1980. 10 December.

Henry, P. 1983. Decolonization and the authoritarian context of democracy in Antigua. In *The newer Caribbean*, P. Henry & C. Stone (eds), 281–312. Philadelphia: Institute for the Study of Human Issues.

IMF (International Monetary Fund) 1983. *Antigua*. Washington, DC: IMF.

Lindsay, L. 1981. *The myth of a civilizing-mission: British colonialism and the politics of symbolic manipulation*. Working Paper No. 31, ISER, University of the West Indies, Mona, Jamaica.

Lowenthal, D. 1955. Economic tribulations in the Caribbean: a case study in the British West Indies. *Inter-American Economic Affairs* **9**(3), 67–81.

Lowenthal, D. & C. G. Clarke 1980. Island orphans: Barbuda and the rest. *Journal of Commonwealth and Comparative Politics*, **18**, 293–307.

McIntyre, A. 1966. Some issues of trade policy in the West Indies. *New World Quarterly* **2**(2), 1–20.

Ministry of Overseas Development 1967. *Report of the tripartite economic survey of the Eastern Caribbean*. London: HMSO.

Nicholson, M. 1976. *The TUC and the West Indian Commission*. Discussion paper, Institute of Commonwealth Studies, London: Mimeo.

Richards, H. 1964. *The struggle and the conquest: twenty-five years of social democracy in Antigua*. St Johns: Antiguan Trades and Labour Union.

Simon, J. 1980. The Antigua and Barbuda independence constitution 1981: a Westminster model with a difference. *Bulletin of Eastern Caribbean Affairs* **7**(8), 1–6.

Thorndike, T. 1980. Associated statehood: quo vadis? In *The Caribbean yearbook of international relations 1977*, 59–82. Augustine, Trinidad: Institute of International Relations.

Thorndike, T. 1985. Antigua and Barbuda. In *Latin America and Caribbean Contemporary Record, 1983–4*, 649–59. New York: Holmes Meier.

Workers Voice (Antigua) 1978. 19 March.

World Bank 1984. *Economic memorandum: Antigua and Barbuda*. Report No. 4695–CRG, International Bank for Reconstruction and Development. Washington, DC.

7 *Fiji*

WILLIAM M. SUTHERLAND

History is replete with instances of attempts to undermine the sovereignty of nations and to frustrate the self-determination of peoples for the purposes of economic or strategic gain. The brunt of recent experience has been borne by Third World countries, and the US invasion of Grenada brought into sharp focus the fragility and vulnerability of small island states. Now that the world's centre of gravity is increasingly shifting away from the Atlantic to the Pacific, consideration of the economic development and geopolitical orientation of island states such as Fiji has taken on a new urgency. These two themes provide the focus for this chapter, and I shall attempt to demonstrate their interrelationship in the Fijian context.

Economic base

The ability of small states generally to achieve their development goals can be expressed in terms of the productive capacity required to enable the wishes and aspirations of the population to be satisfied (Doumenge 1985). This broad and useful conceptualization of the economic viability of small island states would probably find wide agreement and is adopted here. But it is somewhat limited in that it lacks any inherent distinction between social groupings. Consequently, it cannot address the crucial bases of internal social differentiation, which are integral to an adequate understanding of why and how it is that the consequences of smallness affect the various sections of society differently. Put simply, the burden of having to cope with the developmental problems associated with smallness does not fall equally on everyone and the main reason for that is the way in which, historically, social relations have been constituted. This applies as much to the Fijian case as it does to any other. However, before taking up that issue in relation to Fiji, I shall first examine the purely economic dimensions and consequences of Fiji's smallness.

Fiji's total land area is 18 272 square kilometres, but only 10% of the 300 islands of the archipelago are inhabited. The nearest metropolitan capital, Auckland, is about 1900 kilometres away, and the bulk of Fiji's main export, sugar, goes to Europe. By Third World standards, Fiji's economic performance is reasonable. Its per capita gross domestic product (GDP) of Fiji $ 1750 (approximately £1160 at the present rate of exchange) in 1980, for example, was more than twice the figure for all developing countries, and among the Pacific island countries the Fijian economy ranks as one of the most developed. Apart from the larger American and French territories in the region, which rely heavily on metropolitan aid, Fiji's per capita GDP was the highest in 1980. Yet Fiji shares with the other Pacific island countries all the structural disadvantages which come with smallness and severely constrain its ability fully to realize its developmental priorities.

Agriculture is the most important of the productive sectors and its present contribution to GDP (around 24%) is about twice that of the second most important sector, manufacturing (about 12%). Despite the inordinate importance which has long been attached to the tourist industry in Fiji, its contribution is about the same as that for manufacturing industry. In official statistics, tourism is included in the distribution sector as a whole, which makes it difficult to ascertain precisely its particular impact. A recent official estimate for the period between 1980 and 1984 did put it at about 12% of GDP. However, not only is the tourist industry reliant on imports, it is also dominated by foreign capital (Britton 1983, Sutherland 1984), and that is why it has the highest leakage factor, officially estimated at 66% (Government of Fiji 1985), of all the major economic sectors. Notwithstanding these qualifications, gross tourist earnings since 1982 have overtaken sugar revenue as the largest foreign exchange earner. In that year, they stood at 27.3% of the total, compared with 24.6% for sugar, and the latest estimates for 1985 are 28% and 18.7% (Fiji Bureau of Statistics 1985). It is not surprising, therefore, that claims about tourism's supposed central importance to the economy have been made with increasing frequency over the last few years. Moreover, these claims have been accompanied by calls for greater diversion of state resources to the industry so as to hasten its supposedly much needed expansion.

There are good reasons to doubt the wisdom of such redistribution of state resources. In addition to the industry's low internal linkages and its high rate of external leakage, which have already been noted, there can be added the point that sugar employs far more people than tourism. Finally, sugar's poor showing recently has been largely due to the extremely low prices on the international market, and it may well be that the recent upturn in the free market price will restore the industry to its former ranking as the country's largest foreign exchange earner. But even if it does not, Fiji is constantly searching for long-term supply arrangements on reasonably fair terms. Presently, about 38% of Fiji's sugar is sold at a favourable price under the Lomé Convention, and there are similar agreements with several other countries. So despite the greater attractiveness which has apparently come to surround the tourist industry, it seems likely that sugar will continue to be the mainstay of the economy.

This highlights another important feature of the Fijian economy, which is that its structure has remained relatively constant. It is true that the primary sector's contribution to GDP fell by 6% between 1970 and 1984. It is also true that the fall was compensated for largely by proportionate increases in two other sectors: Government and Other Services and Transport and Communication. There is some substance, therefore, in the official view that the country 'has shifted from being a mainly primary based to a more service oriented economy' (Government of Fiji 1985:2). Furthermore, with a slightly greater contribution to GDP by the manufacturing sector, there may be legitimate grounds for claiming 'some success in Fiji's import substitution programmes, particularly in food supply' (Government of Fiji 1985:3). Both of these claims need qualification, but even if they were to be fully accepted, it is still the case that the primary sector, particularly sugar production, remains the backbone of the economy.

What this points to is the relative failure of attempts at economic diversification, at least in respect of productive activity. The one productive area on which high hopes had been placed is commercial tuna fishing. Fiji's exclusive economic zone is about 1.2 million square kilometres, but the initial expectation that the country's increased tuna resources might lay the foundation of a successful industry has not been realized. Indeed, production levels in the fisheries sector fell from just under 10 000 tonnes in 1981 to about 5500 tonnes in 1985. So, though fishery has earned valuable foreign exchange (about Fiji $18 million in 1985), it has not produced any significant change to the structure of the economy's productive base.

Related to this structural continuity is the increasing importance of the state sector, which accounts for about one-quarter of GDP and employs about 30% of all wage and salary earners. Perhaps, therefore, the view that the economy is becoming increasingly 'service oriented' is valid. But there is another side to this. With limited employment opportunities existing in the other sectors, the state is looked upon increasingly as a source of jobs, and the continued viability of the state depends on how well it responds to that need. Burdened therefore with increasing responsibility for meeting the aspirations of growing numbers of people, especially in the face of persistent pressure on a narrowly based and externally oriented economy, the state has come under more and more strain. And this it clearly recognizes. Witness, for example, this official account:

> The government sector, which played a leading rôle in the first decade of Independence, has come under severe strains since 1981. The operating budget deficits widened, mainly due to increases in personal emoluments and debt servicing which rose at a faster rate than general revenue. The rising deficits forced Government to borrow more, partly from external commercial sources, which in turn have further increased its debt service obligations. Capital expenditure fell, in real terms, because of the completion of major projects and also because of measures to curb the widening overall government deficit. Overall central government deficit rose from 4.8% of GDP in 1980 to an estimated 5.5% in 1985. The balance of payments

also came under pressure after 1980. The decline in export receipts as world sugar and other commodity prices collapsed was only partially offset by lower petroleum prices and higher receipts from tourism. Private capital inflows, on the other hand, fell considerably (Government of Fiji 1985).

Economic openness and indebtedness

As this catalogue of problems makes clear, much of the stress stems from the heavy external orientation of the economy. Sugar is still by far the most important export commodity. In 1984, for example, it accounted for 55.7% of all exports and was followed by gold (10.4%), coconut oil (9.4%), tinned fish (7.2%), and other minor items (Government of Fiji 1985). But the country's exports have not been sufficient to meet import costs and persistent trade deficits have weighed heavily on the economy. Between 1980 and 1984, for example, the deficit increased progressively from Fiji $153.2 million to Fiji $206.8 million. The bulk of Fiji's imports fall into five categories and their proportions of the total in 1984 were as follows: petroleum products 22%, manufactured goods 18.7%, machinery and equipment 17.8%, food items 15.4%, and raw materials 11.7% (Fiji Bureau of Statistics 1985). Most of the imports came from Australia (34.6% in 1984), Asia (17%), Japan (16.2%), and New Zealand (16.1%); and the main export destinations were Britain (28.6%), Australia (13.7%), and the US (10.1%).

These figures indicate a significant change in Fiji's pattern of international trade. Traditionally, Fiji's main trading partners were Australia, Britain, and New Zealand (Sutherland 1984), and although Australia has retained its pre-eminent position, Asian countries are now featuring more prominently. In 1984, for example, just six countries accounted for the bulk of Fiji's trade deficit: Australia, Japan, New Zealand, Singapore, Hong Kong, and West Germany.

Alongside the continuing trade imbalances stands the problem of increasing indebtedness. Not only has the state's budget deficit continued to climb, reaching Fiji $67.5 million in 1984 (Reserve Bank of Fiji 1985), but also the country's level of indebtedness has progressively worsened. External debt has more than doubled since 1979 and in 1984 the figure stood at Fiji $116.8 million. The level of domestic debt in 1984 was Fiji $324.2 million. As was noted above, the state is extremely concerned about the level of indebtedness and the way in which it has sought to cope with the mounting financial pressure is therefore worthy of note. For it appears that the state has chosen to rely less on external finance and more on local sources to meet its financial needs. However, in the ten years between 1975 and 1984, for example, its annual financing requirements increased more than fourfold from Fiji $14.5 million to Fiji $67.5 million. In that time, the proportion of funds raised from local sources increased from 56.6% to 72.4% whereas the proportion from external sources (most of which has come from the open market) correspondingly decreased from 43.4% to 27.6%. Clearly this change owed much to differential interest rates, but more significant is the fact that the single most important source of funds has been the Fiji National Provident Fund (FNPF). Between 1975 and 1984, the FNPF's contribution to the state's financial needs increased from 33.1% to 47.4% (Reserve Bank of Fiji 1985).

Although this increasing reliance on internally generated funds might be welcomed as something of an exercise in self-reliance, and hence a positive development, it is clear that the FNPF has become more a source of finance for the state than an organization which might serve as the basis for a comprehensive system of social security in the country, which is what it was originally intended to be. Against this, of course, it could be argued that the state's use of FNPF funds has increased its capacity to respond to the needs of the population. Cheaper local finance, it might be argued, has facilitated significantly higher levels of social, infrastructural, and productive expenditure and thus significantly higher levels of employment. Just how much truth there is in this is extremely difficult to gauge, but the very fact that the state has sought to effect a degree of self-reliance and yet is still confronted with major financial difficulties underscores the extreme difficulty of coping with the structural disadvantages of smallness. What is more, there is a racial aspect which compounds the problem further.

Smallness and racial factionalism

Fiji's population, estimated to be 699 000 in 1985, is growing at an annual rate of about 2.2%. With slightly over 40% under 15 years of age, greater pressure can be expected on the current rate of unemployment, which officially is put at around 10.2%. In 1982, for example, 71% of unemployment both in the urban and rural areas occurred in the 15–24 age group (Government of Fiji 1985). The seriousness of that situation is heightened by a significant change in the racial composition of the unemployed. About 50% of the population are Indo-Fijian, 45% are Fijian, and the remaining 5% are of various other races. Between 1976 and 1982, however, the proportion of the unemployed who were Indo-Fijian increased sharply from 48% to 62% whereas the figure for Fijians fell from 46% to 34% and that for all the other races combined similarly fell from 7% to 4% (Government of Fiji 1985). These figures underscore the importance of a certain racial dynamic in the political economy of Fiji which serves to complicate the task of coping with the disadvantages of smallness.

Political organization since the 1960s has centred largely around the Alliance Party and the National Federation Party. The former, which has always been led by Ratu Mara, Fiji's only Prime Minister since independence in 1970, draws most of its support from Fijians whereas the latter draws its support primarily from Indo-Fijians. In the period leading up to independence much was made of Fijian under-representation in economic life. That grievance, coupled with a racially based system of electoral representation and later a racially oriented constitution, opened the way for Fijian domination of the postcolonial state. When Fijians assumed state power, a whole series of measures were introduced with a view to improving the lot of the Fijians: various Fijian economic enterprises were set up; Fijians were encouraged to take up directorships in private companies; leading positions in parastatal organizations were given to Fijians; soft loans were made available by the Fiji Development Bank; the Business Organization and Management Advisory Service was established to help 'Fijians in business'; a policy of 'racial balance' in employment in the public sector was introduced; fully 50% of state scholarships were set aside for Fijian students; and later additional annual sums were made available to the Ministry of Fijian Affairs to provide further scholarships for Fijians.

Such forms of preferential treatment have been the source of much discontent and ill-feeling, but they need to be understood against the historical background of colonial capitalism. In large part, the capitalist-dominated colonial economy depended for its success on a broad convergence of race and class which has usually been described, rather simplistically, as European capital, Indian labour, and Fijian land. Not surprisingly, therefore, racist ideology and practice became potent weapons for the containment of underlying class tension, and they have remained so to the present day. Racial hegemony has meant that social identification and attachment on the basis of class is minimal, especially among the disadvantaged. What this means is that when the consequences of smallness threaten internal stability, it is unlikely that the defence of interests within the country, particularly among the disadvantaged, will be organized on class lines. But even if they were, the state could still employ racial forms of containment; and it is their very effectiveness that explains the high degree of political stability for which Fiji is so renowned. The significance of this argument extends also to Fiji's external relations (Sutherland 1986).

Geopolitical prospects and pitfalls

Fiji has always been a strong ally of the West. In addition to its political and ideological alignment, the country is also important both for its strategic location in the South Pacific and its reasonably developed infrastructure, especially in the field of communications. All this, combined with the recent rift between New Zealand and the US over the port visits by nuclear armed or powered ships, gives Fiji an even more special place in the wider geopolitics of the region. A major shift in US foreign policy towards the region in the mid-1970s led to a higher American profile and marked the onset of 'strategic denial' as the lynchpin of the Western alliance's security strategy in the Pacific. Fiji and Papua New Guinea were identified as 'key regional states' around which policy links would be focused (Dorrance 1980); their subsequent performance has certainly justified Washington's confidence in them, and President Reagan has been quick to show his appreciation.

In 1986, Fiji was the region's first recipient of direct US bilateral assistance, an offer which was made 'in recognition of Fiji's strong pro-Western stance on several regional and global issues, its contribution to UN peacekeeping forces, and its allowing the visits of US Navy ships' (Alves 1985:16). Moreover, for its 'responsible rôle' in world affairs, which incidentally included support for the US invasion of Grenada in 1983, the US has also 'implemented a military aid programme with Fiji that includes money for training assistance and funds to be applied to the purchase of a new Fijian Army standard rifle – the US M-16A2' (Alves 1985:18). Total US military assistance to Fiji in 1985 was worth US $400 000, and the same level is expected for 1986. Small though these figures are in comparison with US aid to other countries, they are none the less important. For not only do they represent an important 'first' for the region, they also mark the beginnings of what will probably be a long-term programme of material support for a small Pacific island state which is strategically important for, and has shown itself to be a solid supporter of, the West. Should that be the case, then the capacity of the state in Fiji to cope with the disadvantages of smallness will increase at least marginally, perhaps significantly.

This scenario is likely only if future governments continue to follow the present Alliance government's pro-Western policies. Here there is uncertainty. It is very unlikely that the predominantly Indian National Federation Party (NFP) will become the government in the foreseeable future, but the same cannot necessarily be said of the Fiji Labour Party, which was founded in mid-1984. For so young a party, it has done remarkably well electorally. It now dominates the capital's municipal council, holds the balance of power in another council, and has significant numbers of seats in others. Although it did not win the parliamentary by-election in December 1985 for a seat previously held by the NFP, its performance was creditable. Coming second behind an Alliance candidate (who won by the slender majority of 241), the Labour candidate beat his NFP rival by well over 2500 votes (Naidu 1986).

How much better the Labour Party will do in the next general election, which is due in 1987, is difficult to tell, but there can be little doubt that its impact will be considerable. More importantly, should Labour win, it appears from available evidence that a Labour government would be more progressive than the present Alliance government, and would follow a more independent line in the area of foreign policy. How the Western powers will respond to such an eventuality could well have direct consequences for the country's political stability. At one extreme would be the possibility of armed external intervention; at the other might be less blatant forms of destabilization designed to undermine such a government. The likelihood of armed intervention against an independent Pacific island state is probably remote (Kiste & Herr 1984), and in the case of Fiji, in particular, a major reason for this is that the deeply conservative nature of Fiji's political culture and major political institutions makes it unlikely that a radical government would survive very long even if it were to be elected. A rather more likely scenario, however, is the use of 'softer' and more insidious means to undermine the viability of a maverick government. And here trade and aid relations form the basis for highly effective options.

As noted above, Australia is Fiji's main trading partner and, with the present Hawke government firmly committed to safeguarding Western security interests, Australian–Fijian trade relations provide a ready means for keeping Fiji in line. The same also applies to aid. Australia is Fiji's largest aid donor. Of the Fiji $31.2 million aid which the country received in 1983, Australia provided about 35%, which is almost twice as much as that received from the next largest donor, the European Economic Community (Government of Fiji 1985). It is significant that Fiji is seeking preferential access to European markets for its fish products. New Zealand too is a major donor country; in 1983 it provided 12% of all aid to Fiji. As is the case with the US, both the Australian and New Zealand aid packages include a significant level of military assistance. Finally, some idea of the fiscal importance of aid can be obtained by comparing it with the level of state expenditure. Again taking 1983 as the base, total aid received was equivalent to 8.5% of the government's budget and the figure for Australian aid alone was just under 3% (Government of Fiji 1985).

These, then, are the sort of economic ties which serve to bind Fiji to the Western powers. Should there be a change of government and should the new régime be viewed by the Western powers as a threat to their interests, then the kind of economic relations identified here would be vulnerable to a campaign of destabilization. Perhaps, however, the need for such a campaign will not arise, at least in the foreseeable future. The Alliance government has held office since independence and the chances are that it will continue to do so for a while yet.

Conclusion

It is likely therefore that Fiji will remain politically stable. The mechanisms of class containment will continue to operate; but should the consequences of smallness, which will continue to be felt most heavily by the disadvantaged classes, seriously threaten stability, external assistance may well be made available in order to defuse tension. Containment is the other side of the coin to stability, and in the case of a small and strategically important island like Fiji, they are both tied in a fundamental way to two broader and related issues – economic vulnerability and Pacific geopolitics.

References

Alves, P. 1985. *The South Pacific islands: new focus needed for US policy.* Georgetown University: Asian Studies Center Backgrounder.

Britton, S. G. 1983. *Tourism and underdevelopment in Fiji.* Monograph 13, Australian National University Development Studies Centre, Canberra.

Dorrance, J. C. 1980. *Oceania and the United States: an analysis of US interests and policy in the South Pacific.* Washington: National Defense University.

Doumenge, F. 1985. The viability of small intertropical islands. In *States, microstates and islands,* E. C. Dommen and P. L Hein (eds.), 70–118. London: Croom Helm.

Government of Fiji 1985. *Fiji's Ninth Development Plan 1986–1990*. Suva, Fiji: Central Planning Office.
Fiji Bureau of Statistics 1985. *Current Economic Statistics*. Suva, Fiji: Government Printing Office.
Kiste, B. & R. A. Herr 1984. *The potential for Soviet penetration of the South Pacific: an assessment*. A paper prepared for the US State Department. Honolulu: mimeo.
Naidu, V. 1986. *The Fiji Labour party and the by-elections of December 1985*. Working Paper No. 2, University of the South Pacific, Suva.
Reserve Bank of Fiji 1985. *Quarterly Review*, March.
Sutherland, W. M. 1984. *The state and capitalist development in Fiji*. Unpublished PhD thesis, University of Canterbury.
Sutherland, W. M. 1986. *Vulnerability in the South Pacific: economic dependence, geopolitics and the postcolonial state*. Unpublished paper, United Nations University conference on Peace and Security in Oceania.

8 *Mauritius*

Martin Minogue

Mauritius is small, remote, and relatively poor (Minogue 1983). It appears to suffer from crippling economic and geographical disadvantages of a kind typical of small islands (Selwyn 1978). With a population of 980 000 it falls within the definition of small states as those with less than 1 million population. These people also inhabit a small space of about 1860 square kilometres. Situated in the Indian Ocean between Africa and India, the nearest land mass, Madagascar, is 800 kilometres distant. The per capita national income of US $1008 (Lloyds Bank 1985) lifts it out of the category of poorest states, but the economy of the island is open, vulnerable, and erratic in its performance. At first glance, then, Mauritius seems unremarkable by small state standards.

Yet Mauritius can lay claim to economic and political achievements atypical of small dependent states. In the 1970s its annual economic growth rate, measured by per capita gross national product, was one of the highest in the developing world, averaging around 8%, but in the best years showing increases of up to 20%. Politically, it has frequently been referred to as a model of democratic participation, characterized by regular elections which determine changes in political control and by a political executive which is limited both by its need to command a majority in a single chamber legislature, and the existence of a written constitution replete with checks, balances, and safeguards (Minogue 1983). Socially, although divided into several communities distinguished by differences of race, colour, language, and religion, there has been a high degree of ethnic collaboration and relative social stability. According to an experienced journalist writing in 1981, Mauritius could, with its free trade unions, active and free press, able, educated public service, and highly literate population, be regarded as a calm, sane, and civilized place (Keatley 1981).

Is Mauritius, then, some kind of success story in a harsh world of underdevelopment littered with economic and political failures? The evidence of this case study produces an equivocal reply. Undoubtedly, though, the colonial and post-independence experience of Mauritius shows deviations from the typical pattern of development in small dependent states (Toussaint 1972). An explanation of these atypical features will focus on the balance of ethnic forces which lies at the heart of the island's political economy, and upon the political and strategic linkages which provide Mauritius with a measure of autonomy and stability within the global economy.

The economy

At first sight the rise and fall in Mauritian economic fortunes since independence was achieved in 1968 illustrates well the classical dilemmas of open, monocrop, export-based economies, exacerbated in this case by the small size of the domestic market. Dependency theorists would certainly find ample evidence to support the contention that Mauritius is a clear case of a political economy characterized by economic and political relations of dependence upon external 'metropolitan' institutions, within a framework of external capitalist exploitation linked to internal control by a metropolitan-oriented local élite. But in reality such a model sits uneasily with the character of economic development and political events in Mauritius. A model of political economy is necessary, but it is not sufficient to explain the totality of Mauritian economic and political relationships (Selwyn 1977).

Interestingly, for a people who are regarded outside as inhabitants of a subtropical paradise, Mauritians are markedly unwilling to stay there. A French research report in the mid-1970s indicated that 85% of Mauritians would leave Mauritius if they could. Emigration rates are not high, but this is mainly because of restrictive immigration policies in receiving countries, especially in Britain; even so, net emigration has averaged 3600 per annum over the past decade and averaged 5000 per annum in 1980 and 1981 (Government of Mauritius 1982). There are many contributing factors, but the principal cause is overpopulation. In the first third of the 20th century the population appeared to stabilize at around 400 000. But by 1962, with a growth rate in excess of 3% per annum, it had expanded to 681 619; and it is now, despite reductions in the birthrate, just short of 1 000 000 inhabitants, with a density of 2600 per square kilometre.

The population explosion in mid-century caused considerable alarm to the island's policy-makers: the economy simply could not sustain such a rapidly growing population. Special reports were commissioned from British experts, notably by Meade on the economy and specifically by Abel-Smith on population policies (Titmuss and Abel-Smith 1960). The problem was easily diagnosed: a large annual rate of increase due to high birthrates and significant reductions in crude death rates and infant mortality rates. Abel-Smith pointed to the obvious solution, namely, restrictions on the birthrate, particularly through family planning policies. The idea was taken up and in the next 20 years remarkable reductions were achieved in the annual rate of population increase, largely through successful implementation of family planning for which government assumed direct responsibility in the 1970s.

But solving the problem of population increase is not the same thing as coping with the consequence of overcrowded populations. Naipaul (1972) spelled out the likely consequences of social and political instability in his polemical piece *The overcrowded barracoon*. The percentage of the population living in urban areas in Mauritius is 42.5. In 1972, 62% of the population was under the age of 25 years; in 1982, the equivalent figure was still 55.6%; in addition, a third of the population was between the ages of 15 and 29 (Government of Mauritius 1982). In these circumstances, economic and social policies must be addressed in particular to the provision of food and jobs. Mauritius meets its food needs mainly through importing, which is one of the factors contributing to more or less permanent adverse trade balances and balance of payments deficits. Major subsidies on food – principally on rice and flour – add further burdens to public expenditure, but do at least have the political effect of buying off economic discontent. It is much less easy, however, to do the same with respect to unemployment, which has been referred to as the 'social time bomb' that constantly threatens the stability of Mauritian politics.

A clue to the political sensitivity surrounding this issue is provided by the difficulty in obtaining from official documents adequate statistics relating to unemployment. The first real exercise in national economic planning, the Four Year Plan of 1971–5, faced the problem squarely in principle; estimating that 130 000 additional jobs would have to be created by 1980, it set a job creation target of 52 900 by 1975. This target was reached in the economic boom conditions of the early 1970s, and new job creation averaged more than 7000 per annum, with peaks of 10 000 in some years; total unemployment, judged by official figures, actually fell from some 16% of the labour force to around 7%. The second plan for 1975–80 set a job creation target of 76 000 by 1980, but subsequently published government documents were notably vague on the subject of the labour force and employment requirements. These documents and the annual statistical digest give no clear figures on unemployment or the extent to which jobs need to be created.

Only with the electoral defeat of the Mauritius Labour Party (MLP) government in 1982 was it possible to obtain an official figure for unemployment, estimated by the new government at 22% of the labour force (Government of Mauritius 1983); subsequent investigation set the unemployment level at about 70 000 in a total labour force variously estimated between 280 000 and 340 000 and assessed the level of required job creation at 10 000 per annum. Of those unemployed, about 55% were estimated to be between the ages of 15 and 24 (*Mauritius Economic Report* 1985). The Mauritian economy proved able to absorb some of this surplus labour in its best years, but not in normal times or in decline. The estimate of new jobs which must be created in the five years up to 1988 has been put at 120 000 (*The Times* 1983). The best estimate a decade before, in 1972, was 128 000 (Wilson 1982). In other words, after running hard for ten years in pursuit of employment creation, the Mauritian economy turns out to have been standing still.

As is well known, Mauritius has always been a monocrop

economy, dependent upon sugar exports to pay for its food imports and provide employment. It is this sugar economy which has had to bear the burden of the Mauritian population explosion. When sugar prices are high, the burden is manageable: the 'good years' of the late 1960s and early 1970s brought strong economic growth and a sharp rise both in standards of living and public welfare spending. But when sugar prices fall, or crop production is low because of cyclones – a perennial hazard – or import prices rise, then the economy is vulnerable; and when all those things occur together, the chickens of the open, dependent economy come home to roost. As a consequence the economy has progressed erratically. Growth rates averaged 10% per annum in the first few years of independence, but fell back after 1975 and in 1980 GDP actually declined by 10%. Better years after this did no more than return GDP to approximately the level of 1979. As national income stagnated, import bills and public expenditure continued to rise. The results of this inexorable squeeze were high inflation, estimated at 48% in 1979–80 (*Guardian* 1981), constantly widening balance of payments deficits, and sharp rises in unemployment. Only intervention by the IMF and a private European consortium, accompanied by devaluation, rescued a desperate financial position, although it should be said at the cost of heavy increases in Mauritian indebtedness.

A principal feature of economic policy in the postindependence period has been export diversification, associated with a structural shift towards manufacturing. This policy recognized implicitly that sugar could not be expected to generate further growth and in the long run was vulnerable to both external and seasonal variations. In terms of securing markets, Mauritian politicians were notably successful, playing their strong diplomatic cards of strategic significance in the Indian Ocean, cultural relationships with both France and Britain, and offering themselves as a valuable link between French- and English-speaking overseas territories anxious to establish privileged access to the European Economic Community. After independence a market was assured for Mauritius under the Commonwealth Sugar Agreement, but this agreement did not survive Britain's accession to the EEC. Mauritius's membership of Organization Commune Africaine et Malgache (OCAM) secured favourable entry for most Mauritian products to EEC markets, but sugar was specifically excluded. However, under the Lomé Convention, which replaced Yaoundé II, Mauritius was assured a market (mainly British) at a high guaranteed price for 500 000 tonnes annually, more than one-third of the total African, Caribbean, and Pacific quota for the EEC. Any excess could be sold freely on the world market. This agreement coincided with a sugar shortage and high world prices, thereby creating 'a bonanza beyond the dreams of either the planters or the government' (Houbert 1981:91). This underwrote the Mauritian economic boom of the early 1970s and gave a much needed impetus to internal investment in manufacturing and service industries. Mauritius, which is unusual in that most of its capital is locally owned by the white French plantocracy, had been a net foreign investor in the 1950s and 1960s: now capital surplus was to be reinvested locally with some 22% of sugar industry capital investment, according to one report, going into tourism and manufacturing (*Financial Times* 1976). But after 1976 decline set in with deepening world recession and lower sugar prices: the EEC guaranteed price in 1978 was reported to be below the costs of production (*Financial Times* 1979). In 1980 a severe cyclone reduced production to less than the EEC quota of 500 000 tonnes and in 1983 the harvest, at 610 000 tonnes, was again below the target production figure of 700 000 tonnes per annum.

Domestic consumption accounts for only 5% of annual sugar production, underlining the export orientation of the industry and Mauritian dependence on this source of export earnings (around 60% of the total). Exports in 1984 decreased by 12%, and world prices hit their lowest level for 12 years. Since the US quota for Mauritius sugar has steadily been reduced to the present low level of 25 000 tonnes, the dependence of Mauritius upon guaranteed exports to the EEC is manifest (Lloyds Bank 1985). The sugar industry has also been shedding labour throughout the 1970s, first through mechanization and later because of poor production. In 1973 it employed 33% of the 'main sectors' labour force, in 1977 28%, and in 1982 24% (Government of Mauritius 1982). It is clear, therefore, that a solution to the fundamental problem of unemployment cannot lie in this direction.

Yet diversification, the obvious answer to monocrop exporting, is difficult to achieve for an open, dependent economy with a limited domestic market. Certainly in Mauritius efforts at agricultural diversification through tea and tobacco have been disappointing. The Agricultural Marketing Board is widely believed to have done little apart from providing jobs for its officials (Selwyn 1983). The tea industry initially declined, despite much government support, though in the past two years high world prices have meant that its contribution to exports was significant.

The principal effort, though, was made in the manufacturing sector, mainly through the well tried device of an export processing zone (MEPZ) incorporating a variety of tax and other incentives to industrialists. They included low site rents, duty-free raw materials, tax holidays, few restrictions on the repatriation of profits, a guaranteed supply of cheap and capable labour, and access to EEC markets. The MEPZ was a distinct success; in 1970 it had five companies employing 64 people, by 1977 91 companies were employing 18 200, and by 1984 197 firms were employing 35 600 people. Most of the employment generated was, however, for women, which meant that the diversification into manufacturing made only a moderate impact on unemployment in general. Moreover, the MEPZ stagnated in the recession years, and little new investment has been forthcoming from either internal or external sources, partly because rising local incomes have reduced the competitiveness of Mauritian industries against the 50 or so other export zones around the world (*The Times* 1983).

Tourism also experienced rapid growth in the boom years, but has since levelled out. The result has been a modest structural shift, with manufacturing responsible for around 17% of GDP and for some 28% of exports, pushing sugar's share down in a decade from 90% to about 60%. But, like sugar, industrialization has been export directed and has made little contribution to import substitution. In short, the path recommended by Meade 20 years ago has neither led to greater self-sufficiency nor reduced external dependence nor made an appreciable impact on unemployment (Selwyn 1983).

The pattern of export-led boom conditions followed by recession and decline only emphasizes the unpredictable and erratic course of development in an open, dependent economy. Economic growth which is rooted in external commodity price movements carries the seeds of its own disaster, for it creates a euphoric atmosphere in which consumption expands, wages and prices (and inflation) rise quickly, imports – by both volume and value – increase rapidly, and public welfare spending may be unrestrained. When export prices turn down, the high levels of consumption and welfare spending, and of inputs, cannot be so readily reduced. This is a recipe for the adverse trade balances and substantial balance of payments deficits which Mauritius experienced in the 1977–85 period. In 1982, for example, foreign exchange reserves could only pay for two weeks of imports. Total debt stood at Rs7785 million (£1 = Rs18 approximately) and more than 70% of it was external debt. Debt repayments also accounted for 29% of recurrent government expenditure. These figures are not really surprising. Mauritius imports 90% of its fuel and 50% of its food requirements, and the average price of imports is almost twice the average price of exports (*The Times* 1983).

Current economic policy in Mauritius is now closely tied to the financial support – and preferred policies – of the IMF and the World Bank. The objectives of the economic structural adjustment programme which began in 1981 are to stimulate the export-oriented manufacturing sector, diversify agricultural production to increase domestic food supply and reduce 'sugar dependence', and improve the overall quality of economic management. The budget deficit has been reduced from 16% of GDP in 1980–1 to 8% in 1983–4. The rate of inflation fell from 42% in 1980 to 7.4% in 1984. The IMF appears to be well satisfied with the results of its intervention, and released further substantial loan funds in 1985, while insisting (perhaps optimistically) that the budget deficit should be held around 5% of GDP. But by the end of 1983 external public debt was still US $543 million, and debt servicing commitments in 1984 were estimated at 34% of merchandize export earnings. Political leaders of all parties and persuasions have been compelled accordingly to bend to the necessities of IMF support, with concomitant loss of decision-making autonomy and uncertain long-term political consequences.

Politics

Economic policies and structures have been a dominant factor in Mauritian politics; in a small, overpopulated island the urge to ensure the survival of the whole society is primary. But political economy alone cannot explain the political system: for Mauritian politics are, above all, ethnic politics. The 15 years after independence were dominated, as in the pre-independence period, by the Hindu-based Mauritius Labour Party (MLP). The MLP had won the 'independence' election in 1967 in alliance with a smaller Hindu party, the Independent Forward Bloc (IFB), and the Muslim party, the Muslim Committee for Action (MCA). The white plantocracy had little to fear, however: as Houbert says, 'The Indo-Mauritian middle class, with its own sugar interests, has been as staunch a defender of private property as its Creole counterpart' (Houbert 1981:87). After independence there was a realignment of political groups in which the Hindu MLP joined forces with the Creole Parti Mauricien Social et Democrate (PMSD) in a government of 'national unity'.

But the coalition was not popular. Unemployment continued to escalate, and the fruits of such economic growth as there was benefited by relatively few people. The government seemed to many people of all communities to be a cynical expression of political opportunism, not least in its manipulation of the constitution to prevent national elections, postponed in effect from 1972 to 1976. In this atmosphere a young white Creole, Paul Berenger, having acquired some experience in street politics in Paris in 1968, built up a new political movement, the Mouvement Militant Mauricien (MMM). The economic boom of the early 1970s staved off widespread political discontent for a while, but by the time the 1976 election came it was at an end. The Prime Minister and MLP leader, Sir Seewoosagar Ramgoolam, had, meanwhile, broken the coalition with the PMSD, possibly hoping to clear the ground for an alliance with the more popular MMM. The election results indicated a decline in communal affiliations. The Creole-based PMSD saw its votes and its seats halved, and its leader, Duval, defeated. The Muslim MCA failed to gain a seat. The MLP held its rural Hindu vote and probably an 'urban-middle-class' vote. The MMM, appealing to urban workers, the unemployed, and the educated young, categories which cut across all ethnic groups, won more votes and seats than any other party, an amazing performance for a party launched only seven years before, even given its electoral alliance with a small Hindu party, the Parti Socialiste Mauricien (PSM). But it was a hollow victory, for the MMM could not command a parliamentary majority. A coalition was necessary, and to no one's great surprise, the old team of the MLP and PMSD was resurrected (though without Duval) and enjoyed a further six years in office.

Even Berenger could not have prophesied the actual result of the June 1982 elections, in which the MMM won every one of the 62 directly elected seats. But as surprising were the political developments of the next year. For by October 1983 the MMM found itself fighting another election, and losing it to an electoral alliance masterminded by Ramgoolam and Duval in a clear reassertion of the rôle of communal parties in Mauritian politics. The explanation for this reversal lies both in external economic influences and the factional nature of Mauritian politics. The MMM, for all its preoccupation with class, political organization, and political ideology, could not escape the factional and communal characteristics of the Mauritian political system. Its problem was that it was not a coherent class party, but rather a fragile alliance of minority groups: Tamils, Muslims, 'intellectuals', disaffected Creole and Hindu politicians.

The reality of Hindu electoral domination influenced both MMM organization and the shape of its government. Berenger, founder and leader, was Secretary-General of the party, but only Finance Minister in government. Squabbles broke out between Berenger and Jugnauth, the Prime Minister, and also with Harish Bhoodoo, Deputy Prime Minister and leader of the PSM. In March 1983 Berenger and ten of his cabinet colleagues resigned, leaving Jugnauth to preside for a time over a minority government in what was eventually a new Hindu-based alliance between a new party formed by Jugnauth, the Mouvement Socialiste Mauricien (MSM) and the PSM. Elections were held again in August 1983, and were in essence fought between the Berenger-led MMM and a Jugnauth-led coalition of the MSM with the old 'enemies', the MLP and PMSD.

Much of the electoral campaigning turned ostensibly on differing views of how to restructure the sugar industry. Jugnauth, however, had already recognized the inevitability of IMF intervention which had so discomforted Berenger: 'We shall pursue the same economic policy for we have no other choice.' In effect, 'the bitter "hate Berenger" campaign served to cover the ethnic realignment of forces in the political class, for this was really what the crisis was about' (Houbert 1985:256). The results showed how damaging the resurgence of ethnic politics was for an MMM using 'class' and 'nation' as political counters, for they lost all their rural seats and won only 22 in total, compared to 46 won by the coalition.

The new 'political class' controlling the state was based on a reunification of the various Hindu factions, coupled to what had become a traditional political–ethnic alliance between the Indians and the middle-class Creoles – a political formation more acceptable than its predecessor both to economic interests in Mauritius and overseas governments and investors. But such alliances are fragile in the hothouse of Mauritian political life, and will not easily resist the urban, class-oriented challenge of the MMM, which was accurately described in 1985 as 'the only well-organised trans-ethnic party implanted in the towns as well as the countryside; its "national" strategy orchestrates the stirring of Mauritianness within the diversity of ancestral cultures' (Houbert 1985:264). The death of Ramgoolam, the old MLP leader and 'father of independence', late in 1985 may thus stand as a symbol for the death of 'high caste' politics in Mauritius.

International relations

For a small, remote state, Mauritius has achieved a remarkable degree of international support and recognition: it is, for example, a leading member of the ACP group affiliated to the EEC through the Lomé agreements and has in its time chaired the Organization of African Unity (OAU). Cultural links with the United Kingdom, India, and France have also produced valuable aid resources. But the most interesting, if disquieting, episode in

Mauritian external relations has centred on the question of Diego Garcia.

This tiny island, part of the Chagos Archipelago, some 2400 kilometres distant from Mauritius, was detached from Mauritius at independence in what has been alleged to be a deal struck in 1965 between Ramgoolam and the British over the granting of sovereignty. Compensation of £3 million was paid. Diego Garcia was then leased to the United States for use as its major strategic base in the Indian Ocean – the British receiving in return a rebate of US $14 million on Polaris. This involved the forced deportation to Mauritius of some 1400 inhabitants – the Ilois – although the British initially denied this and Ramgoolam subsequently claimed not to have known that the island would be used as a military base.

In 1973 the British government agreed to pay £650 000 compensation to the Mauritian government to meet relief and resettlement costs, but no money was actually distributed until 1978. Both governments were increasingly embarrassed by international publicity for the degraded and desperate circumstances of the Ilois in Mauritius. Mauritius reasserted a claim to sovereignty over Chagos, which was resisted by the British government. In March 1982 a final compensation agreement was reached worth £4 million (in addition to the initial £650 000). The MMM had, in the 1982 electoral campaign, asserted that Diego Garcia should be returned to Mauritius, within the context of a policy for the demilitarization of the India Ocean.

The new 1983 coalition government, led by Jugnauth, Ramgoolam, and Duval (all participants in the 1965 independence negotiations in London), reversed gear and played down the Diego Garcia issue: they were rewarded by a quickly assembled British aid package. In an interview in September 1984 Prime Minister Jugnauth said: 'There is no Ilois issue anymore' (Minority Rights Group 1985:11). Diego Garcia illustrates to some extent the inability of small states to defend their interests, and even their territory, in the face of irresistible 'big power' pressures, but it also shows how strategic issues linked to global cold war politics can be used by small states to lever aid and other types of support out of richer patrons.

Conclusion

The dependent nature of the Mauritian economy is pronounced. Mauritius would appear to fit very easily into the dependency view of metropolitan–periphery relations, yet it does not. There is no gainsaying the external dependency of the economy, locked into a world system of commodity control which determines both the market and the profitability of sugar. But Mauritius simultaneously shows some contradictory features. The ownership and control of capital is not primarily foreign, but local; and local capital has shown some propensity to invest in the local economy, contributing to at least a modest level of diversification and industrialization. Profits and benefits may be very unequally distributed in Mauritian society, but this is a product of the local operation of local capital, not the local operation of international capital; and here we must remember that there were no pre-colonial relations of production upon which the imperialist economy imposed itself: the Mauritian economy was *created* by imperialism. All in all, Mauritius would seem to provide stronger evidence for Warren's thesis of successful capitalist development than for the dependency school. If economic progress has been erratic and uneven, that too is an inherent tendency of capitalist economies (Warren 1980).

The economy has had two significant effects on the political system. First, local political leaders have been relatively helpless in the face of adverse external economic factors, regardless of their particular ideology: in 1982–3 a self-proclaimed Marxist Minister of Finance was forced to preside over a substantial IMF intervention in local economic and financial decision making. The second effect has been upon political stability within the system: the prosperity of the early 1970s reduced the simmering political tensions of the immediate post-independence period and in the end maintained in office a political leadership which in 1969–72 had appeared to be utterly discredited. Economic decline brought a sharp political swing with an apparently radical party winning office; but this party was completely undone by its inability to resist the logic of economic decline, and was rejected by the electorate only a year later. Economic and political instability are seen to have a close relationship.

It is not a simple matter, however, to tease out the 'political economy' of Mauritius, for the relationship between economic ownership and political control is not straightforward. The concept of ethnicity is at least as powerful as the concept of class. In a small island, with a literate and highly urbanized population, politics are characterized by intense interest and factionalism. Political networks form on a patron–client basis, but within factions which tie personal networks to ethnic identity. Parties are merely loose agglomerations of factions, and are constituted for little more than electoral purposes. They are initially based on ethnic communities, but even communities are divided. Mauritian politics, as a result, is a complex weave in which the threads are clear but the ultimate shape of the garment indeterminate. The influence of the electoral process certainly stands out, for apart from the period between 1967 and 1976 elections have been a regular feature of the political system. But on the other side of the coin is the predominance of coalition government, which has resulted when the electoral process has been overturned by the manipulations of party leaders intent on keeping a stake in government for themselves and their communities.

The stability of coalition explains, in part, why Mauritius, small, insignificant, and remote as it is, commands an influence in international arenas. The explanation also hinges on the concessions wrested from stronger international forces due to strategic and geopolitical factors. Two features have been significant. Firstly, the Indian Ocean is a highly sensitive focus for superpower confrontation, since a deadly serious cold war is being waged to control the strategic zone in which Mauritius is located. In particular, the issue of sovereignty over Diego Garcia has been a useful card for Mauritian leaders to play in their dealings with the big powers. Secondly, there is the French connection. As Houbert (1981, 1985) demonstrates, France has always taken a close interest in Mauritius, not only because of the wish to foster and support French culture and pro-French interests there, but crucially because France does not wish to lose control of political and economic developments in Réunion, which is constitutionally part of France and near to Mauritius. There is no doubt that both factors underlie the concessions France was prepared to make in allowing Mauritius and other sugar producers favourable access to European markets. The core–periphery relationship is not, in this instance, a one-way exploitation.

The Mauritian case should counsel us to take account of the uniqueness of particular social and cultural experiences, and to be less obsessed with economistic interpretations of development and underdevelopment. Class forces are emerging in Mauritius and the logic of uneven capitalist development may one day assert itself, but not yet. Traditional social patterns and conflicts show great persistence and significantly shape both political institutions and political behaviour. External economic interventions have a habit of becoming grist to the internal political mill; and in a small state, within small-scale society, it is evident that the personalist, factionalized nature of politics is at least as compelling a force as the structure and operation of the economy. The two factors are brought together in the perpetual struggle between antagonist social groups for control of the power and patronage of the state.

References

Financial Times 1976. Report on Mauritius. 18 June.
Financial Times 1979. Special survey on Mauritius. 6 December.
Government of Mauritius 1982. *Biannual digest of statistics*. Port Louis: Government Printing Office.
Guardian. 1981. Mauritius: a special report. 26 March.
Houbert, J. 1981. Mauritius: independence and dependence. *Journal of Modern African Studies* **19**(1), 75–105.
Houbert, J. 1985. Mauritius: politics and pluralism at the periphery. *Annuaire des pays de l'Ocean Indien* **9**, 225–64.
Keatley, P. 1981. Mauritius: a special report. *Guardian*. 26 March.
Mauritius: economic report 1985. London: Lloyds Bank.
Minority Rights Group 1985. *Diego Garcia: a contrast to the Falklands*. Report 54, Minority Rights Group, London.
Minogue, M. 1983. Economic, social and political development in a small island. *Manchester Papers on Development* **8**, 31–76.
Naipaul, V. S. 1972. *The overcrowded barracoon*. London: André Deutsch.
Selwyn, P. 1977. External dependence of small plantation islands. In *Characteristics of island economies*, V. Nabobsing & R. Virahswamy (eds), 1–22. University of Mauritius.
Selwyn, P. 1978. *Small, poor, and remote: islands at a geographical disadvantage*. Brighton: Institute of Development Studies, University of Sussex.

Selwyn, P. 1983. Mauritius: the Meade Report twenty years after. In *African islands and enclaves*, R. Cohen (ed.), 249–75. Beverley Hills, Calif.: Sage.
The Times 1983. Special report on Mauritius. 24 October.
Titmuss, R. M. & B. Abel-Smith. 1960. *Social policies and population growth in Mauritius*. London: Methuen.
Toussaint, A. 1972. *Histoire des Iles Mascareignes*. Paris: Berger, Editions Levrault.
Warren, B. 1980. *Imperialism, pioneer of capitalism*. London: New Left Books.
Wilson, D. F. 1982. *Manpower development in Mauritius 1972–82*. Port Louis, Mauritius.

9 The Gambia

Arnold Hughes

By any of the conventional criteria used to define smallness among states the West African country of The Gambia must rank among the smallest of non-island units. At independence in 1965, an event barely deemed credible by political pundits at the time, its population was a mere 315 000, which has since grown to about 700 000, and its land area an almost impossibly attenuated 10 400 square kilometres. Apart from a short coastline, it is entirely surrounded by neighbouring Senegal. It is mainland Africa's smallest country by area and its third smallest in terms of population. As will be shown in this chapter, The Gambia shares a great many of the characteristics of small states as identified in the general literature on the subject. This survey does not claim to offer a detailed account of the country's evolution since independence (Hughes 1982–3, 1983); instead, it seeks to extrapolate from The Gambia's short experience of statehood the manifestations of smallness, the advantages and disadvantages posed by lack of size, and the means adopted to try and overcome or mitigate the constraints of smallness. The economic, political, and security aspects of smallness as they affect The Gambia will thus be examined in turn.

Economic aspects

Reference has already been made to the small size of The Gambia's territory and population, to which may be added a number of other typical disabilities of small-scale economies. They include peripheral location; small industrial markets cramping industrialization programmes; narrow specialization of products, though this is as likely the result of a monocrop pattern of development under colonial rule as of smallness; the taxation of external trade as the main source of government revenue; trade imbalance and an attendant foreign exchange shortage; a modern economic sector dominated by trade and non-indigenous entrepreneurs; a shortage of skilled manpower because of limited local work opportunities; and the pervasive influence of social obligations and political connections on economic activity in 'small-scale' societies.

All of the constraints itemized above are to be found in The Gambia. Its smallness is not restricted to population and territory: at independence in 1965 annual revenues were only £1.7 million, which necessitated a Grant-in-Aid from Britain to balance the budget over the next two years. Since then these grants have increased to an estimated *dalasi* 199 million for 1985–6 (approximately £19 million at the present rate of exchange). GDP, although it has risen since independence, was still only an estimated *dalasi* 625 million in 1984–5. Real income per head has been declining for the past ten years or more.

The economy is totally dependent on the production and export of groundnuts, which may comprise as much as 95% of export earnings in a good year. This extreme specialization is made worse by the fluctuations in output and price of the groundnut crop. Over the past decade the tonnage available for export has ranged from about 50 000 tonnes to 133 000 tonnes. The vagaries of weather and crop infestation play havoc with economic forecasting. The 1984–5 harvest turned out to be only one-sixth of that forecasted by government planners. The revenue and income derived from groundnuts are subject to equally uncertain ties in the world price as well. Thus from year to year government has no means of determining the size and value of its major resource. Because the Gambian output is less than 5% of total world groundnut production and because groundnuts have to compete with other sources of vegetable oil, the government cannot manipulate the market single-handedly and there is little prospect of a producer cartel for such a weakly placed commodity.

Severely limited land area and a tiny population militate against economic diversification. Apart from abandoned ilmenite workings and deposits of sand and clay for brickmaking, the country lacks any mineral resources (in common with other countries in the region, The Gambia has engaged in offshore oil exploration but with no success to date). Alternative forms of employment and wealth creation have equally run into difficulties deriving from smallness. Although some forms of manufacturing are not affected by the smallness of the market, any significant expansion of the country's tiny industrial sector is held back by the size of the domestic market. Manufacturing accounted for only 5% of GDP in 1977–8 and is located largely in the area around the capital, Banjul, and confined to light industrial activities such as brewing and bottling of soft drinks, small-scale metal fabrication, and furniture making. The groundnut oil mills are the largest manufacturing enterprise but they employ only a relatively small number of people and their activities are seasonal and tied to the fortunes of the farming sector.

Tourism has enjoyed a boom in the past four years and 65 000 tourists were recorded in 1984–5. But here again a narrow coastline must set absolute limits to beach-centred resorts. Virtually all the hotels are located in the Banjul area and employment is again largely seasonal – the European winter holiday traffic. Fishing is also being pursued as an alternative to agriculture, but a small country such as The Gambia finds it difficult to modernize its fishing fleet and safeguard its offshore fishery grounds from poaching. Its coastal patrol boats are quite incapable of policing the new 320-kilometre offshore economic zone.

As for agriculture, in which some 80% of the population is involved directly or indirectly, and which accounts for some 50% of GDP, a restricted land area occupying the lower reaches of the River Gambia, some 400 kilometres long by 24 kilometres wide, allows for very little climatic and geographic variety. The impact of such natural calamities as drought, pest infestation, or disease tends to be more uniform than in larger countries where soil and climate may be more varied and agricultural disasters more localized in their damage. Non-island small states also run the added risk of cross-border infestation or infection, as has been the case with cassava production in The Gambia.

The Gambia relies heavily on foreign trade and on external

sources for investment and aid. Half of the government's revenue derives from external trade and its development budget is even more dependent on the outside world. The First Five-Year Plan (1975–80) obtained two-thirds of its funding from overseas grants and loans, and an estimated 83% of the funding for the Second Five-Year Plan (1985–6) is expected to come from external sources. Gambian success over the years in obtaining substantial amounts of foreign aid, and from a large number of donors, principally Western Europe, conservative Arab states, and international financial agencies, supports the claim that is often made that smaller countries tend to attract a disproportionate amount of aid. It should be noted, though, that the goodwill enjoyed by The Gambia in this respect probably derives more from the reputation of its government for sound economic management and political tolerance than from smallness as such. In the past five years mounting economic difficulties have brought the administrative competence and political reputation of the government into question, and problems of economic management have affected relations with several aid donors.

The difficulty in servicing external debt, particularly with a growing trade imbalance as exports decline in volume and value while imports continue to increase, is particularly evident in The Gambia. Loan repayments increased 300% in the period 1981–4 and an estimated one-third of export earnings are required to service external debts. At the same time imports are racing ahead of exports by a ratio of 2:1, making it impossible for the country to generate sufficient foreign exchange to meet its increasing financial obligations. Despite trying to adhere to its loan conditions, the Gambian government was forced to default on repayments on a US $28 million loan from the IMF in the spring of 1985. Neither could repayments to three other major donors be maintained. As a result the African Development Bank, the Saudi Fund for Development, and the Islamic Development Bank temporarily suspended further disbursements. This is a familiar problem facing small states with economies distorted by reliance on foreign trade.

The domination of the local economy by expatriate business is also familiar in small economies. In The Gambia the initial domination was by British and French trading houses, but in recent years these have given way to Lebanese and Mauritanian enterprises. Relatively few Gambians have the necessary capital or expertise to compete successfully, even with financial assistance from the state. The government itself has sought to take a more active part in the economy through the creation of numerous parastatal organizations, most of which have incurred losses.

Gambian experience also tends to bear out the fears that have been widely expressed about the problems of nepotism and 'familism' in small states. Since independence in 1965 there have been numerous political–financial scandals involving prominent figures in politics, government, and the business community. Several Cabinet ministers have been forced to resign following accusations of misuse of office for financial purposes, and major public institutions have been harmed by large-scale corruption and peculation. Instances of the latter are the perennial scandals within the co-operative movement, frequently regarded in developing countries as a key institution for achieving equitable economic development; the problems associated with the Agricultural Development Bank, which had to be closed down within a few years of its founding because its funds were being misused by senior employees; the corruption revealed in the implementation of Rural Development Programme I; and the scandals involving officials in other parastatal organizations, the Central Bank and the Customs Department.

How has the Gambian government tried to cope with the constricting facets of smallness? Gambian political leadership has always followed a liberal–capitalist economic policy. In recent years, as it has become increasingly dependent on the IMF, its guidelines in respect of reducing public sector employment, devaluing the currency, encouraging farmers, and promoting the private sector have been faithfully followed, despite the political cost entailed in reducing urban subsidies and cutting back on civil service jobs.

Greater self-reliance in the face of inadequate domestic resources and the difficulty in servicing external borrowing lies behind the decision to promote *Te Sito*, the philosophy and practice of self-help. *Te Sito* projects are usually small-scale activities involving local communities, official agencies and non-governmental organizations (NGOs). Local communities are encouraged to define, contribute to, and manage such self-help activities as food production, provision of infrastructural, health and educational facilities, and technology transfer. Government is concerned with the harmonization of the several hundred individual projects with overall national needs and also provides some financial and professional support. It has turned increasingly to the NGOs, of which some 30 exist in The Gambia, to contribute funds, expertise, and materials to *Te Sito* activities (Hughes 1982). Considerable success has been achieved in attracting NGOs to The Gambia, principally major world charities, such as Oxfam, Action Aid, and the Freedom from Hunger Campaign, and international development agencies including UN affiliates. Bilateral aid from friendly governments such as Britain and the US has also been earmarked for self-help projects. Although their achievements vary, there is no doubt that the myriad self-help activities make a visible contribution to official rural development objectives as well as easing the external debt burden. They diversify further the sources of external aid received by The Gambia.

As indicated earlier, and as the reference to NGOs aid above demonstrates, over the years The Gambia has been remarkably successful in attracting foreign grants and aid. Initial dependence on the British Exchequer has given way to multilateral reliance on a range of external patrons, official and non-governmental. A reputation for political as much as economic liberalism has ensured a steady flow of development funds, principally from Britain, the EEC, the US, and moderate or conservative Arab states. Maintaining the widest possible diplomatic representation has brought in assistance from less likely sources such as China, Libya, and the USSR. The actual amount of aid obtained from individual benefactors is trifling in terms of their gross disbursements, but in terms of the needs of small countries such as The Gambia, the aggregation of such financial 'crumbs' may be substantial and make a major contribution to development funding.

Apart from following orthodox advice in respect of fiscal prudence and economic diversification, The Gambia has turned to that other favourite 'solution' to the financial difficulties of small states – regional co-operation. This operates at several interlocking levels. First there is co-operation with Senegal, its immediate neighbour and protector. Between 1965 and 1976 alone, no less than 23 agreements were signed, covering such subjects as foreign policy and defence, but mainly concerning economic and technical co-operation. As the agreements proliferated it was decided to establish a Senegambian Inter-State Ministerial Committee in 1967, and the following year a Senegalo-Gambian Secretariat came into being to service the increasingly frequent meetings between the heads of state, ministers, and technical specialists. In 1978 an additional body was created, the River Gambia Development Organisation (OMVG), set up to handle interstate relations appertaining to joint development of the river basin. Finally, in the wake of the abortive *coup d'état* in The Gambia in the summer of 1981 the two countries agreed to enter into a confederal association aimed at mutual defence, closer political union, and integration of the two economies.

Monetary and economic union is regarded as central to the aims of the Confederation and numerous advantages to the beleaguered Gambian economy have been claimed. Advocates of closer ties with Senegal anticipate a more effective and rational utilization of scarce resources and the creation of a larger domestic market with attendant advantages to trade and manufacturing. Artificial constraints on the communications system of the region are expected to be removed to the advantage of The Gambia. The harbour at Banjul is expected to gain additional business from the Senegalese hinterland with the removal of trade barriers and the closer integration of the transportation systems of the two states. Joint exploitation of the waters of the River Gambia for irrigation and electricity generation is also held out as a benefit of closer relations. A bridge–barrage at Balinhgo in central Gambia will be financed jointly as the bridge element of the scheme will afford a short and continuous link between north-west Senegal and the relatively remote province of Cassamance. The Senegalese also expect to see an end to smuggling between the two countries, encouraged at present by the lower import duties operative in The Gambia.

Notwithstanding these potential benefits, both the Gambian government and populace express serious misgivings about the total integration of their tiny economy into the much larger and more developed economy of their confederal partner. Doubts, which have given rise to delays in signing any agreement, centre on the need to raise trade tariffs to Senegalese levels, with an accompanying increase in the cost of living in The Gambia, and on the exposure of the vulnerable and small Gambian manufacturing sector to Senegalese competition, from which it is at present protected by trade barriers. The ending of cross-border 'unofficial' trade would also reduce government income from import duties. No accurate figures of the extent of 'smuggling' into Senegal exist, but transit trade to Senegal and other neighbouring countries constitutes some 10% of total imports. Consequently, despite Senegalese urgings, the Gambian government has delayed entering into any form of economic agreement until the full cost has been determined and suitable compensatory terms worked out. A less restrictive free trade zone seems the most likely arrangement at present.

Doubts about the actual as opposed to the imagined advantages of economic integration with Senegal have promoted interest in a second level of regional integration. With only about onetenth of the population of Senegal, The Gambia feels that economic and other forms of national bargaining may be entered into more equitably if other countries are involved. It is also recognized that the waters of the River Gambia can only be exploited with the agreement and participation of Guinea, the third riparian state and source of the river. Guinea joined OMVG in 1980, since when additional dams in the Guinean section of the river have been agreed to. It is apparent that the integrated economic development of the subregion cannot be restricted to those countries straddling the river. In 1984 Guinea–Bissau, a non-riparian state, joined the OMVG. Leaving aside political considerations, there are sound economic reasons for its membership of the organization. There are strong trade and communications links between it and the other three countries, as evidenced by its use of the port of Banjul and the joint approach to the funding and construction of the Dakar–Banjul–Bissau highway.

Finally, there is The Gambia's relationship to the West African region itself. The Gambia was a founder member of the

Economic Community of West African States (ECOWAS) in 1975 and hopes eventually to benefit from regionally focused plans to create a customs union and integrated economic development. The Gambia also belongs to a number of specific regional organizations, such as the rice development agency (WARDA) and the antidrought committee (CILSS). Beyond the region The Gambia is a member of the Organization of African Unity (OAU), the Islamic Conference, the Associated States of the European Economic Community (ACP grouping), the Commonwealth, and the United Nations and its specialized agencies. Membership of some of these groups reflects historical, sentimental, or idealistic factors, but in other cases, the EEC, Islamic Conference, and the IMF/World Bank for example, membership reflects the Gambian government's attempts to spread the net of economic support as widely as possible.

Political aspects

Political aspects of smallness are more difficult to quantify than economic ones, but a number of general sociopolitical characteristics have been advanced, which may be seen to operate in The Gambia. On the positive side, however, smallness has undoubtedly helped to create a sense of 'Gambian-ness', despite the plural nature of society. Communalism has never threatened the political integrity of the state and the political system has proved adept at working through ethnic groupings. Social pluralism has been managed by an 'élite cartel' akin to that represented by the 'consociational model of democracy'. Under a dominant political party, the People's Progressive Party (PPP), and the personalist presidential leadership of Sir Dawda Jawara, state patronage and clientelist social networks have forged a trans-ethnic political community. Although starting life in the 1950s as an ethnic–regionalist party dedicated to shifting power from urban groups to the Mandinka rural majority, the PPP has subsequently turned itself into a coalition of all Gambian ethnic groups, held together by an alliance of communal leaders sharing political office and selectively redistributing economic patronage to their constituencies.

As a consequence, the PPP has not lost a single general election since 1962, and rival parties have been disbanded, merged with the ruling party, or consigned to a permanent minority rôle in political life. There has been no need to introduce a one-party state, and under the qualified liberalism of the Jawara administration The Gambia came to enjoy a reputation for political tolerance quite unusual in postcolonial Africa. This democratic reputation aided the country's attempts to secure international aid, which in turn further strengthened the position of the government. Under this system of government, the manipulation of the characteristics of smallness helped provide The Gambia with some 15 years of unusual tranquillity and tolerance, but over time the ideological caution and administrative *immobilisme* of the government, together with its limited ability to accommodate the political and economic aspirations of its critics, themselves negative features of small societies, generated new forms of opposition.

A section of Mandinka society resented Jawara's policy of turning the PPP into a national party open to all ethnic communities, and in 1976, under the leadership of Sherif Dibba, the dismissed former Vice-president, created a breakaway political movement, the National Convention Party (NCP). Seen by the electorate primarily as a communal party and as a means for the advancement of Dibba's own political career, the NCP failed to make more than local inroads into PPP territory. Personal allegiances and clientelist networks were effectively mobilized by the ruling party to defeat the NCP in two subsequent general elections in 1977 and 1982 and in local government elections.

The conservative and élitist policies of the PPP also aroused a more radical and violent opposition from alienated urban youths in the vicinity of Banjul. Personal frustration resulting from exclusion from political office and economic opportunities and the attractions of Marxist prescriptions for resolving the problems of underdevelopment resulted in the formation of several small political societies dedicated to the violent overthrow of the government. One of these, the Gambia Underground Socialist Revolutionary Party (GUSRP), plotted the attempted coup of 30 July 1981. Factional and personal rivalries within the paramilitary

Field Force led disaffected policemen to join the civilian plotters; other opportunistic elements also joined the insurrection once it had broken out. Initially successful and meeting with a measure of public approval, at least in the Banjul area, the rebellion quickly descended into disorder and was put down within a week by a large contingent of the Senegalese army, summoned by the temporarily exiled Jawara under a 1965 defence agreement between his country and Senegal.

A period of political repression followed the suppression of the coup, with many alleged as well as actual opponents of the government, including Dibba and other NCP activists, being detained without trial under a state of emergency. The detainees were subsequently investigated, released, or put on trial. Though several dozen individuals were sentenced to death for treason, no sentence has been carried out. The government's reluctance to execute its opponents, it may be suggested, again reflects the 'familist' nature of Gambian society. In other respects, though, the easygoing nature of Gambian political life may have been permanently changed. Although the NCP is free once more to oppose the PPP and has been recently joined by a new opposition movement, the Gambia People's Party, restrictions remain on radical groups and members of these proscribed organizations continue to seek the government's overthrow from exile.

The breakdown of political order in The Gambia in 1981 exposes the weaknesses of politics in small-scale societies. Decision making had become restricted to no more than a few dozen persons in the party and state apparatus with access to the President. Constituency politics were allowed to wither away and insufficient attention was given to the interests of youth by a gradually ageing and entrenched leadership. In its actions it behaved more as a 'consociational oligarchy' than a 'consociational democracy'. Mismanagement and corruption persisted, even flourished, opponents of the system would claim, because of the protection provided by the personal and clientelist connections of the ruling élite.

Security aspects

National security, rather than régime survival, is the concern of the last section of this chapter. Before independence, Gambian security was guaranteed by the British, who maintained an intercolonial defence force in West Africa, the Royal West African Frontier Force (RWAFF). The RWAFF was territorialized following the granting of independence to the four separate colonies, but in the case of The Gambia its local batallion was stood down in 1958 on grounds of economy, a striking illustration of how the economic poverty of small states can affect their security. It was replaced by a smaller and less expensive paramilitary police unit (Field Force) of some 600 men, whose function was to provide back-up support for the civil police during the occasional riot, strike, or election clash. The Field Force had no sophisticated military equipment. Britain helped train Gambian personnel and in return enjoyed limited training facilities for its own forces in The Gambia. However, no defence pact existed between the two countries when The Gambia attained independence, unlike the situation in several neighbouring francophone states where France continued to maintain a direct protective rôle.

Instead, the new Gambian government turned to Senegal and a defence agreement, the precise details of which were not revealed, was signed between the two states on Independence Day, 18 February 1965. Although it was unusual at the time for an African state's sovereignty to be underwritten by another African country, the agreement allowed for cooperation in defence matters and for mutual assistance in the event of external aggression. As at this time the only conceivable threat to The Gambia came from Senegal itself, the 1965 defence agreement and membership of the United Nations and the Commonwealth were regarded as adequate protection for its newly acquired autonomy.

In the early 1970s cordial relations between The Gambia and Guinea, then in contention with Senegal, aroused Senegalese disquiet. Smuggling from The Gambia also led to minor border incidents, but it was the activities of local dissidents in the Gambia in the later part of the decade which caused concern to the Senegalese as well as the Gambian government. In particular,

Senegal feared Libyan involvement among opposition groups in The Gambia, as well as within its own boundaries. The Senegalese government shared an apprehension common at that time that the Gadafy régime was bent on destabilizing pro-Western governments in black Africa. Muslim fundamentalists as well as secular radicals were suspected of receiving Libyan funds, and migrant workers from both countries were alleged to have been conscripted into an 'Islamic Legion' as a condition of obtaining work in Libya. The admittedly large Libyan diplomatic mission in Banjul was closed down in October 1980, following rumours of a coup and the murder of a senior Field Force officer. At the same time, a detachment of some 150 Senegalese troops was briefly stationed in the Gambian capital to support loyalist Field Force personnel.

The insurrection of July–August 1981 led to the return of the Senegalese army on a much larger scale. An estimated 3000 troops were brought in as part of Operation Foday Kabba II (the previous October's support measure was code-named Foday Kabba I) to restore order and return Jawara to power. This time several hundred Senegalese troops remained to ensure no further action on the part of the radical dissidents. The Treaty of Confederation included protocols on defence and security which legitimized the Senegalese army's permanent presence on Gambian soil. In a series of subsequent agreements, the composition of the confederal forces and the regulations relating to them were set out. These comprise army and gendarmerie units from both countries seconded for confederal duties in a ratio of two Senegalese to one Gambian. The Senegalese have also helped train a new paramilitary force, the National Gendarmerie, a unit of several hundred men closely modelled on its Senegalese counterpart. Gambian security is not confined to the gendarmerie. The British were invited in once again to help train a small Gambian army, established as a counterweight to the gendarmerie. The Gambia has no air force, and it has only two coastal patrol boats to ensure its maritime security.

Senegal has now replaced Britain as the protecting power in The Gambia, though three British SAS personnel did accompany the Senegalese army during the 1981 operation, mainly in order to rescue the 80 or more hostages taken by the rebels. The Gambian government expressed its gratitude by allowing the

Royal Air Force to use Yundum airport for refuelling during the Falklands War. The use of British instructors to train the small Gambian army may reflect the country's desire to multilateralize, to an extent, its defence arrangements, in the same way as it has sought to broaden its international economic support. Apart from Senegal and Britain, other countries are helping, or have indicated a willingness to help, in small ways with Gambian security. France, as Senegal's own protector, has made available military equipment and, in addition, the US, Morocco, and Pakistan have also agreed to help with training and supplies.

The Gambia has also used diplomacy to improve its security. Relations with Libya have now improved and diplomatic relations have been restored. Likewise, relations with Guinea–Bissau, initially suspected of being involved in the 1981 coup attempt, have improved markedly. Kukoi Samba Sanyang and other organizers of the 1981 coup fled to Bissau when the insurrection failed, and requests for their return were denied. Subsequently, though, they were deported to Cuba, and Guinea–Bissau now enjoys good relations with Banjul and Dakar. The decision to invite Guinea–Bissau to join the OMVG put the seal on the improved relationship. Finally, The Gambia is an active participant in the regional defence arrangements of ECOWAS.

Conclusion

Despite its inadequate and unreliable resource base, The Gambia has survived independence rather better than sceptics forecast in the early 1960s. In recent years, though, limited economic progress has been set back by factors beyond the control of its government. Politically, and in matters of security, the government has been severely tested. Taking advantage of the breathing space afforded by Senegalese military assistance, the government has sought to overcome some of its sociopolitical problems, but the outcome remains uncertain.

British colonial hegemony was not transformed into neocolonial dependency; instead, Senegal has emerged as the country's military patron. But in return The Gambia has had to accept a confederal union with its neighbour, the ultimate outcome of which remains unclear. Senegal is too poor to meet Gambian economic needs; this, and a desire to diversify sources of aid, has led The Gambia to use diplomacy to obtain economic assistance from a wide range of sources. Although this continuing external dependence has necessarily imposed constraints on policy choice in The Gambia, so far it has not seriously impinged on its sovereignty. Multilateral dependency would seem to be the most the country can expect under present circumstances.

References

Hughes, A. 1982. *Grass-roots, self-reliance and broad-based local participation in support of employment promotion and basic needs objectives in The Gambia*. Geneva: International Labour Organization.

Hughes, A. 1982–3. The limits of 'consociational democracy' in The Gambia. *Civilisations* **22**(2)–**23**(1), 65–95.

Hughes, A. 1983. From colonialism to confederation: the Gambian experience of independence, 1965–82. In *African islands and enclaves*, R. Cohen (ed), 57–80. Beverley Hills, Calif.: Sage.

10 *Swaziland*

Anthony Lemon

Swaziland is not only small, but, alone among the states considered in this volume, landlocked. Its peripheral position in the southern African economy and marked dependence on South Africa have long been recognized; Swaziland has been variously characterized as a 'hostage' (Halpern 1965) and a 'colony' (Marquard 1961) of South Africa, a position of particular delicacy given the latter's pariah status in the community of nations. Dependence remains a dominant characteristic, although its detailed pattern has changed radically since Doveton (1937) wrote her pioneering monograph, and even since independence in 1968. This chapter concentrates on the 'royalist decade' (Booth 1983) in Swaziland, the period since King Sobhuza's suspension of the constitution in 1973. But smallness and dependence were not the only factors influencing the nature of Swaziland's economic and political development in these years, as comparisons with South Africa's other hostages, Botswana and Lesotho, make clear (Daniel 1984).

Swaziland had an estimated population in 1982 of 634 000 and an area of only 17 363 square kilometres. The Swazi nation which emerged during the *mfecane*, the 'time of crushing', when new nations were forged out of the remains of old societies uprooted during the Zulu wars of expansion, was more than twice as large, and included much of what is today the eastern Transvaal. This compaction has left Swaziland with a degree of ethnic homogeneity unusual in Africa: 90% of the population are Swazi, 6% non-Swazi Africans, 2% European, and the remainder Eurafrican. Tribe and state by no means coincide, however: some 750 000 Swazis live in South Africa, one-third of them in their designated 'homeland' of KaNgwane on Swaziland's northern border.

It was the desire of another landlocked state, the Boer republic of Transvaal, for access to the sea which effectively led to Swaziland's colonization. It was directly administered by the Transvaal from 1894 until the latter's defeat in the Anglo-Boer War in 1902, whereupon Britain assumed the rôle of protector. Eventual incorporation in South Africa was long seen as likely by both Britain and South Africa, and the Tomlinson Commission (South Africa 1955) reported that the incorporation of Bechuanaland, Basutoland, and Swaziland into the Union was essential for the long-term success of the Bantustan programme. Lord Hailey's writings reflect changing views about the future of the three territories; at first he argued that the question of incorporation should be decided by a legislative representative of the Swazi (Hailey 1953:429), but by 1963, the direction of South African policies having ruled out incorporation, Hailey (1963:128) opted for continuation of 'the solid fact of liberty under British rule', rather than 'the fantasy of independence'. Even in 1967, a year after the independence of Botswana and Lesotho, Spence (1967:110–1) speculated about the possibility of either a UN presence to guarantee Swaziland's integrity or the reservation of defence and foreign policy to the British government. Such fears for Swaziland's ability to survive as an independent state were soon brushed aside, however, and Swaziland became fully independent in 1968.

The new state differed from most others in Africa in two vital respects: the power of the monarchy and traditional institutions, and the pattern of land ownership. Swaziland suffered extensive land alienation in the late 19th century when King Mbandzeni recklessly granted land concessions, many of them overlapping, over virtually the whole of present-day Swaziland. A British proclamation in 1907 set aside one-third of the land for Swazi occupation, but granted freehold title to white concession holders over most of the remainder (Daniel 1966). Britain added over 120 000 hectares in 1946, and with subsequent purchases Swazi Nation Land (SNL) now constitutes nearly two-thirds of the total. SNL is held by the King 'in trust for the nation', and is distributed to the people in usufruct only through the chiefs, placing a premium on loyalty to them and to the King (Booth 1983:85); it is the greatest single source of royal strength.

That strength was dramatically demonstrated when the monarchy formed its own political arm, the Imbokodvo National Movement (INM), in 1964. The INM won all the Swazi seats in elections two months later and went on to win all seats in the 1968 independence election. King Sobhuza thus became a notable exception to the decline of traditional authority which has usually accompanied decolonization. In 1972, however, the INM lost one of the eight three-member constituencies, Mphumalanga, where an opposition party proved its appeal to the Swazi *petit bourgeoisie* in an area which included the Commonwealth Development Corporation's Vuvulane Irrigated Farms scheme for Swazi smallholders and two major sugar complexes (Booth 1983). Even this limited challenge to royal authority was considered too much, and in 1973 Sobhuza suspended the constitution and began to rule by decree, thereby inaugurating the so-called 'royalist' era.

The economics of dependence

Swaziland's natural resource endowment is disproportionate to its size. The well watered highveld in the west has proved particularly suitable for afforestation, and over 120 000 hectares have been planted with conifers (especially pines) and eucalyptus since the 1940s, resulting in Africa's largest man-made forests. Wood pulp accounted for 14.5% of Swaziland's exports in 1982. Swaziland's five perennial rivers represent considerable hydroelectric potential and their exploitation for irrigation in the drier middleveld and lowveld has greatly assisted commercial agriculture, largely on European land where sugar cane, Swaziland's leading export, is the major crop. Pineapples, citrus fruit, cotton, rice, and tobacco are also grown. Not all white land is well farmed; Whittington & Daniel (1969:456–60) emphasize the problems of absentee landlords and 'treksheep' farms in the highveld and middleveld where land is used for winter grazing by its Transvaal owners, whose land-use practices have caused concern.

Nearly half the population lives in the more densely populated middleveld, which has some of the best soils, but the SNL is relatively poor, with only 28 000 hectares out of over 800 000 hectares being classified as having good irrigable or dryland soils (Daniel 1966). Maize, the staple food crop, occupies more than half the ploughed land, but sorghum, vegetables, nuts, fruit, wattle, cotton, and tobacco are also grown. The middleveld is usually self-sufficient in maize, but Swaziland as a whole has had to import an increasing proportion of its needs in recent years, a trend accentuated by drought in the early 1980s and a cyclone in 1984. More than 70% of Swaziland (including 30% which is rocky and steep) is used for grazing. The SNL tenure system effectively allows free grazing of unlimited numbers of cattle, which is a fundamental impediment to improved productivity.

Although the Swazi nation has regained all the mineral concessions made in the 19th century, the contribution of mining to the GDP has declined from 10% in the 1960s to 3% in 1982. This is unusual among African economies and largely reflects the exhaustion of high-grade iron-ore deposits mined between 1964 and 1978 by Anglo-American at Ngwenya; surrounding deposits of low-grade ore do not justify exploitation at present. Asbestos, once Swaziland's leading export, was mined at Havelock, but the company of Turner and Newall ceased mining in 1986. Lowveld coal is the main hope for the future; at present a single Anglo-American mine, Mpaka, produces about 140 000 tonnes per annum, mainly for export, but reserves exceed 200 million tonnes, much of it anthracite.

Of all Africa's landlocked states, Swaziland is the closest to the sea (Reitsma 1980). Its eastern border is only 74 kilometres by rail from Maputo, and no part of Swaziland is more than 250 kilometres from the sea. Swaziland's transport costs do not greatly exceed those of coastal states, and indeed they are below those of large areas in its coastal neighbours' territory. Its problem for much of the 20th century was, like most of the South African 'homelands', the lack of rail connections. Thus Green & Fair (1960:205) stressed that Swaziland's development could 'depend very much on the degree to which its communication system and economy can be integrated into those of South Africa as a whole'. This has occurred rapidly since they wrote, and the problems arising from Swaziland's landlocked situation are now those of dependence rather than inaccessibility or distance. The railway to Maputo, opened in 1964, is a legacy of iron-ore export to Japan, but serves the country's major industrial estate at Matsapha and the Mpaka coalfield (Whittington 1966). Although Mozambiquan willingness to accept Swazi transit traffic is not in question, the port of Maputo is partly dependent on South African technical assistance (Azevedo 1980), and in the event of congestion Swazi traffic does not receive priority.

South Africa was unwilling to link Swaziland to her rail system unless it was allowed to incorporate Swaziland. With Swazi independence in 1968 and the coming to power of an avowedly Marxist government in Mozambique in 1975, the geopolitical situation changed dramatically and South Africa became positively eager to integrate Swaziland into its railway network. Thus a southern link to Richard's Bay, the major new port in northern Natal, was completed in 1978. Work on a northern link from Mpaka to Komatipoort began in 1983. This will not only create development opportunities in north-east Swaziland but will also shorten the route from the eastern Transvaal to Richard's Bay, thus reducing South African dependence on Maputo and providing transit revenue for Swaziland (Goudie & Price Williams 1983). Swaziland has thus *chosen* to increase its dependence on the South African transport system. This decision makes good geographical sense given Swaziland's close trading links with South Africa, but is directly contrary to the aims of the nine-nation Southern African Development Co-ordination Conference (SADCC), to which Swaziland has belonged since its inception in 1979.

Swaziland has less choice concerning other aspects of its dependence on South Africa. The Republic is the market for 25% of its exports and the source of 90% of its imports, although many of the latter originate elsewhere. Swaziland's tiny domestic market means that most forms of industrial expansion depend in practice on South Africa's markets. In normal years Swaziland's maize deficit is made up with South African imports. Labour migration to South Africa remains significant, although the volume has dropped from over 20 000 in the mid-1970s to just over 13 000 in the early 1980s, four-fifths of which is employed in the mining sector. All Swaziland's major rivers are international, and water usage schemes thus involve negotiation. Expansion of coal mining is partly dependent on South African agreement to buy thermal power from Swaziland, whose own demand is tiny; currently almost two-thirds of its electricity requirements are imported from South Africa (over 80% during the drought of the early 1980s), although a new hydroelectric station in the Ezulwini valley will reduce imports. Oil is imported from South Africa in refined form, mostly via Maputo. South African capital plays a leading rôle in Swazi mining, manufacturing, and especially wholesale and retail trade (Booth 1983). The Swazi tourist industry is also largely capitalized by South African interests and depends on South African tourists.

Swaziland joined the Rand Monetary Area when it was formed in 1974. The *lilangeni* (plural *emalangeni*) is therefore pegged to the value of the rand, giving South Africa effective control over monetary policy and rendering Swaziland unable to reduce the spillover effects of South African inflation on its own economy. By contrast, Botswana has shown the feasibility of monetary independence: the *pula* has consistently outpaced the rand. The dramatic fall of the latter in mid-1985 will perhaps prompt Swaziland to reconsider its position.

Swaziland shares its peripheral, dependent position in the regional economy with Botswana and Lesotho. The position of the three BLS countries is institutionalized by their membership of the Southern African Customs Union (SACU), which dates from 1910. Renegotiation of the agreement in 1969 markedly increased the revenues accruing to BLS, and more than half Swaziland's recurrent revenue derives from SACU. The revenue-sharing formula seeks to divide the common revenue pool among the four countries in proportion to the value of their imports and their production and consumption of dutiable goods. For BLS this figure is raised by 42% as compensation for the disadvantages of being in a customs union with a more developed country – principally the well-known polarization effect of development – and the loss of fiscal discretion (South Africa alone determines excise taxes and import duties for the entire region).

Much criticism of SACU rests upon the effects of the agreement on trade and industrial development in BLS. Although some goods could be obtained more cheaply from outside South Africa, practical opportunities for diversifying import sources are severely limited by the small quantities involved, the non-local ownership of importers, and the fact that many Western multinational corporations have South African subsidiaries with sole distribution rights in the SACU area (Cobbe 1974, Crush 1979). Despite SACU constraints on BLS states entering other trade agreements, they have in practice been able to do so. They receive preferential access to the EEC under the Lomé Convention, and their products also enter the US, Australia, and the Middle East on concessionary terms.

The 1969 agreement specifically called for the development of BLS and the diversification of their economies, but little has been achieved in this respect. The agreement contains no machinery for distributing industry among the four countries, and the establishment of such measures is effectively precluded by South Africa's essentially political concern with her own decentralization programme. Yet industrial polarization in southern Africa is certainly not the result of SACU. The small domestic markets of BLS limit their potential for competition with South African industries, which probably means that they have less to lose than larger countries in the region from preferential trade relationships with a far more developed neighbour (Maasdorp 1982).

Much has been made of South African actions against new BLS industries, but they have not hindered the establishment of import replacement industries. Retaliation has been taken only against industries attempting to penetrate the South African market by avoiding non-tariff barriers imposed by South Africa on its own industries, as in the case of the Swaziland fertilizer factory quoted by Kowet (1978). Maasdorp (1982) suggests that BLS governments have not always made use of the provisions of the 1969 agreement to promote industrialization.

Membership of SACU is internationally embarrassing for BLS, given South Africa's world image. At present, however, all three governments perceive membership to be economically beneficial if not absolutely vital. It seems unlikely that any of them – least of all Swaziland – will leave the Customs Union before political change in South Africa brings that country into a wider economic relationship with all southern African countries.

Generally speaking, Swaziland has a more balanced economy than most small developing countries, but the dramatic growth of the sugar industry poses problems. Sugar accounted for 46% of export earnings in 1980, but low world prices reduced this to 33% in 1982. Recent completion of a third sugar mill increased potential output, so that Swaziland ceased to qualify for minimum price support as a small producer under the hardship clause of the International Sugar Agreement. Production in 1982–3 was 380 000 tonnes, of which 120 000 tonnes is protected by Lomé quota agreements and exported to the EEC at agreed prices which are about twice prevailing world prices.

Attempts at economic diversification have chiefly involved manufacturing and tourism, both of which illustrate the constraints under which Swaziland operates. Like most small developing states, 'the country takes what it can get in the way of industries' (Maasdorp 1976:180). Both industrial and tourist development must compete with South African black 'homelands' which offer substantial incentives to companies locating at their growth points, especially since the introduction in 1982 of a 'co-ordinated regional development strategy' which is more politically than economically motivated (Zille 1983). Since then Swaziland has lost several small firms which relocated in Transkei. Tourism was hit by South African fuel restrictions in the mid-1970s, but more seriously since 1980 by the expansion of hotels and casinos in the 'independent homelands', especially at Sun City, Bophuthatswana; these take advantage, as had Swaziland hitherto, of the illegality of gambling in South Africa (Wellings & Crush 1983).

Swaziland has established two parastatal organizations to promote industrial growth (Selwyn 1975). The National Industrial Development Corporation promotes development through loans, grants, and capital investments to industries whose equity is greater than E 100 000, and the Small Enterprises Development Company (SEDCO) assists smaller, locally owned enterprises, concentrating on commercial service and manufacturing (including handicraft) industries which will create rural employment and reduce imports.

Overall manufacturing output expanded, from a small base, by an average of 7.4% annually between 1977 and 1982, when it contributed 23% of the GDP. Manufacturing suffered a major blow in 1983 with the liquidation of Swazi Chemical Industries in circumstances which underlined Swaziland's dependence on outside forces. Producing mainly fertilizers, this concern accounted for 16% of total exports in 1982. Its demise was attributed to both regional and world recession, as well as inefficient management, corruption, and developments in the South African fertilizer industry.

Of course, to a very large degree, the dependence highlighted in the foregoing discussion is to be expected in a small developing country bordering a powerful neighbour with a semi-developed economy which constitutes a secondary core in the world capitalist economy (Wallerstein 1974). But it does not end discussion. The second half of the chapter seeks to explore the choices Swaziland has made both domestically and internationally, choices which have promoted internal stability and economic growth within a framework of reinforced dependence.

The politics of choice

Sobhuza's suspension of the constitution in 1973 created a 'no-party state'. Despite labour strikes and teacher–student boycotts in the late 1970s, the new 1978 constitution confirmed the ascendancy of traditional institutions. Parties continued to be banned, and voting was by public ballot in the *tinkhundla* (community or tribal councils) for candidates approved by the King, who himself appointed 10 out of 50 deputies to the lower chamber of Parliament and 10 out of 20 to the upper chamber. When Sobhuza died in 1982 the traditional instruments for the transfer of power were employed for the first time since 1899, and the 15-year-old Prince Makhosetive was chosen.

The struggle that followed was so internalized as to have little immediate impact on the lives of ordinary Swazis; nor did it seriously dent the outward image of political stability which Swaziland presents to the world, although its eventual outcome will affect the course of both domestic and foreign policy. More than three years of almost continuous intrigue, coups and countercoups were marked by the imprisonment at various times of leading political figures as members of the royal family waged a Byzantine struggle for power. The desire to legitimize Queen

Ntombi's position as regent was clearly a major factor in Makhosetive's early coronation. The crown prince must normally wait until he is 21; Makhosetive's birth date has never been made public, but it appears that pre-coronation rituals were considerably speeded up to allow him to be crowned (as King Mswati III) on 25 April 1986, when his probable age was only 18. King Mswati's political abilities are as yet untested; it remains to be seen whether, either influenced by his mother or through his own inclination, he will follow the traditional path of Sobhuza in domestic and foreign affairs.

The conservatism of the régime is reflected in its close relationship with foreign capital through the national Tibiyo fund and in the promotional literature of NIDC, which stresses low wages and the absence of unions. It is debatable whether Swaziland has crossed the line between development and exploitation but, as has been seen, it would have little hope of attracting industry on other terms. Agricultural investment has appeared to favour the largely European individual tenure farms at the expense of Swazi Nation Land (Booth 1983), whereas the government appears to view any rural development outside the traditional framework of leadership as potentially destabilizing (Magagula 1978).

Much has been written about the inevitable dependence of Botswana, Lesotho, and Swaziland on South Africa. The conventional view is a pessimistic one which sees little possibility of sustained independent action, given the geography of dependence in southern Africa (Hailey 1963, Hill 1972). The reality is more complex, and a useful corrective is provided by Henderson (1974), who demonstrates with reference to Botswana the opportunities opened up by formal status as an independent state. Botswana maintains an essentially accommodationist stance towards South Africa, but 'a liberal ideology coupled with certain practical development possibilities establishes claims on international resources. The manipulation of these claims and the opportunities created by them in turn strengthens the institutions of statehood and makes possible further plays of the game' (Henderson 1974:49). Botswana's status as a 'frontline state' on the Zimbabwean and Namibian questions is one of the fruits of its international standing.

Chief Leabua Jonathan, the former Lesotho Prime Minister,

also realized the possibilities of statehood. Lacking Sir Seretse Khama's stature as a liberal statesman and facing domestic pressures (he had cancelled the 1970 election as the results showed that he was losing), Chief Jonathan developed a militantly anti-apartheid stance to gain sympathy for his impoverished country. In Lesotho's case a minimal resource base and a land-locked situation completely surrounded by South Africa could at least be used to justify high levels of international aid. Lesotho's relationship to South Africa has been one of confrontation rather than accommodation (Daniel 1984): considerable economic and some military pressure was needed to force Chief Jonathan's government to act against the African National Congress (ANC). In the end South Africa's determination to achieve a non-aggression pact led it to impose a virtual economic blockade on Lesotho in January 1986; this brought domestic pressures to a head and led to a coup. The new military government of Major-General Lekhanya has vested considerable power in the King, Moshoeshoe II, and early indications suggest a far more compliant attitude to South Africa.

Swaziland's own relationship with South Africa has been essentially consensual for most of the time since independence. Integration with the South African railway system has already been noted. Of more direct political significance is Swaziland's pragmatic attitude to the 'homelands'. Swazi princesses have, with Sobhuza's blessing, married prominent figures in Transkei and KwaZulu, including the Zulu King Zwelithini; and both Zwelithini and President Matanzima of Transkei have visited Swaziland (Daniel 1984). The latter's criticism of apartheid has been restrained, and relations between the two governments have been good, reflecting some similarity at least in their ideological world views. Swaziland responded not unwillingly to diplomatic pressure and sharply increased its harassment of the ANC at the end of 1981. In February 1982 it signed a non-agression pact with South Africa, which remained secret until the latter signed the Nkomati Agreement with Mozambique in March 1984. Since the Swaziland pact, the ANC presence there has been reduced to a token one.

Swaziland's willingness to act at South Africa's bidding was probably influenced by the enthusiasm of Sobhuza and the traditionalists ascendant in his government for border changes. Discussions with South Africa in 1982 concerned the incorporation of the KaNgwane 'homeland' and the Ngwavuma district of KwaZulu in Swaziland. This would have enabled the latter to regain some of the territory lost in the Pretoria Convention of 1881, albeit relatively unproductive land with few resources. It would also have given Swaziland a coastline. But the price envisaged by South Africa was a heavy one: the 750 000 Swazi in South Africa would exchange South African for Swazi citizenship, although two-thirds of them lived outside KaNgwane. Swaziland would thus have approached Lesotho in its dependence on labour migration. It would also have incorporated 135 000 unwilling non-Swazis in Ngwavuma.

Swaziland's foreign relations also reflect its ideological stance. It has no relations with socialist states apart from Mozambique (with whom a trade agreement was signed in 1978), but maintains diplomatic links with Taiwan, which gives aid to Swaziland. For nearly a decade after the Yom Kippur war in 1973, Swaziland was the only black African country retaining diplomatic ties with Israel (Daniel 1984). Its position on international issues is more akin to the West than the Third World, as its voting record at the UN bears out.

This stance is certainly not unhelpful to Swaziland in attracting foreign aid, which has also been encouraged by its position *vis-á-vis* South Africa. Small size may be an advantage in the eyes of donors, presenting tangible objectives for a relatively limited financial outlay. Much of Swaziland's foreign aid currently supports Rural Development Area schemes. It also benefits from membership of the Lomé Agreement and received payments from the European Development Fund to offset the loss of export earnings consequent upon the decline and closure of the Ngwenya iron-ore mine.

Conclusion

Swaziland is thus unusual among the many small states produced by African decolonization. The monarchy and traditional institutions have emerged stronger than before from both independence and subsequent constitutional changes. It has not sought to resist the implications of dependence, despite the political system of its powerful neighbour, but has in many respects chosen to reinforce them. This seems to reflect not only economic motives but the ideological inclinations of a conservative, traditionalist government which, despite the emergence of frustration amongst middle-class elements of the Swazi, continues to enjoy the support of the majority of its people.

References

Azevedo, M. J. 1980. A sober commitment to liberation? Mozambique and South Africa, 1974–1979. *African Affairs* **79**, 567–84.

Booth, A. R. 1983. *Swaziland: Tradition and Change in a Southern African Kingdom*. Aldershot: Gower.

Cobbe, J. H. 1974. The South African trade control system and neighbouring states. *South African Journal of Economics* **42**, 438–42.

Crush, J. S. 1979. The parameters of dependence in Southern Africa: a case study of Swaziland. *Journal of Southern African Affairs* **4**, 55–66.

Daniel, J. B. McI. 1966. Swaziland: some problems of an African rural economy. *South African Geographical Journal* **48**, 90–100.

Daniel, J. 1984. A comparative analysis of Lesotho and Swaziland's relations with South Africa. In *South African Review Two*, South African Research Service (ed.), 228–38. Johannesburg: Ravan.

Doveton, D. M. 1937. *The human geography of Swaziland*. Institute of British Geographers Publication No. 8. London: George Philip.

Goudie, A. S. & D. Price Williams 1983. *The Atlas of Swaziland*. Lambamba: Swaziland National Trust Commission.

Green, L. P. & T. J. D. Fair 1969. *Development in Africa*. Johannesburg: Witwatersrand University Press.

Hailey, Lord 1953. *Native administration in the British Territories Part V: The High Commission Territories: Basutoland, the Bechuanaland Protectorate and Swaziland*. London: HMSO.

Hailey, Lord 1963. *The Republic of South Africa and the High Commission Territories*. London: Oxford University Press.

Halpern, J. 1965. *South Africa's Hostages: Basutoland, Bechuanaland and Swaziland*. Harmondsworth: Penguin Books.

Henderson, W. 1974. Independent Botswana: a reappraisal of foreign policy options. *African Affairs* **73**, 37–49.

Hill, C. R. 1972. Botswana independence: myth or reality? *The Round Table* **245**, 55–62.

Kowet, D. K. 1978. *Land, labour migration and politics in Southern Africa: Botswana, Lesotho and Swaziland*. Uppsala: Scandinavian Institute of African Studies.

Maasdorp, G. 1976. Industrialisation in a small country: the experience of Swaziland. In *Strategy for Development*, J. Barratt, D. S. Collier, K. Glaser and H. Mönning (eds), 179–89. London: Macmillan.

Maasdorp, G. 1982. The Southern African Customs Union – an assessment. *Journal of Contemporary African Studies* 2, 81–112.

Magagula, G. T. 1978. Rural development area programs: the case of Swaziland. *Journal of Southern African Affairs* 3, 433–67.

Marquard, L. 1961. *The peoples and policies of South Africa*. London: Oxford University Press.

Reitsma, H. A. 1980. Africa's landlocked countries: a study of dependency relations. *Tijdschrift voor Economische en Sociale Geografie* 71, 130–41.

Selwyn, P. 1975. *Industries in the southern African periphery*. London: Croom Helm.

South Africa 1955. *Report of the Tomlinson Commission on the socio-economic development of the Bantu Areas*. Pretoria: Government Printer.

Spence, J. E. 1967. The High Commission Territories with special reference to Swaziland. In *Problems of smaller territories*, B. Benedict (ed.), 97–111. London: Athlone Press.

Wallerstein, I. 1974. Dependence in an interdependent world: the limited possibilities of transformation within the capitalist world economy. *African Studies Review* 17, 1–26.

Wellings, P. A. & J. S. Crush 1983. Tourism and dependency in Southern Africa: the prospects and planning of tourism in Lesotho. *Applied Geography* 3, 205–23.

Whittington, G. W. 1966. The Swaziland railway. *Tijdschrift voor Economische en Sociale Geografie* 57, 68–73.

Whittington, G. W. & J. B. McI. Daniel 1969. Problems of land tenure and land ownership in Swaziland. In *Environment and land use in Africa*, M. F. Thomas & G. W. Whittington (eds), 447–61. London: Methuen.

Zille, H. 1983. Restructuring the industrial decentralisation strategy. In *South African Review One*, South African Research Service (ed.), 58–71. Johannesburg: Ravan.

11 *Malta*

James Craig

The Maltese Islands, with a population of 330 000, represent a classic case of smallness in the context of international politics. Throughout the centuries Malta has been desired for its position at the centre of the Mediterranean and its superb natural harbour. British dominance over the islands was merely the last phase of a long history of subordination which gave rise to Malta's designation as a 'fortress colony' (Frendo 1979). In the formal political sense independence was achieved in September 1964, but Britain retained military facilities on the islands until 31 March 1979.

During this 15-year period successive Maltese governments have had to face similar developmental problems – above all, how to manage the transition from being a fortress and a base for British defence needs into a viable economic unit where defence expenditure was no longer of crucial importance. Even today when Malta is no longer a base for foreign military activity, the relative lack of natural resources poses important policy problems in relation to development. To achieve some room for manoeuvre Maltese political leaders have had to use the international political setting as a key resource for economic and social development (Selwyn 1975). The theme of small state manoeuvrability is the focus of this chapter.

In discussing small states it is too easy to conclude that relationships of dependency imply a problem. At least as far as the Maltese case is concerned, it can be argued that dependence on Britain and its NATO allies also provided policy opportunity. Britain was clearly more powerful in every political and economic sense, but the relationship provided successive Maltese governments with an opportunity to bargain and indeed, as will be shown below, to win important concessions on a number of fronts. The case of Malta does provide at least one general lesson for the future of small states, namely that the application of political skills in international relations can provide tangible advantages to a small country and that power in international politics is not just about economic strength or military might. Political leadership is very much a part of the equation (Craig 1983). Certainly in Malta there is no doubt that personalities have played a key part in recent political history. Borg Olivier, Prime Minister from 1962 until 1971 as leader of the Nationalist Party (PN), and Dom Mintoff, Prime Minister from 1971 until 1984 as leader of the Malta Labour Party (MLP), so dominated internal politics that their policy preferences were rarely challenged.

To illustrate these general propositions, the period 1964–86 has been divided into two phases. Dependent sovereignty can be said to characterize the Borg Olivier years, and the military rundown crisis of 1966–7 encapsulated the PN strategy for Malta until the party's defeat in 1971. Positive neutralism summarizes the MLP approach, which is highlighted by an examination of the 1971–2 crisis and the post-1979 era. Despite the very different approaches of Borg Olivier and Mintoff there are areas of similarity. Both sought from their different perspectives to further Maltese interests against difficult odds. The economic and social progress of the 1960s and 1970s testifies to some successes.

Dependent sovereignty, 1964–71

On the successful completion of independence negotiations in September 1964, Malta and Britain signed a Defence and Financial Agreement, designed to facilitate economic development within the security of a British and NATO presence. The Agreement reflected much of the political thinking of PN under the leadership of Borg Olivier with regard to Malta's future development. At first sight Malta's policy options looked painfully curtailed by Britain's declining rôle in the Mediterranean area. As far back as 1959, the colonial government had recognized the need to bring together a battery of policy proposals to strengthen and expand sectors of the economy such as tourism, light industry, and agriculture in order to achieve diversification away from British services-related expenditure and employment. All parties concerned, Britain, the PN, and the MLP, were united in the conviction that economic viability would only be achieved if Britain and its NATO allies were prepared to assist Malta and harmonize their own defence planning and Malta's interests for long-term development. The PN and the MLP disagreed fundamentally on how this was to be achieved, though a UN mission visited the islands in 1963 and stated that economic viability was likely to take 15 to 25 years to achieve, a conclusion which was accepted by Britain as a realistic assessment.

The Defence and Financial Agreement negotiated by Borg Olivier and the British Commonwealth Secretary, Duncan Sandys, stated that Britain would provide a sum of £51 million over a ten-year period, 75% of which was to be in the form of a grant and 25% a loan at current UK interest rates (Colonial Office 1964a). These financial arrangements were to last for a five-year period and then be subject to further review in 1969. A parallel defence agreement was also signed which gave Britain considerable control over key installations and the use of property and land for military purposes (Colonial Office 1964b). Britain also agreed to train and assist generally with the development of Malta's own small defence forces.

What emerged emphasized the PN commitment to a solidly pro-Western foreign and security policy. Borg Olivier had strong backing from the Cabinet and party for this position. Although a nationalist, Borg Olivier was cautious in his approach to policy. He held to the view that the aim of economic viability required the security of a British and NATO presence. He was aware that, in 1964, 13% of all gainfully employed Maltese worked for British services departments and that the wages and salaries paid to Maltese employees of the services constituted 23% of the total wage bill (Pirotta 1974).

Although services expenditure was falling at a rate of £2 million per year from a peak of £22.3 million in 1961 and such falls were likely to continue, the pace of that decline was of the essence. The Defence and Financial Agreement remained the main pillar of PN thinking for the rest of the decade, even though it was fully realized that Malta had to use the ten-year period to good effect. Defence, security, and the economy were thus interwoven. The presence of British forces provided defence of an order that Malta could not provide for itself; Southern HQ of NATO provided a security network and a stage on which Malta might play a part in wider European and North American concerns; and the entire relationship could be translated into tangible economic benefits.

This may appear, on the surface, to be a curious form of nationalism. However, it will be argued later that Borg Olivier's defence of Malta's interests in his negotiations with Britain in the second half of the 1960s did not suggest a neocolonial puppet. With great determination and considerable political skill he fought to extract the best out of the increasingly retreating British. The election of a British Labour government under Harold Wilson soon after Maltese independence in 1964 proved difficult for the PN government. Wilson and the Defence Secretary, Denis Healey, were determined to extract defence cuts and reduce the commitments of British forces. Malta was unlikely to escape the effects of this policy. Whatever the benefits of the Financial Agreement, cuts in British forces were bound to result in reduced economic activity and consequent unemployment in Malta.

Two connected themes then emerged that in effect set the parameters of development policy for the rest of the 1960s and the 1970s. The first, as mentioned, was how to operate the British connection to minimize the effects on Malta of Britain's Mediterranean withdrawal; the second was how to widen the NATO connection from security to economic development. This latter goal was another aspect of Borg Olivier's conservative nationalism. His leadership of the PN had seen the party scuttle its Italianate past so that Italian language and culture had all but disappeared as a political force. This was replaced by a desire on the part of the Maltese middle and professional classes, from whom the PN obtained much of its support, to be seen as part of wider European culture. Borg Olivier spoke frequently of the island's attachment to Europe, the West, and NATO. In a 1966 speech to the House of Representatives (the Maltese one-chamber Parliament) he declared that Malta's place was with the West, with NATO, and all they stood for. Throughout his premiership and beyond he held a consistent view on this matter. He believed that Maltese national interests and Europeanism were complementary; NATO, for Borg Olivier, was a defence, security and political expression of his intellectual and emotional attachment.

The question that has now to be asked is how successfully did Borg Olivier manage to weave together his defence, security, and economic policies to achieve tangible development for Malta until his narrow defeat at the hands of the MLP in 1971. The critical test was the dispute with the British government which arose in 1966–7 over proposed reductions in British forces in Malta and the consequent employment effects upon locally engaged workers. The issue came to a head after the PN government had been returned to office in 1966 at the end of an election campaign dominated by the continuing dispute between the MLP and the island's Roman Catholic bishops. Controversy surrounds the benefit derived by the PN from the dispute, but the economic indicators do suggest that Borg Olivier's claims, that the economy was expanding, the tourist industry growing, and gross production rising, played at least some part in the victory (*Times of Malta* 1966).

However, improved economic performance was to prove double-edged for Malta. In the middle of the election campaign the British government published its Defence Review that stated, 'we shall continue these responsibilities and obligations (in the Mediterranean) while making substantial economies in our contingents in Cyprus and Malta' (Defence Estimates 1966). Britain adopted the view that substantial savings could be made in defence expenditure in the Mediterranean in general and in Malta in particular, while still fulfilling the basic demands of NATO and the agreement with Malta. It also considered that Malta's growing economic prosperity meant that the financial and employment effects of a British rundown would not be devastating. For the Maltese the issue looked very different. Here was Britain sacrificing Maltese interests on the altar of economy only two years after granting independence and signing a defence agreement. Not only was Malta's defence and security in question, but the economic gains of the last few years were likely to falter as Maltese workers were made redundant as the economies were carried out (Craig 1983).

The situation posed a real and difficult dilemma for Malta. Mintoff's MLP asked repeatedly, and with devastating effect, what was Malta really achieving by sheltering so closely under the British and NATO umbrella. The 1964 agreement stated quite clearly that Malta would be consulted before any major changes were contemplated, but Borg Olivier denied that he had been consulted prior to the publication of the defence review. The word 'consultation' is, of course, conveniently ambiguous. In the House of Commons it was stated that the Maltese government had been informed of that part of the review referring to Malta. But it is difficult to regard information of a decision already taken as constituting consultation. Borg Olivier's reply to the British was clearly intended to give him time in which to see his party safely back in power at the 1966 general election and to begin the type of negotiations which he regarded as his right under the Defence Agreement.

By the second half of 1966 it was clear that there were major differences between London and Valletta. Lord Beswick, the Parliamentary Under-Secretary of State for Commonwealth Affairs, visited Malta in August 1966 with proposals to put into effect the objective outlined in the Defence Review. Borg Olivier went to London for the Commonwealth Prime Ministers' Conference and had discussions with Wilson and other ministers. Borg Olivier refused to state publicly what the British government's proposals were, but he left no doubt as to his hostility. The London *Daily Telegraph* (1966) reported that the British position was to save £8 million by cutting British servicemen in Malta and discharging local personnel. It warned that Britain would have no one to blame if the Maltese decided to abrogate the Defence Agreement, expell the troops, and sell to the highest bidder; this was a clear reference to the *Telegraph*'s interpretation of the policy of Mintoff and the MLP.

There followed months of bargaining in which Borg Olivier played a dominant rôle. At first he tried to convince Britain that severe reductions in service personnel would harm vital strategic interests. The growing Soviet presence in the Mediterranean showed the importance of Malta for Britain and NATO. There was probably some pressure on the Wilson government from the US and Italy to proceed gently with troop reductions in Malta;

hence the willingness of the British government to continue to negotiate. Borg Olivier certainly visited the US and Italy to gain support for his position. The Secretary of State for Commonwealth Affairs, Herbert Bowden, in turn, visited Malta in January 1967 with revised proposals designed to win the support of the Maltese government. His concession was that the proposed rundown of British forces would be phased over four years instead of two, but this, he stated, was Britain's last offer (*Times of Malta* 1967). With the full approval of his Cabinet, Borg Olivier accused Britain of breaking the 1964 Defence Agreement and declared that Britain could not undertake her treaty obligations to Malta with such reduced forces.

There was a period of maximum pressure on the British government in the early months of 1967. Malta was increasingly regarded as a pained innocent fighting a moving battle against overwhelming odds. Wilson's treatment of Britain's ally was even attacked by the pro-Labour weekly magazine, the *New Statesman*. This was precisely the kind of comment which the Maltese government wanted to see. It had unofficially accepted the principle of the rundown, but somehow concessions had to be extracted from Britain. To do this, leverage had to be created, and Borg Olivier was at the forefront of efforts in this respect. On visits to Britain and elsewhere he rarely missed an opportunity to use the press and television to further the Maltese case. He frequently spoke of the historic link between the two countries and utilized pro-Maltese feeling to try to drive a wedge between Wilson's government and public opinion.

With hindsight, it is probably accurate to say that Borg Olivier knew that he had got about as much movement out of the British as he was likely to achieve, at least as far as the principle of a rundown was concerned. What he required was a settlement in circumstances that would give his government maximum political mileage. Accordingly, he mobilized every conceivable group within Malta in a wave of protest – the church, voluntary organizations, the trade unions, business, commerce, and the professions. Even British residents (mostly retired servicemen) held a silent march through the streets of Valletta protesting against British policy. The largest trade union, the General

Workers Union, joined in, much to the annoyance of Mintoff and the MLP. The Maltese High Commission in London was flooded with letters from all over Britain attacking the British treatment of Malta. Finally, the Maltese government informed Britain on 27 Janaury 1967 that facilities available to British forces under the Defence Agreement could no longer be used and that it was introducing into the Maltese Parliament a Visiting Forces Bill to change the status of service personnel on the islands.

On 13 March 1967 an agreement was officially announced. The British obtained their broad aim enshrined in the 1966 Defence Review. The rundown was to be phased over a four-year instead of a two-year period, with the concession that Malta could seek a review during the rundown if Maltese unemployment was to rise dramatically. A joint mission of British and Maltese experts was to start work on a plan for job creation and strengthening the Maltese economy to cope with local discharges. This latter point was considered an essential ingredient of the agreement, as a loss of 6500 jobs by the end of the rundown period would leave Malta with an unemployment rate of 17%. Britain also agreed to pay some £2 million in gratuities to discharged Maltese workers and further conceded that £3 million from the Agreement in Financial Assistance spent since the dispute started should not revert to the British Treasury but be carried over for the use of the Maltese government.

For the better part of a year Borg Olivier was engaged in protracted negotiations with Britain. How is one to evaluate the final outcome? At one level the conclusion reached by the Maltese opposition led by Dom Mintoff has a clarity that is both seductive and appealing. Malta, he argued, would always face dire economic problems when Britain changed her defence policies. Britain must therefore be told what the price was for Malta's facilities and, if it was unwilling to pay, then it must be told to leave and another power found which would.

To the cautious Borg Olivier this was too radical and risky. Who would substitute for Britain and NATO if the asking price was too high? In opposition Mintoff could pose the question without having to provide a policy answer, and he tantalizingly spoke of the US and others without directly clarifying his position. There can be little doubt that by the mid-1960s Mintoff was well on the way towards developing a strategy that would put a time limit on the British presence and substitute a foreign policy of non-alignment. These ideas were only evolving in 1966–7, but the dispute with Britain represented a watershed in Mintoff's thinking which will be discussed in greater detail later.

The government under Borg Olivier was assisted in selling the 1967 agreement locally by the fact that the years 1966–9 witnessed considerable economic progress in Malta. The worst fears of many for the future did not materialize and many sectors of the economy showed distinct signs of health. Unemployment, which stood at 8.2% (7859) at the beginning of the period, fell to 3.7% (3813) at the same time as emigration was falling (Cassar 1972). A boom in tourism, construction, and light industry accounted for the expansion and employment.

The Central Bank had been created in 1968 and the Malta Development Corporation had been established shortly afterwards to provide aid and practical help for investors. Tourist arrivals in 1969 rose to 186 084, with a planned target of 250 000 by 1972. The restrictions imposed by Britain on travel outside the sterling area were welcomed by the Maltese tourist trade as tourist arrivals were overwhelmingly from Britain (a situation that continues despite attempts at diversification). Financial incentives attracted light manufacturing and numbers gainfully employed rose from 86 080 in 1966 to 100 460 in 1969 (Cassar 1972). The construction industry operated at a high level of activity, despite criticisms of lack of implementation of planning regulations. By 1968, 9290 persons were employed in construction and there was a dramatic rise in the number of construction firms on the Islands (Spiteri, n.d.). The Joint Mission reported in July 1968 and set as a major objective the creation of 15 000 jobs by 1972. The Mission's chairman appeared reasonably happy with progress to date particularly as the number of people discharged by the services had not been as great as predicted (*Times of Malta* 1968).

To sum up, then, the Anglo-Maltese dispute of 1966–7 demonstrates many of the features of Maltese security and development policy under Borg Olivier and the PN government. Another serious dispute arose over the second phase of the

Financial Agreement in 1968–9 (Craig 1983). Characteristically, Borg Olivier used similar tactics to gain concessions, and the election of a British Conservative government in 1970 saw him achieve all that he had asked.

Positive neutrality, 1971–84

In June 1971 the Maltese people went to the polls to elect a new House of Representatives. In a poll of 92.6% Mintoff's MLP gained power by a majority of one seat and thus formed the new government. By 1971 the Maltese economy was in considerable difficulty. The boom of 1967–9 had run out of steam, unemployment was rising, and tourist arrivals were falling. Underlying the Mintoff approach to Malta's economic problems lay the conviction that the arrangements on finance and defence negotiated by Borg Olivier in 1964 required fundamental reappraisal.

There were two major strands to Mintoff's thinking, which he had publicly developed in speeches throughout the 1960s. In the first place, he considered that the Borg Olivier agreements gave too much to the British, considering Malta's independent status. Malta needed to reclaim her identity from years of subservience to Britain. Mintoff was determined to assert Maltese identity and, by so doing, give Malta a pride in itself. In this sense, Mintoff's nationalism was more strident and angry than the 'softer' approach of Borg Olivier and the PN. Mintoff felt strongly that the British had always patronized Malta and its people, and he was determined that Malta should be treated as a free and independent nation. Secondly, he held that the British paid far too small a sum for the facilities offered. He regarded the £5 million per year given in financial assistance to be nothing like the amount that Malta was worth to Britain and NATO – and to add insult, 25% of that sum was in the form of loans. Throughout the 1971 election campaign and before, he made perfectly clear that a fundamental renegotiation of the relationship with Britain would be the top priority for an MLP government. Despite his narrow election victory, Mintoff believed that he had a mandate for such a move. It was thus the battle over renegotiation which occupied Mintoff in the first months of his government.

At first sight it might appear that Malta had little with which to bargain. The strategic value of the island had declined, as was aptly demonstrated by the events of the 1960s; therefore, if Britain was pressed too hard, it might simply leave. However, Malta's position in the Mediterranean had noticeably changed with the increasingly competitive nature of the presence of naval forces of both superpowers. Malta was useful (if not critical) for NATO's system of shadowing Soviet naval activity. It is clear that the US and Italy were concerned to avoid a break between Britain and Malta. Both countries used their efforts to keep the two sides talking and were willing to help financially in a final settlement.

Although the question of the level of payment that Malta enjoyed from the relationship with Britain was a major factor in Mintoff's thinking, other factors require analysis. Mintoff was extremely suspicious of British governments in their dealings with Malta and his distrust was voiced frequently and in public. To an extent, these expressions were part of a political game with small Malta kicking the pants of big brother Britain, an entertainment which his supporters loved. More seriously, though, Mintoff had come round to the view that Malta would be best served by adopting a policy of non-alignment. Therefore, if there was to be a new agreement with Britain, it must include a time limit beyond which Malta would no longer have foreign troops on its soil. Malta must also achieve a level of what was to be termed 'rent' sufficient to make a substantial contribution to economic independence. A renegotiated settlement with Britain and a foreign policy of non-alignment were of a piece, for Mintoff was convinced that many leaders of non-aligned countries would be willing to help Malta build its economy by granting economic aid.

Throughout the 1960s, Mintoff had established strong links with a number of countries in the non-aligned group, particularly with Libya under Colonel Gadafy. There can be little doubt that Gadafy had promised economic support for a policy of limiting Britain's presence in Malta: Mintoff's willingness to take negotiations with the Heath government to the very edge of failure was testimony to the probability that Libya would assist if the British pulled out.

Like Borg Olivier before him, Mintoff entered a period of negotiations with Britain which stretched over a number of months. A combination of threats, staged walkouts, and visits to London and Rome were used to extract a settlement which Mintoff considered acceptable to his long-term aims (Davies 1975). Press speculation was considerable as to Mintoff's demands, and a well connected local journalist put the figure at £30 million per year as the opening bid (*Bulletin* 1971). A shot had been fired across the bows of NATO by the virtual expulsion of Admiral Birindelli, NATO's naval commander in Malta, and the transfer of Southern HQ to Naples. If NATO was in any doubt as to Mintoff's determination, this aptly demonstrated the seriousness of purpose of the new Maltese government.

During the months of negotiation, Mintoff's skill and his willingness to take risks were valuable assets. In December 1971, Malta imposed a deadline for the withdrawal of all British forces by the end of the month, because of the failure to reach agreement. This deadline was then extended and talks restarted. A final agreement was signed in London on 21 March 1972. Britain was to rent facilities in Malta for a period of seven years, but on 31 March 1979, Malta was to end its long history as a 'fortress'. Britain and NATO were to meet an annual rent of £14 million payable in advance in two instalments of £7 million. This was a major economic gain for the Maltese economy, as it was an outright payment to the Maltese exchequer and contained no loan element (Davies 1975).

The departure of the British forces in March 1979 did to some extent leave Malta exposed. This can best be demonstrated by examining the relationship with Libya and the question of oil exploration. The friendship with Libya was a cornerstone of Mintoff's personal political credo. But it had within it a number of potential problems, not the least of which was the distinct possibility that oil might be found on the continental shelf separating the two countries. During the 1971 general election campaign Mintoff had attacked Borg Olivier for indolence in not pushing ahead with the exploratory work. Ironically, it was not until 1980, by which time negotiations between Valletta and

Tripoli had failed to produce any agreement on the division of the area, that Malta decided to go it alone and charter an oil rig to begin exploration. No sooner was the rig in place than a Libyan gunboat appeared alongside and ordered the cessation of activity. Operations were halted and relations between the two countries cooled noticeably until 1982 when the matter was finally taken to the International Court.

In 1980 and 1981 Mintoff secured Italian and Soviet guarantees for Malta's neutrality, accompanied by agreements on economic co-operation and assistance. The final years of Mintoff's premiership saw a continuation of the search for friends and economic assistance in the Arab World, China, North Korea, Eastern Europe, and latterly the USSR. Yet despite the signing of many government-to-government agreements, Malta's economic fate still lies solidly with its Western trading partners. This has not been substantially altered by the years of effort to diversify, though West Germany has replaced Britain as the major recipient of Maltese exports. The problem is that Malta possesses little that the USSR desires or needs apart from ship repairing and bulk oil storage facilities, and even these are not critical to Soviet Mediterranean policy.

Conclusion

Mintoff retired in December 1984. Just as in the final years of the Borg Olivier era, the early 1980s were economically difficult for Malta. The new Prime Minister, Dr Carmelo Mifsud Bonnici, has decided to seek closer ties with Europe while maintaining the edifice of positive neutrality. Despite Mintoff's controversial style and the considerable doubts raised about a number of internal developments, dependent sovereignty for Malta is dead and positive neutrality is now accepted even by the opposition PN.

References

Bulletin (Valletta) 1971. 30 June.
Cassar, L. M. 1972. *Unemployment and the Maltese economy 1959–1969*. Unpublished BA economics dissertation, University of Malta.

Colonial Office 1964a. *Proposed agreement on financial assistance.* Cmnd 2423. London: HMSO.
Colonial Office 1964b. *Proposed agreement on mutual defence and assistance.* Cmnd 2410. London: HMSO.
Craig, J. A. 1983. The politics of economic development: the Maltese experience. *Manchester Papers on Development,* **8**.
Daily Telegraph (London) 1966. 29 August.
Davies, L. 1975. *Malta versus the NATO powers 1971–72.* Unpublished BA History dissertation, University of Malta.
Defence Estimates 1966. *The defence review.* Cmnd 2901, Part 1, para 21. London: HMSO.
Frendo, H. 1979. *Party politics in a fortress colony: the Maltese experience.* Valletta: Midsea Books.
House of Representatives 1966. *Report.* (Translation).
New Statesman 1967. How not to cut defence. 3 February.
Pirotta, M. 1974. *The British services sector in Malta, 1946–69.* Unpublished BA economics dissertation, University of Malta.
Selwyn, P. (ed.) 1975. *Development policy in small countries.* London: Croom Helm.
Spiteri, L. n.d. *Aspects of the property boom.* Valletta: Mimeo.
Times of Malta 1966. 6 January.
Times of Malta 1967. 18 January.
Times of Malta 1968. 19 July.

12 Cyprus

Floya Anthias

Cyprus may be a small country (640 000 population) but it is not a small issue. In the past 30 years it has endured an anticolonial revolutionary war, a military coup, and a foreign invasion and occupation. Cyprus is a small state, but it contains within it two ethnic and religious groups which are divided territorially, six armies, a no-man's-land, and an illegal second state which purports to represent the Turkish-Cypriot community. It is the only country in Europe in recent times to have been invaded and recolonized by a larger state – Turkey in 1974. Cyprus is the only country whose boundaries have been forcefully changed by a member of NATO. The Cyprus case demonstrates how small countries are discounted and used by the superpowers in the pursuit of their own interests. It also illustrates effectively how internal ethnic divisions respond to economic and political forces, both external and internal, and how ethnicity and nationalism continue to be of salience in the modern world.

To a student of Cypriot politics it came as a shock but no great surprise that Turkey, a larger power with a substantial military force, invaded the island in 1974, on the pretext of restoring the *status quo* in the aftermath of a coup led by the extreme right-wing EOKA B and the Greek junta. The intervention was within the boundaries imposed by the Treaty of Guarantee which formed part of the independence arrangements for the island in 1960, Turkey being a 'guarantor' power, along with Greece and Britain. The subsequent annexation of approximately 40% of the island's territory resulted in the displacement of a third of the population and a movement of Greek-Cypriot refugees to the south together with a movement of Turkish-Cypriot southerners to the north. As Hitchens (1984) points out, since 1948 no member of NATO or the Warsaw pact has sought to change the boundaries of an existing state. Turkey redrew the map against much overt international opposition but with a great deal of implicit US support. The fact is that a larger power suited itself by altering geography and demography, thereby demonstrating, as again Hitchens (1984) notes, the way in which small countries and peoples are discounted or disregarded by the superpowers.

In the case of Cyprus, however, it is not at all clear that smallness has been a decisive characteristic in accounting for its turbulent political history, although it has had important effects on internal political and social life. In small face-to-face societies clientelistic politics become central: when individuals are organized in communities where they interact with one another in either a direct personal way or in some other way 'know' each other, identification and consciousness tend to be more locally based and social control is vested in the practical management of affairs as opposed to larger moral claims. However, patron–client relations are found in the larger societies of the Mediterranean such as Greece and Italy, and are effective not only in small societies such as Cyprus (Gellner & Waterbury 1977). It may be possible, though, that they are more resistant to change where societies are small, and this certainly has been the case in Cyprus.

As regards the form of nationalism generated by small states, the main characteristic of modern nationalist movements is that they are secessionist and aim to produce an autonomous political unit. As a general rule the weaker and smaller the state and the greater the ethnic or religious heterogeneity it experiences, the greater the problems posed by secessionism. The myth of common origin in such cases has to be constructed or revised. Where this proves impossible or where such common origin is denied by struggles for dominance between ethnic groups, there may be conflict concerning the territorial boundaries of the nation. In the case of Cyprus this led to a form of nationalism that saw Cyprus as part of an already existing larger national unity – Greece on the part of Greek-Cypriots and Turkey on the part of Turkish-Cypriots – the two visions embodied in claims for Enosis (Union with Greece) and Taksim (Partition) respectively (Attalides 1979). In this sense the form of nationalism that arose ran counter to the modern secessionist strain.

The form of the state

In Cyprus, the form of the state was externally imposed and satisfied the perceived needs and desires of neither of the two main ethnic groups on the island, the Greek-Cypriots and the Turkish-Cypriots. Indeed, what put an insurmountable obstacle in the way of the formation of a common national consciousness within the state structure was its thoroughgoing commitment to bicommunalism in political representation, education, and family law – all those processes that can act, where they are common, to cement a national state. The 1960 independence constitution created one unified national state, but two separate communities were formally designated, the Greek-Cypriot and the Turkish-Cypriot, with their own specified political representation (Kyriakides 1968). The Turkish-Cypriots were given 30% of the representation in Parliament, which was considerably in excess of their share of the population. The President was always to be Greek and the Vice-President Turkish; each was to be elected by his own community, to derive authority from it, and to be responsible and accountable to it. Both had the right of veto in foreign affairs and defence and security matters, and could thus block the decisions of the other. Bicommunalism was also written into the structure of the civil service, the security forces, the army and, indeed, at every level of government and administration.

The dominant rôles played by Britain, Greece, and Turkey in the independence talks that were to form the basis of the constitution and related treaties naturally ensured that their interests were represented. In fact, their ability to 'resolve' the Cyprus issue in the interest of NATO was made easier by those internal developments on the island which had led to the growth of ethnicity and ethnic conflict. The Zurich–London agreement of 1959 established the form of the constitution and also set up three treaties allowing the retention of colonial rule, albeit in a different form. Through the Treaty of Establishment Britain was to retain 250 square kilometres of Cyprus territory and 32 other points all over Cyprus and to establish two military bases in the south, thus retaining overall some 3% of the island.

The Treaty of Alliance provided for the permanent presence of

Greek and Turkish troops on the island, and the Treaty of Guarantee prohibited both union and partition and gave Britain, Turkey, and Greece the right to intervene with the sole aim of re-establishing the state of affairs created by the Treaty (HMSO 1960). It thus specifically linked constitutional developments in Cyprus to the interests of the guarantor powers. In addition, the development of Cypriot ethnic consciousness was made difficult by the presence of Greek and Turkish troops whose purpose was to protect their own communities. This Treaty also had the significant effect of establishing Greek rights in Cyprus and formally re-establishing those Turkish rights which had been ceded in 1923 at the Treaty of Lausanne when Cyprus was formally handed over to Britain. In summary then, although formal state power was passed into indigenous hands, the three treaties curtailed the autonomy of local politics and gave the right of interference to three foreign powers. The prospects for nationalism in Cyprus had been sacrificed to the wider political interest of the Western alliance.

Clearly such constitutional provisions required a great deal of collaboration and agreement on both sides of the ethnic divide within Cyprus if they were to work; within three years they had broken down. One of the problems was that the Greek-Cypriot and Turkish-Cypriot political representatives defined the constitution differently. The Turkish-Cypriots endowed it with a federal character and, since they saw it as protecting their rights, argued for its total implementation. The Greek-Cypriots saw it as representing the interests of Turkey and other foreign powers and as giving unfair representation to Turkish-Cypriots; they wanted an integrated unitary state instead. In 1963 President Makarios proposed certain constitutional amendments which resulted in intercommunal fighting and the withdrawal of Turkish-Cypriots into their own enclaves, thus beginning the fateful physical separation of the two communities (Anthias & Ayres 1983).

In the next section I shall examine the development of nationalism and ethnic conflict in Cyprus in order to show that this was the result of the conjunction of internal political forces and external manipulation and intervention. It is not possible to see these developments as merely externally imposed, as Hitchens

(1984) does; nor is it adequate to see them as resulting from generic ethnic antagonism (as much of the received wisdom on Cyprus does). Rather, as Attalides (1979) shows, it is the unique interaction of factors, both internal and external, that is important.

Nationalism and ethnic conflict

It was the British colonial era from 1878 to 1960 which gave the impetus to the growth of polarized ethnicities in Cyprus. Prior to British rule, passive ethnicity characterized the two communities, which had traditionally tended to live in mixed villages. Britain formalized ethnic divisions under the 1882 constitution when proportional representation was given to Greek-Cypriots and Turkish-Cypriots, with the British maintaining ultimate control. By encouraging a rapid expansion of schools along religious lines it also forced the two communities to become dependent for personnel and literature on Greece and Turkey respectively. However, for much of this period the two communities continued to live in mixed villages and, as peasants, shared the trials and tribulations of the agricultural economy and the substantial poverty and economic uncertainty that were attendant (Kitromilides 1977).

These trans-ethnic commonalities found their most effective organizational expression within the syndicalist movement. For example, both Greek-Cypriots and Turkish-Cypriots participated in a number of strikes, the most famous of which was against the American mining company at Mavrovouni in 1948 (AKEL 1976). Both communities were also represented in the Communist Party of Cyprus (KKE) which was set up in 1928, to be banned in 1931 under the direct rule of Sir Richard Palmer, re-emerging in 1941 as AKEL (the Progressive Party of the Working People) (Anthias & Ayres 1983).

Although both (Turkish) Moslems and (Greek) Christians (the latter being the categories used at the time) tended their crops side by side and shared a common rural life, they had their own separate cultural practices. They attended each other's festivities and weddings but only rarely did they intermarry. Mixed marriages were not regarded as desirable by the Greek Orthodox church. For Muslims, on the other hand, they were possible between Moslem men and non-Moslem women, but not the other way round. As William Turner, a local commentator, noted: 'They [the Turks] frequently marry the Greek women of the island, as their religion permits a Turkish man to marry an infidel woman, though to guard against the abandonment of Mahometanism it forbids a Turkish woman to marry an infidel' (cited in Aimilianides 1938:32).

Intermarriage also took place between Christians and the sect of *Linobambakoi* (linen/cotton) who were crypto-Christians, that is, they were Moslems who spoke and dressed like the Greek-Cypriot population. They had either converted to Islam to avoid the taxation that non-Muslims paid or were Latins who were forced to convert to avoid being expelled (Papadopoulos 1965), for they had Christian names and celebrated Christian religious feasts. Until 1889, mixed marriages, like all marriages, were not the concern of civil law but of religious law. After this date, if one of the parties was a British subject, it was a case for civil law and by the 1920s all mixed marriages came under civil law.

Given the existence of what has been termed 'traditional co-existence' and a history of other commonalities – even the development of a shared Cypriot dialect – the question remains as to how 'two virulent nationalisms have been generated in one small island in so many decades' (Worsley 1979:3). I have already mentioned that when Britain took over the administration of the island it assumed by implication that the two religious groups had separate interests and were extensions of Greece and Ottoman Turkey respectively. Along with the practice of separating the two groups educationally, this exacerbated already existing differences and gradually fostered political élites who were primarily concerned with protecting the interests of their own communities.

The development of passive ethnicity into active nationalist consciousness occurred first within the majority Greek-Cypriot population. It involved an identification with Hellenism and a pan-Hellenic ideology which had been fired by the Greek War of Independence of 1821; an opposition to British colonial domination; and the growth of territorial claims to unite Cyprus with the 'motherland', Greece. The increasing identification of Greekness with Greek Orthodoxy was important (Carras 1983), as was the assertion of a common linguistic, historical and cultural heritage uniting the island with the mainland. The Turkish-Cypriots were defined as extraneous to the 'real' Cyprus national collectivity; at best they were only seen as an ethnic minority who did not have specific rights to separate political representation.

The factors responsible for the emergence of the Enosis movement (union with Greece) and the subsequent national liberation struggle led by the right-wing EOKA urban guerrilla group, under the leadership of the virulent anti-communist Grivas, are complex. Suffice it to say that the rôle of the Greek Orthodox church was of fundamental importance, as was the failure of the socialist movement to harness some of the genuinely anticolonial and liberationist tendencies that existed (Anthias & Ayres 1983). The material conditions for the growth of nationalism can be found in the extreme oppression of the Cypriot peasantry and the discrimination against indigenous capital displayed by the British administration. This latter gave the Cypriot bourgeoisie a specific economic reason to oppose colonial rule. The peasantry under British rule were at the mercy of the merchants and intermediaries who were likely to be Greek-Cypriot, were crippled by colonial taxation, and were particularly hard hit by the crisis in the world economy in the 1930s (Attalides 1979). Economic discontent found its expression, in part, in the 1931 riots when the Governor's house was burnt down, after which direct rule was imposed until 1941.

Enosis became the dominant ideology of the church and the Greek-Cypriot bourgeoisie and spread to large sections of the peasantry and the new urban proletariat, thereby emerging as the dominant form of Greek-Cypriot ethnic consciousness. As regards the EOKA movement which began to be active in April 1955, the leadership came from the church and broadly bourgeois elements in society, but the fighters were young workers and children of the peasantry. They were drawn in through church and school and were fired by the vision of union with Greece.

There can be no denying the disastrous impact which Enosis had on the development of ethnic conflict. Turkish-Cypriot anti-Enosists had existed in the early part of the century, but came mainly from the Turkish-Cypriot urban élite which favoured the continuation of British rule. Turkish-Cypriot nationalism had not developed, and Headlam Morley, a commentator at the time, noted that 'the Mahometan population showed no tendency to identify themselves with the Turks' (cited in Kyrris 1977:37). However, in the 1930s, and particularly in the 1940s, as the Enosis movement gained in strength, there grew a concomitant Turkish-Cypriot nationalism fostered by Turkish right-wing extremists. Developments in Turkey were also significant; indeed, events on the island have generally to be seen in the context of broader processes at work in Greece, Turkey, and the Western alliance (Attalides 1979).

Turkey's reputation as the strongest power in the Middle East was enhanced during the 1930s, and it was inevitable that the Turkish nationalist movement in Cyprus would be boosted by the success of Ataturk's revolution. Turkish-Cypriot nationalism was also purveyed by the educational system organized through Turkey. The 1940s witnessed the growth of separate Turkish-Cypriot political parties and trade unions. Although many Turkish-Cypriots belonged to AKEL (the Communist Party) and PEO (the Communist trade union), the pro-Islamic Turkish National Party gained in strength, partly as a result of AKEL's equivocal stand over Enosis (Attalides 1979). Yet the process was slow: even by the mid-1950s there were fewer Turkish-Cypriot workers in the Turkish trade unions than in PEO (AKEL 1976).

It was not until 1955 that the Turkish national cry for partition of the island took over as the main Turkish-Cypriot demand, though ironically this possibility was first raised formally by the British. It was on 1 April 1955 that EOKA – the Union of Cypriot Fighters – the Greek-Cypriot rightist guerilla movement, launched its attack on British rule. This had dramatic implications for the growth of ethnic conflict. During the EOKA struggle of 1955–9, the British used Turkish-Cypriots as auxiliary policemen and commandoes, which helped to cement interethnic divisions. More important, by 1958, Turkish-Cypriot nationalists, possibly under the direction and pay of the colonial government (Kyrris 1977), began military activities with their own right-wing organization, the Turkish Resistance organization (TMT). In the ensuing conflict between the two communities, the activities of EOKA and TMT finally split the last tenuous horizontal links that existed between Greek- and Turkish-Cypriots.

The rejection by Turkish-Cypriots of the constitutional amendments proposed by Makarios in late 1963 was followed by violent clashes between the two communities which extended into 1964. During the next three years there was a gradual settling down of the two communities to their respective and separate lives, only for the violence to erupt again in 1967. Threats by Turkey in 1964 and 1967 to invade the island in support of the Turkish-Cypriot minority were effectively removed by the force of international opinion, the latter, however, being conditional on Athens withdrawing illegal mainland troops. In this period, too, US and NATO plans to partition the island were always rejected by the Greek-Cypriots. After 1967, the intercommunal clashes ceased and 1968 saw the beginning of talks.

Nevertheless, the Turkish-Cypriots had already been effectively segregated and their economic position was worsening in relation to that of the increasingly industrializing Greek-Cypriot community. Politically, within the Greek-Cypriot sector, a 'popular unity' movement evolved round Makarios which included within it the large Communist Party. This ethnically based consensus was facilitated by the demise of class politics within the Cypriot left in favour of an ethnically premised unity (Anthias & Ayres 1983). In the Turkish-Cypriot community the activities of the TMT and pressure from Ankara ensured that the Turkish-Cypriots were effectively united in their opposition to the constitutional amendments envisaged by Makarios. Yet there were still important political divisions within the Turkish-Cypriot community which had their origins in pre-independence Cyprus. These found expression in the early 1970s with the formation of the National Unity Party (UBP), which was the pro-Turkish, right-wing party of Denktash and favoured an independent Turkish state of Cyprus, and the Republican Turkish Party (CTP), which was left wing and had informal links with EDEK (the Socialist Party) and AKEL on the Greek-Cypriot side, and favoured a united Cyprus with strong safeguards for the security and rights of the Turkish minority.

After the 1967 intercommunal clashes, Grivas, the former

leader of EOKA, had been forced to leave the island, but he returned in 1971 to campaign for Enosis through EOKA B, an organization less popularly based and more explicitly right wing than EOKA. His death in 1974 did not diminish the activities of EOKA B, which made several attempts on the life of Makarios and probably had the support of officers within the Greek National Guard on the island. In July 1974, after publicly accusing the colonels in Athens of being in league with EOKA B, Makarios demanded that the mainland officers and half the National Guard of 10 000 be withdrawn. A few days later, on 15 July, the Junta-dominated National Guard attacked the Archbishop's palace and took control of the island; Makarios fled, Sampson became President with the support of the Athens Junta, but Turkey invaded a few days later, using the coup as a pretext for intervention and subsequent annexation of about 40% of the island. In the following section I shall explore developments in Cyprus since 1974, with particular reference to the rôle played by the refugee issue in ethnic relations and political life.

Post-1974: ideology, politics, and class

The Turkish invasion created approximately 200 000 Greek-Cypriot refugees (a much smaller number of Turkish-Cypriots were displaced from their homes in the south of the island). Homelessness on a vast scale then became the most pressing problem for the legitimate state on the island (the Greek-Cypriot state in practice). Initially the refugees settled on the open ground wherever they could, but very soon camps were set up, partly with aid from international funds (PIO 1983). The massive displacement of the population and the loss of what has been estimated as 70% of the productive potential, as well as of major ports and airports, led to mass unemployment – initially 39% of the economically active population in the south (PIO 1974). By 1979, however, only 1.8% were employed, though this figure hides underemployment and emigration of the unemployed (PEO 1979).

Housing for refugees has been of three types. The largest proportion have been housed in low-cost government housing estates where they live without paying rent. These have been built mainly in the suburbs of Nicosia and Limassol. The next largest proportion have been accommodated in units on government land, which entails refugees being awarded specified grants, according to family size and other criteria, to build their own houses: a small number in addition are living in self-constructed units on private land. Finally, a substantial proportion occupy Turkish-Cypriot housing, which tends to be the least satisfactory accommodation (PIO 1983).

Although in the new Turkish-Cypriot sector the authorities attempted to eliminate any signs of Greek-Cypriot habitation by renaming roads and villages with Turkish names (King & Ladbury 1982), the reverse was true in the south. Impermanency has been reinforced through the careful maintenance of Turkish-Cypriot shop and road signs and a rhetoric of 'return'. This is part of the concern with re-establishing an independent unified state structure which has as its central purpose the return of refugees to their homes and villages. The pursuit of 'comfortable impermanency', as President Kyprianou has recently called it, has, however, left its mark in a number of ways. One of the most significant is the creation and perpetuation of the 'martyred refugee' syndrome, with the continual retelling of the story of loss and uprooting and the reification in the public consciousness of 'our villages' and 'our homes'.

This construction of a refugee category locked in impermanancy has also functioned to give an artificial unity to the refugee population, whereas in reality class differences are as important as within the population as a whole. This supposed social homogeneity within the category and the reinforcement of the division between refugee and non-refugee militates against class discourse as well as distracting attention from those refugees belonging to the commercial entrepreneurial class, who have been given favourable financial terms by the Cypriot state in order to encourage the restructuring of Cypriot society along the old lines.

Despite the ideology of return, the political debates make problematic the return of the vast proportion of refugees, particularly where they take account, realistically, of the interests of Turkey and the Turkish-Cypriots. This constructs a division between refugees from those regions that are most likely to return in the event of a political settlement (such as those from Famagusta) and the rest, which in turn overlays the effect of class division within the refugee population by that of regional difference. Yet the rhetoric of return remains as a political weapon purveyed by the media, the schools and, to a lesser extent, the political parties, with, I might add, highly contradictory effects for the refugee population itself.

Depression, anxiety, and problems in adjusting to urban life and the anomalous environment, particularly on the larger refugee estates, is compounded by tension created by uncertainty about their return and the future generally. A continuing feeling of loss is experienced, particularly by the older women who are most likely to live in the hope of returning to their homes and communities (Evdokas *et al.* 1976, Phatoura *et al.* 1981). The very real problems of social dislocation and potential unrest which this could bring in its wake have led to an expansion of welfare provision and the passing of legislation designed to deal with problems created more generally by the Turkish invasion. One of the most significant was a change in the abortion law after many women were raped and made pregnant by the invading forces (Social Research Centre 1975). Increased welfare has taken the form of improvements in social services, the creation of youth centres, and a more interventionist policy on the part of state agencies.

The war also created a number of significant changes in Cypriot society. The new differentiation into refugees and non-refugees is not only important at the ideological and political levels but also in terms of economic and class relations. For the first time in Cypriot society a large propertyless urban proletariat was created which could function as a pool of available cheap labour for the light manufacturing service sectors of the economy that were already growing in the pre-invasion period. One might have expected this to have significant effects on political consciousness, but this has not occurred (Anthias, forthcoming), largely because most members of the work-force have remained ideologically within their pre-refugee ethnic identities, despite experiencing loss of economic and social status. This has been facilitated by the way in which the refugee issue has been handled by the state and the political parties, even those on the left. The state quickly rehoused families but, because of the problems of bringing together old communities, many were rehoused among strangers. This has resulted in the growth of individualism which militates against active class participation. An additional factor is that the majority of refugees appear to live within the social relations of the pre-invasion period, adopting an attitude of impermanency to the present that prevents them from committing themselves to new allegiances.

The political parties on the left, particularly AKEL, which has the allegiance of approximately a third of the Greek-Cypriot population and until quite recently was proportionately the largest communist party in Europe, have not wished to make political capital out of the refugees; AKEL and PEO have refused to regard them as a specific section of the work-force, seeing this as antagonistic to the notion of a united working class, and preferring to reaffirm the importance of unity within the population in these difficult times. Refugees have their own pressure groups, however, mainly organized under the umbrella of the Pancypriot Committee of Refugees.

As regards the economy, mention has already been made of the importance of the refugees as an urban labour force. Cyprus has become mainly a service society with this sector absorbing the largest proportion of the economically active population (36%) (Planning Bureau 1982). The restructuring of the society has led to even greater decline in the agricultural sector, which by 1981 employed only 20% of the population. There has been an increase in 'employees', who now constitute two-thirds of the work-force as opposed to a half in the pre-invasion period. A large proportion of poor refugees have been absorbed in manufacturing and the building and construction industry (50%). Expansion in these sectors was helped by the availability of refugees (and women) whose presence has kept wages low (House 1980). The growth of these particular sectors indicates that Cypriot society prefers to consume rather than invest in the productive sphere, which is a significant weakness in terms of the economy as a whole. The growth in the tourist sector also has its negative aspects, especially in the destruction of the environment, which in the long term will make Cyprus less attractive as a tourist centre, and in the consequential failure to invest in productive industries likely to generate long-term economic growth.

Turning now to look at the political changes that have occurred since the invasion, there is no doubt that the most significant effect has been the demise of Enosis. It had been declining in support throughout the 1960s but still remained a romantic ideal, however unattainable. The failure of Greece to intervene in 1974 and the equivocal stand which it took at this time did little to inspire the Greek-Cypriot population in belief in its 'maternal' intentions. This does not mean that the notion of double Enosis – union of the Greek-Cypriot sector with Greece and the Turkish-Cypriot with Turkey – is completely off the political agenda; indeed, there have recently been signs that it is being spoken of more openly. Old-style Enosis, however, is finally dead. There is not only more willingness to discuss that period of Cypriot history critically, but there has also been a reorientation towards the Turkish-Cypriots in the sense that the failure of Greek-Cypriots to consider seriously the economic and social position of the Turkish community is increasingly admitted. In effect, the 'national' problem has been converted from a problem that derived from the conflicting demands and desires of Greek-Cypriots and Turkish-Cypriots (although it was never that simple) to one that is more and more conceived within the Greek-Cypriot sector as an anti-occupation struggle against a foreign invader.

The form of the state was altered with Makarios's death and the assumption of the Presidency by Kyprianou. Makarios had been widely seen as a charismatic leader who was able to achieve an almost unattainable consensus, nation and state being seen as one (despite, of course, the existence of an excluded group in this formulation, the Turkish-Cypriots) (Markides 1977). Since his death, there has occurred a growth of new political parties and an increasing fragmentation of Cypriot political life and opinion.

The old social consensus has been broken. At the beginning, with the threat of disunity within the Greek-Cypriot collectivity, AKEL regarded Kyprianou as best able to pull everyone together, announcing 'that which is most primary today is not the gaining of power or socialist transformation but the united struggle of Cypriots for true independence' (PEO 1979:9). In the elections of 1976, the United Front of the Democratic Party (Kyprianou's party), AKEL and EDEK, the Socialist Party of Lyssarides, took 76% of the vote. AKEL's co-operation in the Presidential elections of February 1982 was a significant factor in Kyprianou's victory, and the Minimum Programme of AKEL and the Democratic Party (DIKOK) was announced in April 1982. In more recent elections, AKEL has lost some of its support and the Minimum Programme broke down in 1984, at which point a great deal of dissent again became apparent in Greek-Cypriot society over the issue of a United Nations peace plan and the way that summit talks in New York had been handled by Kyprianou.

Conclusion

Events since 1974 have led to a stalemate on the Cyprus problem. Attempts by the United Nations to organize intercommunal discussions have repeatedly failed to produce any agreement on a federal structure, though both sides accept that it must be the basis for any compromise. The most difficult stumbling block relates to the withdrawal of Turkish troops from the north of the island, which the Greek-Cypriot leader insists on as a precondition for any settlement. Other important issues to be resolved relate to the rights of movement and settlement for the two communities, territorial adjustments, the terms of a federal constitution, and the precise division of powers between a federal government and the two communities.

While this stalemate exists, nationalism appears to be resurfacing in the south, partly as a result of the resurgence of nationalism under the socialist government of Papandreou in Greece. It is also a reaction to the continuing failure to reach a viable compromise, with frustration and anger growing against both Turkey and all those who might be regarded as wishing to sell out Greek-Cypriot interests. The old and feared vision of double Enosis rears its head, although it is one that most of the population definitely do not want. But until the indigenous political leaders and intellectuals on both sides can provide a critique and an alternative to the received wisdoms that often pass as the history of the last thirty years or so, very little hope exists of overcoming the devisive force of an ethnic nationalism, which is a continuing obstacle to a permanent peaceful solution.

In the north, Denktash's position as leader is not seriously challenged, and the presence of the Turkish Army discourages open debate on the Cyprus problem. But as far as can be gauged, two of the major political parties, the Communal Liberation Party and the Republican Turkish Party, which between them obtained a majority of votes in the 1981 election, are in favour of a federal solution. It is also clear that there is discontent in the north with the lack of economic progress, the high level of unemployment, the uncertainty that Turkish-Cypriot southerners face, the conflicts that have arisen with settlers brought in from Turkey to change the demographic balance of Cyprus, and the continued interference of Ankara in domestic issues. But Turkey and the Turkish-Cypriots are unlikely to want to make too many concessions; they are, after all, in a position of military strength if not moral or international right. And certainly they will not want a return to the old constitutional structures which failed them so early on in the life of the Cypriot Republic.

This chapter has examined ethnic relations in Cyprus with particular reference to the conditions under which nationalism has flourished. The Cyprus case illustrates the way in which ethnic relations respond to both internal and external, political and economic, interests and demonstrates the importance in the modern world of looking at them within a context which includes superpower relations. A satisfactory conclusion to the Cyprus problem, as many of the refugees are willing to admit (Anthias, forthcoming), may in the final analysis depend on the will of America and NATO, although Turkey has an autonomous position that is unlikely now to yield fully to US pressure unless it can gain something in return.

References

Aimilianides, A. 1938. The law relating to mixed marriages. *Kypriakai Spoudai*. Nicosia (in Greek).
AKEL (the Progressive Party of the Working People) 1976. *The Worker's Party: 50 years of AKEL* Commemorative volume. Nicosia: AKEL.

Anthias, F. Forthcoming. *The refugee issue and social change in Cypriot society*.
Anthias, F. & R. Ayres 1983. Ethnicity and class in Cyprus. *Race and Class* 25(1), 58–76.
Attalides, M. 1979. *Cyprus: nationalism and international politics*. Edinburgh: Q. Press
Carras, C. 1983. *3,000 years of Greek identity: myth or reality?* Athens: Domus Books.
Evdokas, T., L. Mylona, K. Paschalis, K. Olimpias, S. Chimona, E. Kalava, N. Thesdoron and I. Demetriadou 1976. *Prosfiges tis Kyprou*. Nicosia.
Gellner, E. & J. Waterbury (eds) 1977. *Patrons and clients*. London: Duckworth.
Hitchens, C. 1984, *Cyprus*. London: Quartet Books.
HMSO 1960. *Cyprus*. Cmnd 1093. London.
House, W. 1980. *Labour market segmentation and sex discrimination in Cyprus*. Nicosia: Statistics and Research Department.
King, R. & S. Ladbury 1982. The cultural reconstruction of political reality in Greek and Turkish Cyprus since 1974. *Anthropological Quarterly* 55(1), 1–16.
Kyriakides, S. 1968. *Cyprus: constitutionalism and crisis government*. Philadelphia: University of Pennsylvania Press
Kyrris, C. 1977. *Peaceful coexistence in Cyprus under British rule (1879–1959) and after independence*. Nicosia: Public Information Office.
Markides, K. 1977. *The rise and fall of the Cyprus Republic*. New Haven, Conn.: Yale University Press.
Papadopoulos, T. 1965. *Social and historical data on population 1570–1881*. Nicosia: Social Research Centre.
PEO (Pancypria Ergatik Omospondia) 1979. *18th conference papers*. Nicosia: PEO.
Phatoura M. et al. 1981. *Psycho-social problems of Cypriot refugees*. Thessalonika: Thessalonika University Press.
PIO (Public Information Office) 1974. *Economic consequences of the Turkish invasion*. Nicosia: PIO
PIO (Public Information Office) 1983. *Cyprus: the refugee problem*. Nicosia: PIO.
Planning Bureau 1982. *4th emergency economic action plan 1982–86*. Nicosia: Department of Finance and Research.
Social Research Centre 1975. *Cypriot women: rise and downfall*. Nicosia: Public Information Office.
Worsley, P. 1979. Communalism and nationalism in small countries: the case of Cyprus. In *Small states in the modern world*, P. Worsley & P. Kitromilides (eds), 30. Nicosia: New Cyprus Association.

PART C

Perspectives

13   *An academic perspective*

Robin Cohen

In the period of decolonization, when many new small states were created, politicians and administrators were preoccupied primarily with the theoretical minima of economic and political viability. Now, as is indicated in the title of this book, the focus has shifted somewhat to the problems of integrated or autarkic development and the threat posed to international security by the political instability of many small states. The security threat is, in turn, derived both from internal political and economic factors and by regional or great-power rivalry for effective control over small countries.

However valid were the earlier considerations of the minima for economic and political viability, the fact is that, for better or for worse, the 19th century doctine of self-determination has triumphed more frequently than any reasonable application of such criteria would have dictated or the most ardent advocates of self-determination could have anticipated. What I want first to establish in this short chapter is why practical considerations were often discounted as small states were established in the postwar world. Secondly, I want to probe the implication of two contrasting characterizations of the problems facing small states. Finally, given the *de facto* existence of small states which would historically have been considered 'unviable', I ask how we would measure 'success'.

The triumph of self-determination or the weakness of empire?

When John Stuart Mill wrote that 'it is in general a necessary condition of free institutions that the boundaries of government should coincide in the main with those of nationalities' (cited in

Kohn 1961:39), it is clear that he considered 'nationality' widely, as a social bond of common sympathy and association that could transcend the bonds of race, language, religion, or ethnicity. Adherents to some of these narrower affinities in the postwar world have none the less sought to clothe themselves in the more ample robes of 'nationality' in their quest for a separate political identity.

This attempt to use 'nationality' as a substitute for narrower loyalties means that the accession to statehood by so many small states in the period after World War II is neither a vindication of classical liberal notions of representative government nor a guarantee of 'free institutions'. Nor again, as I shall argue, can the proliferation of new 'nations' automatically be assumed to have enhanced the sphere of individual or collective freedom against unprogressive or alien tyrannies.

Lest this statement seems like a reactionary response or even an unqualified defence of colonial empire, let me specify more exactly what I mean by suggesting that nationhood is by no means simply a synonym for freedom or liberalism, as 19th-century political liberalism assumed. Virtually every empire, even those that we remember for their despotic or militarist character, had some universalizing principle which regulated the relations between the core society and its peripheral outposts. Long-term conquest, settlement, and trade within an empire would otherwise have been impossible. The Roman system of international law, *jus gentium*, made dialogue and transactions between Roman and foreigner and between provincial and provincial possible and profitable for the first time. The *Code Napoléon* extended these principles and introduced other universal concepts inherited from the revolutionary Jacobin tradition.

Many of the small states that emerged in the period of decolonization were territorially formerly part of the French, British, Spanish, and Dutch empires. These empires also advanced universalizing principles. The *pax Britannica*, the French notion of the *civilisable* colonial subject, and the equivalent Spanish notion of the *asimilativo* 'indiano', however patronising, nonetheless did presage the possibility of a wider association, on more equal terms, with the core society. This possibility survived, residually, in the notion of a 'British' (the adjective was later tactfully dropped) Commonwealth, and more vigorously in the 1954 Charter of the Kingdom of the Netherlands (which gave theoretically equal status to the Dutch Antilles, Surinam and Holland), and in the French *départements d'outre mer* – Réunion, French Guiana, Martinique, and Guadeloupe – whose inhabitants when in France enjoy the same political rights and social security benefits as metropolitan residents.

It would, of course, be absurd to deny that Holland is responsible for Aruba, Curaçao, or Bonaire or that the 'assimilationist path' has not caused bitter controversy in the *départements d'outre mer* (Blerald 1983). Yet, however vigorously one espouses the right to self-determination, it is difficult to argue that the inhabitants of such territories are notably less free, or enjoy less extensive political expression (or indeed are materially worse off) than their 'independent' small state neighbours. It is perhaps easier to see the dead hand of colonialism or the denial of open democratic debate in British dependencies such as the British Virgins, the Turks and Caicos, Hong Kong or St Helena. Yet, none of these territories exhibits an even moderately convincing nationalist movement and most of the residents seem accepting, if not enthusiastic, beneficiaries of reasonably efficient, normally honest (Hong Kong being the exception) colonial administrations committed to equality before the law.

What follows from this apparent (though qualified) defence of the colonial order? First, that the proliferation of small states dismembered from the 20th-century empires represented a *failure* of these empires' universalizing ideals. Here and there, as in the *départements* and dependencies, the founding ideals survived, but more as faded notes on worn-out gramophone records than as a triumphal Elgarian fanfare.

What is often assumed to have taken the place of these ideals is a vigorous alternative nationalism, fuelled by powerful anticolonial sentiment and commanded by leaders determined to allow their enthusiastic followers to walk tall in the comity of nations. Of course there were, and are, many national liberation struggles having precisely that character. Those with a taste for such events might have cheered on the Vietnamese peasantry who demolished the French Empire at Dien Bien Phu, then proceeded to defeat the massive forces of the US, both militarily and ideologically.

But if the armed national liberation struggle mobilizing the bulk of the population in defence of self-determination represents one end of the spectrum, there are many intermediate cases of constitutional decolonization, with a powerful leader at the head of a popular national campaign, which fall short of violent and sustained struggle (Nehru, Nkrumah) and many more, in the small states, where the sanctions and pressures mounted by the nationalist movement were extremely weak. In a number of cases an anti-independence, pro-metropolitan party even developed.

In short, the empires cut many of their peripheral outposts free; when judged in strict military terms they need not have done so. In probing for the reasons why empires were abandoned one also finds a first approximation of the problems of development, political instability, and security that were bound to follow.

The collapse of ideological legitimacy

The simple fact is that the ideological justification for empires had collapsed in the wake of World War II. This was partly because of a serious erosion in morale and pride on the part of the two principal European powers with extensive empires – Britain and France. Whatever the ultimate outcome of the war, French military prowess had tumbled like a house of cards, and the British, subjectively perhaps even more humiliatingly, had been driven from their Asian territories by a *non-white* power, Japan. The fact that some Indian nationalists and Malaysian insurgents were happy to co-operate with the Japanese in order to displace their colonial masters was a further disheartening factor.

There seemed little point in proclaiming the glories of empire when the 'jewels in the crown' wished to glitter on some other head, preferably their own. The founding statement of the United Nations, the San Francisco Charter of 1945, drove the ideological point home, demanding that all colonial powers devolve greater autonomy to the territories they administered.

In Britain the ideological defence of empire was virtually impossible, despite Churchill's blusterings, except in the weak

Fabian terms characteristic of the Attlee government and the period of welfare colonialism. In this, the Colonial Office harked back to prewar days when the notion of a temporary 'trusteeship' underpinned the expansion of the colonial administration. Only this time the beneficiaries felt they had escaped their statuses as minors and demanded that the trust be dissolved. Some longer-sighted administrators sought to make the best of their situation and committed themselves to an imaginative programme of devolution and welfare, hoping thereby to retain the loyalty of former colonial subjects. Other British administrators went through the motions of delivering welfare institutions and installing systems of representative government in their colonial territories without very much belief in their long-term efficacy. For all, sceptics and enthusiasts of British decolonization alike, the question was not whether, but when, 'self-government' would take place.

For the French, the ideological justification for empire was somewhat more tenacious in that their war experience had revealed colonial subjects (in Central Africa and the Caribbean especially) to be more loyal to the founding ideals of the French Republic (as represented by the Gaullist cause) than the metropolitan French citizenry itself. The French notion of *civilisation* also extended to a small, but significant, section of colonial subjects who were tied psychologically, intellectually and culturally to metropolitan ideals.

But these differing circumstances between the French and British resulted in largely the same outcome. The French were rebuffed militarily in Vietnam and Algeria and politically in Guinea, where Sekou Toure organized a 'no' vote to the idea of a French West African 'community'. The last was so galling to the French administrators that they are said to have removed everything to the last sheaf of stationery and the last toilet roll as they stomped from their former colony. 'Now, manage without us', was the message. But it was a fit of pique that did little to delay the extensive dismemberment (at least at a formal level) of the French Empire in West Africa, Central Africa, and the Pacific.

Ignoring some dependencies and *départements* alluded to earlier, what remains of the empires is a commitment to a multiracial

Commonwealth supported by 30–40 specialized agencies in the case of the British and a somewhat more vigorous set of cultural associations and security arrangements in the case of the French. However, at the ideological level, in the space of less than one generation, the universalizing ideals of the European empire have disappeared.

The rise of rival powers

Internal misgivings aside, the political demise of the European metropoles was paralleled by the rise of rival powers (both global and regional) which challenged the hegemony of Britain, France, Portugal, and Belgium in their old colonial 'patches'.

Just as the US had destroyed Spain's imperial projects in the Philippines, Cuba and Puerto Rico in the late 19th century by imperiously proclaiming the death of imperialism, so too did the US in the post-1945 period begin to assume imperial responsibilities through its own military assertiveness and push for economic hegemony. Even the old white Dominions began to fall like ninepins to the juggernaut of US power: in 1950, Australia and New Zealand signed a defence pact with the US to which Britain was not a party.

In the Middle East and the Gulf, US companies began to dominate the oil industry and manipulate the price of oil. The existence of a black population in the US and the country's former status as a colonized nation enabled State Department officials to express sympathy and understanding with nationalist and anticolonial sentiments, while simultaneously rechannelling the movements of trade, the flow of communications, and the lines of dependency away from London, Paris, Lisbon, or Brussels and in the direction of Washington.

The second great global power, the Soviet Union, also sought to influence emerging nationalists, this time in the direction of combining the anticolonial struggle with a commitment to a strategic alliance with the Eastern bloc and an attack on international capital's interests in each territory where they exercised some influence. Military aid to insurgents in Vietnam, Korea, Laos, Burma, and elsewhere in Asia triggered or sharpened a more contested struggle for nationhood than occurred in most parts of Africa, the Caribbean, and the Pacific.

The third power with 'global reach', namely Japan, abandoned its wartime military–imperial dream expressed in the South East Asia Co-prosperity Sphere in favour of a determined and markedly successful effort to penetrate the world's marketplaces with cheaper, and ultimately better, manufactured goods.

While the US, the Soviet Union and Japan carved great slices off the European colonial cakes, significant portions were also claimed by regional powers. Perhaps the point is best illustrated by reference to the cases of Botswana, Swaziland, and Lesotho in southern Africa. Over each of these territories, Britain had proclaimed a 'protectorate'. But the regional power from whom these territories clearly needed protection was South Africa, into whose hands the British delivered them when 'acceding' to their demands for independence.

Let me conclude this first part of my argument by summarizing some salient points. When examining the practical questions of the security, development, and internal political stability of small states, 'an academic perspective' must start by situating these questions within the historical crucible from which they emerged. The elements contained in the mix were characteristically a weakly articulated nationalism covering a narrower set of loyalties; a declining European empire losing its *raison d'être*; a countervailing hegemonic global power undermining what little credibility the old empire still retained; and a regional power ready to trouble the waters and to fish therein as and when the opportunity presented itself.

Characterizing the problems of small states

The foregoing remarks should serve to indicate that I would caution against those characterizations of small states that start only from a morphological classification based on appearances. For example, 'many small states are islands', 'over three dozen have populations under 1 million', 'many rely on a narrow range of exports', 'a number are former plantation economies'. One can go on building a more and more finely graded structure of classification, but such an exercise does have real limitations.

The kinds of generalizations that can be made are unlikely to constitute universal (across all small states) statements, though some striking contrasts can be used as illustrative material. For example, the United Arab Emirates and Oman are (or perhaps were) awash with oil money, and the Sierra Leonean and Jamaican populations are more than twenty times as poor as the top 5% of those with the highest incomes (Kidron & Segal 1981:43). Some states, even with the same colonial heritage, have managed a reasonably orderly and democratic management of régime changes (for example, Mauritius and Barbados); others (for example, Grenada and the Seychelles) have stumbled from rigged election to coup to countercoup to invasion. However, using purely observed characteristics and measurements internal to small states will generate only statistical associations (which will often result in bizarre juxtapositions) or, certainly more positively and usefully, some probabilistic statements about likely trends in carefully grouped or predefined cases.

Another and more plodding route may be necessary to secure a more nuanced understanding of the problems of small states – if only for the reason, already implied, that the phrase 'small states' covers too many diverse cases. Thus a possible way of moving beyond case-by-case empiricism is to insist on setting groups of small states in their historical and regional settings, rather than concentrating on their surface characteristics alone.

Let me take two contrasting statements that are often made of small states to demonstrate how this cautious advance in generalization might work.

Proposition A: 'Small states are too strong'

Such a generalization might be drawn from Alavi's (1976) widely quoted article on the overdeveloped postcolonial state. His thesis was so striking precisely because it seemed to fly in the face of the conventional wisdoms that many states are too weak – either to suppress dissent or defend themselves internationally. On a closer reading, it is clear what Alavi means. Influenced as he is by Marxism, any state was for him an outcome of the efforts of a successful bourgeoisie to manage its common affairs. In many postcolonial states, the bourgeoisie was small or weak, or perhaps even barely existent. The state inherited at independence was neither therefore an authentic state nor one that grew from the strength of an indigenous bourgeoisie. It had been superimposed as part of the superstructure of another country, the metropole, and reflected the interests of *its* ruling class. None the less, this did not prevent the state, in the absence of any other major source of accumulation, from being the major focus for primary capital accumulation (for example through corruption) for the aspirant bourgeoisie. Access to state revenues is a fierce bone of contention between different contenders, as they seek to displace incumbents or prevent competition. Such a depiction also, of course, would serve to explain the level of political instability often found in many small states.

Provided one sets this thesis within the framework of a departing colonial power and an appreciation of the emergence of states in modern European history, the overdeveloped postcolonial small state can indeed be seen as too 'strong'. The European bourgeoisies had to fight their way out of feudalism and aristocratic privilege to create a rational state structure, whereas the colonial power left a ready made structure (courts, parliaments, civil service) which would not otherwise have emerged spontaneously.

On the other hand, exactly the same data could be used to demonstrate the opposite proposition.

Proposition B: 'Small states are too weak'

Such a generalization would flow from the argument that the major problem confronting small states is that they do not have the power or resources to stifle internal dissent or ward off the depredations of regional or global forces. Certainly, if the state of Lesotho, say, is incapable of preventing raids across its border by South African troops or acts of sabotage and subversion from the same source, it is difficult to describe such a state as 'overdeveloped'. It is indeed too weak, relative to the threat presented to it and relative to the ever-escalating demands of national security posed in a world whose economies are fuelled by rearmament and intense confrontation – a confrontation which falls short of war, but is far from peace.

If, again, we can imagine a modern state too remote or small or insignificant to attract the Japanese importer, the US State Department, the Russian ideologue, or a regional 'protector', such a state would more likely than not be 'sufficiently strong' to manage internal change successfully. Small states may therefore be too strong or too weak, or adequate to their task depending on their historical and regional context.

From nations without states to states without nations

By way of conclusion I want to ask how we might gauge the 'success' of a small state. The shortest and clearest answer is a Darwinian one: survival.

To this blunt measure can be added others of a more evaluative kind. How autarkic is the economy of the small state or how dependent? If, as is likely, highly dependent, is there one boss who calls the tune or are there many? In that case some manoeuvrability by a well disciplined ruling class might well be possible. Is the small state implicitly protected by a 'godfather' (thereby preventing regional adventures) or exposed to a potential takeover? The godfather option for a departing power was well described by one astute observer as 'decolonizing without disengaging' in the case of French territories in the Indian Ocean (Houbert 1986). Is there, finally, evidence of progress either in welfare terms or in terms of conventional economic indicators?

Such measures of success will differentiate one small state from another and also help to situate the question, posed earlier, as to whether within its context a state is sufficiently strong to manage internal change, undertake meaningful development initiatives (even if this is only managing the rules of the game for private enterprise), or show a defiant face to rapacious outsiders. In such an exercise no doubt some of the 50 or so small states which have emerged since 1945 will be deemed 'successful' and 'viable'. But many might be considered as extremely vulnerable to takeover or continual internal disorder.

This takes me back to my starting point, which turns on the relationship between 'state' and 'nation'. For John Stuart Mill the major source of injustice and instability was the brutal attempt by old and decaying political entities (like the Ottoman and Austro-Hungarian empires) to hang on to territories inflamed by a passion for self-government and independence. In his view and in his time, we had 'nations without states'. Both liberal doctrine and pragmatic reason dictated that oppressed nations should be permitted to attain statehood.

In the postwar world, I would submit, we have all too many cases of 'states without a nation'. In their haste to abandon their outposts in the face of competition from global or regional competitors and with their own collapse in morale, the European empires gave birth to many premature offspring. The sense of purpose deriving from a sense of common historical oppression, common cultural symbols, and common social aspirations was imperfectly developed when many states arrived at the UN to unfurl their new national flags (designed and made in the metropole) or issued their first postage stamps (some of which showed national heroes like Mickey Mouse, Donald Duck, and Goofy).

It is ultimately a purposive sense of nationhood that will protect the fledgling new states. Where their historical experience was too fragmentary to forge this purpose, it will have to be developed 'after the event', as a form of post-independence nationalism. Failing this development, we shall see the doctrine of self-determination reach an historical *cul de sac*.

References

Alavi, H. 1976. The state in post-colonial societies. *New Left Review* **74**, 59–81.
Blerald, P. A. 1983. Guadeloupe–Martinique: a system of colonial domination in crisis. In *Crisis in the Caribbean*, F. Ambursley & R. Cohen (eds), 148–165. London: Heinemann.
Houbert, J. 1986. France in the Indian Ocean: decolonising without disengaging. *The Round Table* **198**, 145–166.
Kidron, M. & R. Segal 1981. *The state of the world atlas*. London: Pan Books.
Kohn, H. 1961. *Prophets and peoples: studies in nineteenth century nationalism*. New York: Collier Books.

14 *A policy perspective*

NEVILLE LINTON

Since the invasion of Grenada the policy debate in respect of small states has shifted away from issues of economic viability to their security problems. It is a matter of record that many small states in their early years of independence assumed that they did not have the capacity for adequate self-defence against external attack and so simply did not make any provision for such defence. Some indeed did not create a military establishment for quite a while or, at most, had a volunteer 'militia' which was a carry-over from colonial practice. In these cases the police force, with or without a coastguard, was the 'armed' unit, and that force was solely trained for traditional police duties.

The experience of the past few years has brought home to small states that they are full members of the international political community in every meaningful sense and, most of all, that as sovereign states their responsibility for their own defence is total. Furthermore, it is clear that the ramifications of East–West competition are so widespread and complex that no part of the globe is free from it, no area beyond involvement. It is of interest to note in this connection that in February 1985, at a meeting in New Zealand, Pacific small states indicated that they felt that the risk factor of great power rivalry in their region was not great and that they did not perceive any threat of interference by a power outside the region. A year later it is doubtful that these states would be ready to reiterate that view, given the Greenpeace affair; concern over the grant by Kiribati of extensive fishing rights in its waters to the USSR; Vanuatu's plan to provide the same superpower with a deep-water port; and the increased security importance to the US of American trust territories in the Pacific since the fall of Marcos. Small states have, therefore, to have a clear appreciation of their vulnerabilities, a realistic assessment of the potential and actual threats to their security, and a renewed analysis of the question of capacity.

Military threats

In respect of capacity, all small states have come quickly to terms with the need to be self-reliant in dealing with threats of domestic origin. Even those new states which did not originally have a military arm rapidly created such a unit for the purpose of coping with domestic unrest, subversion, or attacks by externally based national dissidents; but this was often seen as the limit of their capacity.

During the last decade, however, the threat from major operators trading in arms and/or drugs, from mercenaries, and from piracy in maritime zones has created a totally new security dilemma for small states. Moreover, in multi-island states, attempts at secession can take a military form and where it does there are few small states which have the sea and air defences for suppressing the insurrection. In respect of direct territorial incursions from larger powers or by national dissidents backed by such a power, there is again little that a small state by itself can do militarily to deter or repel aggression.

The policy options *vis-à-vis* this category of threat therefore must range across the whole gamut of possibilities. Rather than opting out, small states need to use their political and military capacities to the limit. At the political level the options would seem to include the following possibilities:

(a) *The establishment of a collective security arrangement regionally or entry bilaterally into a defence pact with a friendly major power, preferably a regional one.* A security pact which is restricted to regional small states, such as the one involving the Organization of Eastern Caribbean States (OECS) in the Caribbean, can be useful for many of the types of threat with which such units usually have to cope, but clearly not against aggression from a larger power. However, the advantage of such a pact lies in the possibility which could be built into it for a collective approach for assistance either to larger powers or to relevant international institutions, not only at times of crisis but to cover the technical and financial needs of the regional security establishment itself. If that link is formalized, in that a regional great power is known to be a guarantor or at least a sponsor, the relationship could even have a deterrent effect.

(b) *An integral political link with a large power which would look after security needs and external political affairs, for example the Cook Islands with New Zealand and Guam with the US.* This arrangement usually means that the small state does not regularly participate formally in major international institutions of a political nature, although it does do so at the regional level and in functional international bodies. The range of possible action is in fact defined by practice and the case of the Cook Islands demonstrates that this can be a lively relationship, with the terms continually under test.

(c) *A bilateral arrangement with a major power.* This is unlikely to occur without a *quid pro quo* based either on an economic benefit to the larger state or a grant of military or other facilities. In considering such a grant, a small state should always bear in mind its regional and international impact. It should also judge carefully whether, once installed, the power could develop a vested interest which it would later be reluctant to surrender.

(d) *Neutrality arrangements.* This option does not seem a likely prospect given the geopolitical circumstances of most small states. However, the model provided by Malta of unilaterally declaring its neutrality is worthy of note and may be applicable in some other locations, such as the Indian Ocean, if relevant powers could be persuaded to recognize its status. Neutrality, of course, is usually specific to a region or to a limited set of circumstances and does not necessarily prevent a country from playing a vigorous international rôle. A related option is the declaration of a nuclear free zone, as in the South Pacific.

Political aspects

Small states, because of their military weakness, need to apply maximum resources to analysing security problems, assessing interests, possibilities and capabilities, indeed taking security at a new level of seriousness and purposefulness. At the domestic level this means that more attention has to be paid to the security establishment – a coming to terms, belated in some cases, with the real costs of independence.

Whatever the size of the security forces, it seems clear that they should be highly trained and motivated and be as multipurpose as possible. Small states cannot afford the luxury of a conventional approach to military or police rôles: their forces should be able to carry out a diversity of functions, from disaster control through maritime and/or border surveillance to regular military self-defence rôles. The need for versatility cannot be overemphasized, nor can the necessity for keeping morale and motivation as high as possible. Since money, men, and equipment are often in short supply, it is also advisable that security forces be used as much as possible in public works and community service.

It is particularly important in small states that the military be kept at a high level of discipline, for, as is widely recognized, a few armed men can organize a successful coup in a small state or at least cause considerable disruption. This very fear earlier kept some small states from organizing an army. But faced with the necessity of having such an establishment, the political leadership must keep the military under firm control.

The tragic events of Grenada demonstrate that an army can be ideologically overtrained, and that political indoctrination can be a two-edged sword, as much from inexperience as from ambition. Security should not become an end in itself in a small state, as an overzealous military may turn the state into a prison. Rotation of duties between community work and military or police work is one technique for keeping a balanced perspective among young soldiers. Another control mechanism is the strict limiting of the size of the armed units and the reliance, if necessary, upon a military reserve based on ordinary citizens volunteering for part-time service, such as occurs in Switzerland.

The major political decision is, of course, whether there should be any full-time military establishment at all. Increased vulnerability of small states in the current international arena does not automatically mean that they must all follow the conventional practice. The size, scale, and nature of the defence establishment should evolve out of a sober assessment of the national interest. Indeed, small states should be just as ready to reduce or eliminate military forces as to build them up. In making such judgements, access to information is crucial and small states should be careful, particularly in respect of intelligence and other security information, that they do not become too dependent on larger powers and thus possibly subject to manipulation. The development of computer and satellite systems will greatly facilitate the information-gathering capacity of small states, as will the gradual worldwide spread of document centres and data banks. Growing sponsorship of these by international institutions, governmental and non-governmental, and by universities could greatly benefit small states.

Even so, these states need to give far more importance than they are currently doing to the training of information and intelligence specialists. Small states should appreciate that work on security policy requires the skills of professionals. Such advisors in a small state should be trained broadly and flexibly rather than be restricted either to military or political concerns.

The threat to a small state whether internal or external is enhanced if political stability is fragile. Promotion of internal cohesion is thus certain to contribute to security. The link between economic weakness and political instability is too well established to need argument here. Over and above the measures and changes in the international arena which could improve the ability of the governments of these states to cope with their needs, there are many others which are within their capacity to take, including the familiar case for regionalism. Groupings of small states have tended to be rather cautious in increasing regional collaboration in the security sphere, although they all recognize the need to do so: it might well take the experience of a serious threat to hasten closer arrangements. The Eastern Caribbean post-Grenada is a case in point, and developments there are very instructive.

The Grenada case also demonstrates that the terms of a regional security treaty need to be carefully worded. A crucial issue raised by the invasion was whether the security arrangement permitted regional intervention in cases of domestic unrest. There are other security lessons to be learned from Grenada, since even the like-minded states which felt that they needed to intervene to protect their fellow Caribbean citizens were unable to mount the necessary military operation: that was done only through the US. In the aftermath, the Eastern Caribbean states have sought to improve not only their military capacity but to develop their information and intelligence systems. Yet even now this regional alliance is still not able to mount an inter-island sortie of any size without the logistic support of a major power, since the naval and air operations required are beyond their budgets. The limitations of size therefore do set sharp boundaries to what small states can do.

Given such limitations, small states need therefore to rely not only on sober, democratic, and humane domestic policies, which ensure internal tranquility, but on prudent foreign policy and effective diplomacy. The record of small states shows that they are quite capable of conducting their diplomacy ably, and some of the most astute diplomatic operations in international fora have come from these states. Size is no limitation in respect of diplomatic ability, even if a small population and limited resources mean that the size of the diplomatic establishment and its geographical range are limited.

Small states need to maintain few overseas missions, but should seek to maximize their representation in international agencies. Clearly, selected major powers and neighbouring states have priority, but a United Nations presence continues to be of great advantage to small states giving, as it does, unrivalled access to the world community and to technical assistance agencies. The United Nations has also been crucial in cases of real crisis for some small states – Guyana against Venezuela, Cyprus *vis-à-vis* Turkey and Greece, and Belize *vis-à-vis* Guatemala – where, in its absence, state security would have been even more seriously threatened. All of these cases demonstrate the value of diplomacy in defence of the national interest.

It is a great advantage to a small state if its foreign policy can be co-ordinated with that of neighbouring states. This may include bilateral and multilateral postings which provide common facilities; common offices and consular services; joint coverage of committees at multilateral organizations and the sharing of information at conferences; group positions at important fora, such as ACP/EEC meetings, or in mobilizing international support. The Commonwealth Caribbean small states, for example, have had some success in these matters.

Much depends on the actual policy and posture of the state, which raises the issue of the quality of political leadership. Discretion suggests that small states should know their limits and in seeking to play an activist rôle should not involve themselves gratuitously in issues where they are likely to attract the hostility of larger powers. There is no advantge in provoking the suspicion and hostility of other states, particularly neighbouring states and, of course, larger ones, as the case of Bishop's Grenada demonstrates.

Decision-makers also need to bear in mind that domestic political developments can have an impact on their international relations, particularly in their immediate region. This is simply a corollary of being a part of a closely interrelated international system where communication is easy and where political and economic ideas and forces are in constant interaction. Small states therefore should always consider the likely reactions of others to major changes in their domestic politics, particularly with respect to ideology and economics.

International provision

Should the international system make any special provision for the security of small states? Presumably when small states were admitted to the UN it was assumed that they would at least be as secure as other states and there was no recognition of special vulnerability. Indeed, small states have not been the objects of more threats than larger units, and it is their potential vulnerability in the contemporary world which is the cause for concern. But it must be acknowledged that, given the failure of the collective security system of the United Nations Charter, the steady deterioration in international co-operation, and the downturn in world economic conditions there has been over the last two decades a general breakdown in international peace and security and the number of incidents of international conflict has steadily increased.

It is exactly because of this general context of insecurity and the increasing use of political violence that the focus has shifted to the strategic vulnerability of small states. But it would surely be expecting too much to hope that an international system which did not take special measures earlier would now do so in a period when its overall unity and sense of purpose is far weaker. Attempts, therefore, to persuade the United Nations to set up a special security régime for small states are no more likely to be successful than Olaf Palme's abortive proposals for isolating some issues from superpower contention, thus creating specific situations where the United Nations' system for settling disputes and collective security could function as designed.

Failure of the United Nations' system does not automatically remove the mutual responsibility of states for maintaining peace and order. There is surely room for the larger and stronger states to acknowledge that they have some special responsibility for the smallest and weakest ones, since the latter do not have the capacity to fend for themselves. Size is relevant here, for it is true of the states which we have defined as small that a physical threat to a part of the state is automatically a threat to the whole state, and in the case of island states the administrative centre on one island often can do little about an invasion or a secession attempt on an outer island if the adversary forces are of even modest scale. This sense of obligation is arguably clearest in trans-regional associations such as the Commonwealth or among the network of the francophone community. In the absence of such recognition, many small states may be forced, for the sake of basic survival, to resort to patron–client relationships characteristic of a world of pure power politics. At the individual level some may be forced to become wholly subordinate to larger neighbours or regional powers, with their 'independence' becoming a sham, and others may deliberately seek to become client states of larger countries.

The sense that insecurity is the lot of small states would probably discourage those territories which are not yet independent from seeking such status. Already there has been a noticeable slowdown in the rush to independence by the smallest remaining colonies. It is currently unlikely, for instance, that a Bermuda or Curaçao would decide to be independent unless they had a guarantee of a defence link with the colonial power or had an acceptable regional neighbour as protector. Some small states which are already independent are likely in the current international environment to consider seriously the option of granting military-base facilities to a great power as a means of providing security. Although Western powers are not looking for base facilities as much as perhaps they used to be, this is not true of the Soviet Union, which still lacks significant strategic access and leverage in some parts of the world. It is also increasingly possible that new regional powers might seek special facilities or rights from adjacent small states.

There are not as yet pressing enough political reasons for the great powers to instigate major initiatives *vis-à-vis* the security of small states beyond the steps already taken. These include exerting traditional hegemonic control not only in an immediate vicinity (the US in the Western hemisphere) but even beyond; treaty arrangements with former colonies (France in Africa); and continued adherence to colonial or semi-colonial relationships (France in the Caribbean and Pacific, the UK in Bermuda and, albeit reluctantly, Holland in the Netherlands Antilles).

Among the middle powers, Australia has developed, with New Zealand, such a close network of relationships with Pacific small states that the region is often seen as one entity and, so far, these units feel secure even in the absence of formal guarantees. The links here are somewhat paternalistic but are clearly benign, and the extent of Australian presence and interest in these islands, plus the immigration flow from the islands to Australia, justify the feeling in some of the island governments that Australia (and New Zealand) can be depended upon to rally to their support, though not necessarily in military terms, in times of crisis.

In the Caribbean there has long been the hope that Canada would undertake a rôle somewhat like that of Australia in the Pacific. Apart from the distance factor, the dominant rôle first of the UK and now the US has not contributed to fostering this idea. However, against the background of the current international and hemispheric developments there is more than ever a need for Canada to play such a part in the security of the Caribbean region.

Neither Britain nor the US is ready to be linked in security guarantees with small states, save in exceptional cases where there is a strategic benefit. Nonetheless, some small states do see a security advantage in being the 'ward' of a great power. As vulnerability intensifies, the tendency to seek client status could increase, and this has been happening in the Commonwealth Caribbean, particularly since Grenada. The Grenada case, of course, does not imply that the US would always readily intervene, militarily, in the region – the circumstances were unusual.

However, a sense of vulnerability might mean that the bogey of communism could become an important tool for a small state seeking protection in both the economic and political security spheres, and that the patron state might have increased opportunity for penetration. In the face of this reality, there are obvious advantages to a regional security arrangement, both for negotiations and as a buffer against intervention. Such regional mechanisms need substantial financial and technical support from larger powers and international institutions. This support is probably easier and cheaper in the long run than the costs which could accrue to the same sources if there was a major international crisis involving a small state.

Generally speaking, most small states are likely to remain fairly secure from external threats unless they seek trouble. The important rule is to recognize the limitations of their situation. In an arena which does not have a democratic international system of government and where the play of traditional power politics is still the rule, it would be an indiscretion to take the equality of states too literally. The historic accidents which helped to create so many small states do not really imbue these states with inherent rights, and the operative rules of the international arena are managed by those who control the key levers.

With discretion on their part and tolerance on the part of the large states, small states should be able to operate with as much freedom as they need, if not as much as some dynamic leaders might desire. But a small state whose particular location has important strategic implications for a large power or which is located in reasonably close proximity to other states is simply not free, on the grounds of its right of sovereignty, to conduct any foreign policy it likes. A large state could try to do this and may be successful, but a small state cannot. Even in a region of small states, such as the Commonwealth Caribbean or the Pacific, there is the strong feeling that no one member state should be free, in crucial issues, to take independent steps, diametrically against the major stream, in foreign relations. Both hegemonic states and regional neighbours, then, are likely to seek to intervene in the domestic politics of small states, if they feel that their vital interests are threatened.

The postwar thrust to create independent entities has been balanced by the emergence of an increasingly interdependent world. That interdependence and the communications system which goes with it mean that the citizens of small states can have access to information and services way beyond their state's inherent capacity to supply them. The smallness of a state therefore does not automatically impose penalties on its citizens in their private capacities. With luck, judgement, and the adoption of appropriate policies, as set out here, they should be able to enjoy the advantages of smallness while having access, at will, to the wider world.

Conclusion

COLIN CLARKE AND TONY PAYNE

Several of the most important themes discussed in the preceding chapters deserve brief restatement in this conclusion. It is the case that virtually all the small states that have recently become independent have achieved sovereignty through decolonization and the general demise of empire following the end of World War II. Nationhood has been shown to have its own logic separate from the question of viability. Yet many small states still lack a strong sense of identity, due to their long history of imperial subordination and the contemporary realities of ethnic pluralism. They exist, firstly, because of the facts of physical geography, notably insularity, and, secondly, because of United Nations support for self-determination, regardless of the size of the political units produced. The process of small state creation via decolonization appears now almost to have run its course, although there are still a few colonial rocks left as well as several small dependencies which may yet become independent via secession. Against the trend, however, it is possible that in the future a number of small states may seek federation or opt for incorporation in larger units (the double Enosis of Cyprus).

Small states can be defined easily enough in the physical sense as islands or enclaves, but boundary features in every other way are difficult to sustain. In reality there is no sharp boundary around small states: migration allows the community to spill over into other locales; travel back and forth enables a sense of community to transcend state boundaries; return migration breaks down isolation and facilitates innovation. Equally, the boundary between national and international affairs is manifestly unclear. Not only is the continuing impact of British imperialism to be felt in all the small states studied in this book; so also is the pressure of the present international economic structure as revealed in all the familiar characteristics of dependency. From the social point of view too, no sharp boundary separates small states from small entities that are not states: social relations are usually similar, as are ways of coping with a restricted environment.

Politically, small states within the developing world display a greater attachment to democratic practices than is the norm, but this does not necessarily derive from their smallness. The presence in the category of a large number of ex-British colonies is a more relevant explanation. Generally, a particular politics of smallness does not emerge from the study. Personalism, for example, has been a much stressed theme, politicians in small states being said to exercise a dominating influence, based more on personality than party. There is no doubt that several remarkable figures have graced the pages of the country studies in this book – Mintoff, Makarios, Maurice Bishop, to name but three. It is a different matter to argue that this is a feature of politics peculiar to small states. So too with many of the other domestic political characteristics that emerged. From the political point of view it seems that smallness is neither necessarily good nor bad.

However, few economic advantages attach to smallness, as the case studies amply testify. Such success in economic development as has been achieved has a great deal to do with the quality of economic management, both in the governmental and the private sector. The lack of innovation in Antigua and Barbuda and the choice of economic growth within a framework of reinforced dependency in Swaziland contrast very markedly with the energetic multilateralism pursued in The Gambia and Grenada, at least during the revolutionary era. Moreover, the instances of Malta, Mauritius, and Fiji show that geopolitical location backed by skilful bargaining can be used to extract financial support from a regional or superpower patron, especially now that foreign bases have taken on renewed significance. On a more theoretical level it has, nevertheless, to be admitted that the social sciences lack a properly developed political economy of small size; consequently many economists working in this field do not display much understanding of the ideological permutations associated with development strategy in small states, either at the national or regional level.

The problem is that economic weakness has the further effect of making it difficult for most small states to defend themselves from interference by other states. It is not even easy to repel mercenary invasion or contain internal subversion and insurrection. Treaties of assistance can be negotiated to remove some of these threats, and careful diplomacy (as was not evident, for example, in Grenada) can be used to defuse confrontations between the small state and regional powers or superpowers. An additional important factor is the need to develop a political culture to counter militarism. What emerges as critical, however, is the fact that the legitimacy of the political process is a security resource more crucial for small state stability even than the existence of security forces. As already noted, most small states have an estimable record of democratically held elections, and most are reasonably secure unless they look for trouble. Yet the consequences of a dictatorship, a coup, or an armed invasion in a small state are so grave – as the cases of Grenada, Cyprus, and The Gambia demonstrate – that small-state vulnerability cannot be dismissed as being of negligible significance.

It can perhaps be expected that those small states which survive into the next century will develop a stronger sense of nationhood as an expression of their identity and their determination to maintain a separate political existence. But they will only be able to survive if the international system, in theory and in practice, emphasizes the equality of states and insists upon the upholding of the international rule of law. A major danger to small states derives from the predatory activities of regional powers and superpowers: rivalry between the latter bifurcates the world and so easily draws the small state into a conflict with the intensity of which it simply cannot cope.

What, in conclusion, can be said about the concept of smallness in states? We have not been able to detect a firm category of smallness in any of the four dimensions of analysis considered in this book – politics, society, economics, and security. Smallness certainly intensifies, but it is not a characterizing feature. In each real-world case it has been essential to go into the historical, regional, cultural, and geopolitical context of the small country in question. None of the problems discussed in this book are, in fact, unique to small states. Smallness is neither intrinsically ugly nor beautiful. It simply represents an additional set of factors which have to be considered. By skilful political leadership and a policy of diversifying dependency, states can take advantage of its positive aspects and minimize its disadvantages. How they actually do so will vary from case to case according to multiple other factors more important than the fact of smallness.

Contributors

Floya Anthias Floya Anthias is Senior Lecturer in Sociology at Thames Polytechnic, London. She studied sociology at the London School of Economics, Birmingham University, and Bedford College, London, where she took her doctorate. She is the author of a number of articles on Cyprus, gender divisions, Cypriot migration, and ethnicity. She is co-director of the Ethnic and Gender Divisions Project at Thames Polytechnic, and is currently co-authoring a book entitled *Resistance and control–racism and the community* as well as co-editing *Woman, nation, state*.

Colin Clarke Colin Clarke is a university lecturer in geography and an Official Fellow of Jesus College, Oxford. He has taught at the universities of Toronto and Liverpool, where he was Reader in Geography and Latin-American Studies, and he has carried out numerous field investigations in Mexico and the Caribbean. His publications deal with race and ethnic pluralism, urbanization, demography, rural change, and politics. He is the author of *Kingston, Jamaica: urban development and social change 1692–1962* (University of California Press 1975), *East Indians in a West Indian town: San Fernando, Trinidad, 1930–1970* (Allen & Unwin 1986), and *Livelihood systems, settlements and levels of living in 'Los Valles Centrales de Oaxaca', Mexico* (School of Geography, University of Oxford, Research Paper 37, 1986); co-author of *A geography of the Third World* (Methuen 1983); and co-editor of *Geography and ethnic pluralism* (Allen & Unwin 1984).

Robin Cohen Robin Cohen is Professor of Sociology and Director of the Centre for Research in Ethnic Relations, University of Warwick. He was formerly Professor of Sociology at the University of the West Indies, Trinidad. He has written mainly in the fields of international labour studies and ethnic relations, but has also developed a strong interest in the study of small societies. His publications in this area include a book, co-edited with Fitzroy Ambursley, *Crisis in the Caribbean* (Heinemann 1983) and an edited collection, *African islands and enclaves* (Sage 1983).

James Craig James Craig studied politics at Swansea, Birmingham, and the University of Ghana and was a lecturer in politics and administration at the University of Manchester at the time of his death in 1986. He had conducted research and had held consultancies in Ghana, Mauritius, Sri Lanka, India, Malaysia, Malta and Mexico. His particular interests were in public policy, development studies, the politics of economic planning, and the politics of development. He had published articles on Ghana, Malaysia, and Malta and was editor of the journal *Teaching Public Administration*.

Roberto Espíndola Roberto Espíndola lectures in sociology and politics at the University of Bradford. He studied law and political science in Chile and the US. He has taught at the Catholic Universities of Santiago and Valparaíso and at the University of Essex, and has carried out field research in Chile, the Caribbean, and Central America. His current research interests are in the international relations of the countries of the Caribbean Basin and Cuban foreign policy. He was Finance and Commodities Editor of *South* magazine, and has covered the Caribbean for the *Sunday Times*. Currently, he is Editor of *Caribbean Report* and a consultant for the *Independent*.

Arnold Hughes Arnold Hughes was educated at the University of Wales, Aberystwyth, and Ibadan University, Nigeria, where he was a Commonwealth scholar. He is Lecturer in Political Science at the Centre of West African Studies, University of Birmingham. He has travelled and researched widely in West Africa and published on a variety of subjects relating to the political history and current politics of the region. Since 1972 he has been a frequent visitor to The Gambia and has written numerous articles and academic papers on its domestic and external politics.

Anthony Lemon Anthony Lemon is a lecturer in geography at Oxford University and a Fellow of Mansfield College. He specializes in the political geography of southern Africa, where he has held several visiting lectureships, and has twice been a university research fellow at Rhodes University, Grahamstown. His publications include *Apartheid: a geography of separation* (Saxon House 1976), *Studies in overseas settlement and population*, with N. C. Pollock, (Longman 1980) and *Apartheid in transition?* (Gower 1987, in press). He has also published articles on elections in South Africa and Zimbabwe, constitutional change in South Africa, the organization of black labour supplies, 'frontier commuters' and other aspects of the geography of apartheid.

Neville Linton Neville Linton, Assistant Director of International Affairs at the Commonwealth Secretariat, London, is a West Indian academic who was formerly at the Institute of International Relations, University of the West Indies, Trinidad. He has taught in the US, Canada, and Africa, and specializes in the political systems of recently independent states and Caribbean foreign policy problems. He is the author of several papers on these topics, and has also been active as a journalist and broadcaster.

David Lowenthal Emeritus Professor of Geography at University College London, David Lowenthal was previously Secretary of the American Geographical Society and visiting professor at many American universities. His experience with small and quasi-autonomous states extends from Alderney to Tasmania, but his research in this realm has focused on the Caribbean, where he was Fulbright

Research Fellow at the Institute of Social and Economic Research, University of the West Indies, in 1956–7, and subsequently consultant to the Vice-Chancellor. He is the author or editor of ten books, most recently *The past is a foreign country* (Cambridge University Press 1985) and (with Edmund Penning-Rowsell) *Landscape meanings and values* (Allen & Unwin 1986).

Martin Minogue Martin Minogue is Director of the University of Manchester International Development Centre. He has held posts in the Department of Administrative Studies, Manchester, at Kent University and the University of Mauritius, and has been a visiting lecturer at several Mexican universities. His main interest is in comparative public policy studies. His publications include *African aims and attitudes*, co-edited with Judith Molloy (Cambridge University Press 1974), *Documents on contemporary British government* (editor, Cambridge University Press 1977), *A consumer's guide to local government* (Macmillan, for National Consumer Council, 1977 and 1980) and several journal articles. He co-edits, with Paul Cook, *Manchester Papers on Development*.

Tony Payne Tony Payne is a lecturer in politics at the University of Sheffield. He studied history and politics at Churchill College, Cambridge, and did his postgraduate work at the University of Manchester and the University of the West Indies in Jamaica. He lectured at the Polytechnic in Huddersfield for six years before moving to Sheffield in 1985. He has written and edited a number of books and articles on Caribbean politics including, most recently, *The international crisis in the Caribbean* (Croom Helm 1984). He is currently writing a book on Jamaican politics.

William Sutherland William Sutherland is a lecturer in political science at the University of the South Pacific, Suva, Fiji. He holds an LLM in international law from the University of Hull, and a PhD in political science from the University of Canterbury, Christchurch, New Zealand. His publications deal mainly with economic development, politics, and security in the South Pacific, and his most recent works have been on regional responses by the small Pacific island states to the problems of size and vulnerability. He is currently completing a book on race, class, and the state in Fiji.

Paul Sutton Paul Sutton is Lecturer in Politics and Director of the Centre of Developing Area Studies at the University of Hull. His main research interests are in the politics of the insular Caribbean and the application of the Lomé Conventions to landlocked and island developing states. He is co-editor with Tony Payne of *Dependency under challenge: the political economy of the Commonwealth Caribbean* (Manchester University Press 1984), co-author with Tony Payne and Tony Thorndike of *Grenada: revolution and invasion* (Croom Helm 1984), and editor of *Dual legacies in the contemporary Caribbean: continuing aspects of British and French dominion* (Frank Cass 1986).

Tony Thorndike Tony Thorndike is Head of the International Relations and Politics Department at the North Staffordshire Polytechnic in Stoke-on-Trent. He studied international relations at the London School of Economics and specializes in Caribbean politics. He obtained his doctorate from the University of London in 1979. He has taught in Nigeria and London and has spent prolonged periods carrying out research in the Commonwealth Caribbean and Central America. He has published a variety of articles, a major study of the Grenadian revolution, *Grenada: politics, economics and society* (Frances Pinter 1985), and critiques of the Marxist–Leninist perspective on international relations.

Index

Abel-Smith, B. 127
Afghanistan 33, 46, 65
Africa xv, 9, 11, 27, 65, 141, 148, 152–3, 156–7, 158–60, 162, 165, 167, 207, 209, 222
African, Caribbean and Pacific (ACP) States 130, 135, 149, 220
African National Congress (ANC) 108, 166
Alavi, H. 210
Algeria 207
Allen, Sir Colin 21–2
Alliance Party of Fiji 119, 121–3
Amin, Idi 30
Andorra 32, 37, 72
Anguilla 41, 42, 45, 101–2
Antigua and Barbuda 9–11, 20–2, 58, 96–111 (Chapter 6), 226 *See also* Barbuda
Antigua and Barbuda Democratic Movement (ABDM) 105
Antigua Caribbean Liberation Movement (ACLM) 108–9
Antigua Labour Party (ALP) 100, 102–9, 110
Antigua Progressive Movement (APM) 105
Antigua Workers Union (AWU) 105–7
Antiguan Trades and Labour Union (ATLU) 102–4, 106
Arabian Gulf 31, 65, 75, 144, 146, 182
Argentina 66
Aruba 5, 205
Ascension 42, 75
Asia 117, 208
Association of Southeast Asian Nations (ASEAN) 66, 77
Attalides Michael 188
Australia 5, 21, 42, 117, 122–3, 162, 208, 222
Austria 76

Bahamas 9, 10–13, 20–1, 73

Bahrain 13
Bangladesh 33
Barbados xviii–xix, 9, 11–13, 14, 17, 20–1, 28, 42–4, 67, 73, 83, 210
Barbuda 38, 41, 44–5, 96–7, 102, 106–7, 109 *See also* Antigua and Barbuda
Belgium 51, 208
Belize xvii, 9, 11–13, 20–1, 22, 32, 68, 72, 219
Benedict, Burton xv, xvii–xviii, xx, xxiii, 6, 51
Berenger, Paul 133, 134–5
Bermuda 222
Best, L. 54–5
Beswick, Lord 175
Bhoodoo, Harish 134
Bird, Lester 109–10
Bird, Vere 99, 100, 104–6, 107, 109
Birindelli, Admiral 181
Bishop, Maurice 21, 74, 86, 87, 89–91, 92–3, 220, 226
Blair, P. W. 19
Blaize, Herbert 93
Blondel, J. 16
Bonaire 205
Bonnici, Dr Carmelo Mifsud 182
Bophuthatswana 163
Botswana 10–13, 20–1, 32, 156–7, 161, 165, 209
Bowden, Herbert 176
Brazil 66
Britain xiii, 6, 8, 16, 20–1, 27, 36, 68–70, 72, 74, 77, 83, 85–8, 92, 96–7, 101–3, 107–8, 117, 126–7, 129, 135–6, 142, 144, 146, 152, 153–4, 157, 159, 170–81, 182, 184, 187, 188–91, 204, 206–9, 222–3, 225, 226
British Virgin Islands 205
Brunei 9, 11–12, 20, 71–2
Burma 208
Burton, Eric 106, 109

Index

Cabinda xxi
Canada 88, 108, 222–3
Canary Islands xxi
Cape Verde xxi
Caribbean xiii–xv, xx, xxv, 6, 9, 11, 14, 20, 34, 42, 54, 67, 68, 71, 73, 77, 83–5, 87–8, 92, 97, 98, 108, 109, 207, 209, 215, 218–20, 222–4
Caribbean Basin Initiative (CBI) 89, 110
Caribbean Community (CARICOM) 66, 77, 98, 102
Caribbean Free Trade Association 60
Cayman Islands 41
Central America 30, 65, 66
Central American Common Market 60
Chad 65
Chamberlain, Joseph 27
Chenery, H. B. 50
Chile 29, 86
China 110, 146, 182
Coard, Bernard 74, 83, 88, 90–1
Cocos Islands 5
Cohen, Robin xxi–xxii
Comitas, L. 34
Commonwealth xiii–xiv, xxiii, 8–9, 11, 13, 14, 16–18, 20, 22–3, 34, 51, 72, 73–4, 76–7, 83, 92, 129, 149, 152, 158, 175, 204–5, 208, 221
Communal Liberation Party of Cyprus 199
Communist Party of Cyprus (KKE) 188
Comoros Islands xxi
Cook Islands 22, 42, 101, 216
Cuba 46, 58, 66, 72, 74, 87, 88, 94, 154
Curaçao 205, 222
Cyprus, 11, 13, 17, 21, 29, 40, 68, 72, 74, 174, 184–200 (Chapter 12), 219, 225, 227

Dagenhardt, H. W. 18
Dahl, R. A. 7–8, 13
Daniel, J. B. McI. 158
Day, A. J. 18
Demas, W. G. 50, 54
Democratic Party (DIKOK) of Cyprus 198
Demos, J. P. 38
Denktash, R. 192, 199

Dibba, Sherif 150–1
Diego, Garcia xvi, 136, 138
Diggines, Christopher 16, 32, 35
Djibouti 32, 75
Dominica 9, 11, 14, 21, 101
Dominican Republic 70
Dommen, E. C. 10, 31, 56
Doumenge, François 7, 44
Doveton, D. M. 156
Duval, Gaetan 133–4, 136

EOKA 184, 190–1, 193
Economic Community of West African States (ECOWAS) 149, 154
Enosis 185, 190–2, 193, 197, 198, 225
Equatorial Guinea xxi, 32
Ethiopia 33, 65
European Economic Community (EEC) 21, 74, 88, 102, 122, 129–31, 135, 146, 149, 162, 163, 220

Fair, T. J. D. 159
Falkland Islands xviii, xxiii, 154
Faroe Islands 44
Fiji 10–12, 14, 20–1, 40–1, 113–23 (Chapter 7), 226
Fiji Labour Party 121–2
Fiji National Provident Fund (FNPF) 118
Finland 76, 78
France 5–6, 7, 27, 30, 66, 72, 114, 126, 129–30, 135, 138, 144, 152, 154, 204–8, 212, 221–2
French Guiana 205

Gabon 32
Gadafy, Colonel Moammar 153, 180
Gairy, Eric xvii, 16, 45, 84–8, 89, 92, 94
Gambia, The xxi, 10–12, 20–1, 32, 58, 72, 75, 141–55 (Chapter 9), 226–7
Gambia People's Party 151
Gambia Underground Socialist Revolutionary Party (GUSRP) 150–1
Gayoom, President 34
Gellner, E. 29
Germany, Federal Republic of (West Germany) 117, 182
Gibraltar 32

Index

Gluckman, M. 38
Greece 184–7, 188–91, 192–3, 197, 198, 219
Green, L. P. 159
Greenland 5
Grenada xiii–xiv, xvii, xxv, 9, 11, 14, 16, 21–2, 45–6, 64, 65, 67, 74–5, 83–94 (Chapter 5), 100–1, 109, 113, 121, 210, 214, 217–20, 223, 226–7
Grenada United Labour Party (GULP) 87, 92
Grivas, George 190, 192–3
Guadeloupe 7, 206
Guam 42, 216
Guatemala 32, 68, 219
Guinea 148, 152, 207
Guinea-Bissau 32, 148, 154
Guyana 9, 11, 14, 20–1, 40, 42, 72, 73, 83, 219

Hailey, Lord 157
Hall, Robert 105, 107
Harden, S. 31
Hawke, Bob 122
Healey, Denis 173
Heath, Edward 180
Hector, Tim 105, 108–9
Hein, P. L. 56
Henderson, W. 165
Henry, Rowan 105
Hitchens, C. 184–5, 187
Hong Kong xv, 32, 117, 205
Hoogvelt, Ankie 60
Houbert, J. 133, 138
Hughes, Arnold xxi

Iceland 13, 44, 72
Imbokodvo National Movement (INM) of Swaziland 158
Independent Forward Bloc (IFB) of Mauritius 133
India 27, 135, 206
Indian Ocean xv, xxi, 9, 11, 21, 125, 129, 136, 138, 212, 216
Indonesia 29, 66
Institute of Development Studies (IDS), University of Sussex xviii–xix
International Monetary Fund (IMF) 12–13, 22, 99, 129, 132, 135, 137, 144, 145, 149
Iran 75

Iraq 75, 88
Ireland 44
Israel 66, 167
Italy 27, 173, 176, 180–1, 182, 185

Jamaica 83, 210
Japan 117, 160, 206, 209, 212
Jawara, Sir Dawda 149–51, 153
Jersey 37
Jonathan, Chief Leabua 165–6
Jugnauth, Aneerood 134–5, 136

Kampuchea 65
Kaplinsky, Raphael xxi
Khama, Sir Seretse 166
Kiribati 10–11, 20–2, 214
Knox, A. D. xvi–xvii, 51
Kohr, L. 28, 50
Kuznets, S. 50
KwaZulu 166–7
Kyprianou, President 194, 197

Laos 208
Latin America 11
Lebanon 65, 89
Lekhanya, Major-General 166
Lesotho 156–7, 161, 165–7, 209, 211
Levin, Bernard 28
Lewis, W. Arthur 43, 84–5, 87
Libya 66, 88, 146, 153, 154, 180–2
Liechtenstein 32
Lindsay, Louis 103
Lipman, W. 63
Lomé Convention 115, 130, 135, 162, 163, 167
Luxembourg xvii, 13, 32, 44, 75

McIntyre, A. 98
McRobie, C. A. 35
Madagascar 125
Makarios, President 187, 192–3, 197, 226
Makhosetive, Prince (King Mswati III) 164–5
Malawi 33
Malaysia 206
Maldives, The 10–11, 21, 22, 34
Malta 11–12, 20–2, 76, 170–82 (Chapter 11), 216, 226
Malta Labour Party (MLP) 171–2, 174–5, 177, 179
Maniruzzaman, T. 64

Manley, Norman 83
Mara, Ratu 119
Marcos, Ferdinand 214
Martinique 7, 205
Maurice, Bishop Patriotic Movement (MBPM) of Grenada 93
Mauritius xxi, 10–13, 14, 20–1, 125–40 (Chapter 8), 210, 226
Mauritius Labour Party (MLP) 128, 133–5
Max-Neff, M. 35
Meade, J. E. 127, 131
Mediterranean 170, 171, 173–4, 175, 180, 182, 185
Mexico 30, 66
Middle East 162, 191
Mill, John Stuart 203, 213
Mintoff, Dom 171, 175, 177–82, 226
Monaco 32
Montserrat 5, 36
Morley, Headlam 191
Morocco 154
Mouvement Militant Mauricien (MMM) 133–5, 136
Mouvement Socialiste Mauricien (MSM) 134
Mozambique 160, 166–7
Muslim Committee for Action (MCA) of Mauritius 133

Naipaul, V. S. 127
Namibia 5, 32, 165
National Convention Party (NCP) of The Gambia 150–1
National Federation Party (NFP) of Fiji 119, 121
National Unity Party (UBP) of Cyprus 192
Nationalist Party (PN) of Malta 171–7, 178–9, 182
Nauru 9, 11–12, 20, 21–2, 44
Nepal 33
Netherlands, The 70, 204–5, 222
Netherlands Antilles 205, 222
New Caledonia 5, 7
New Jewel Movement (NJM) of Grenada 86, 90–2
New National Party (NNP) of Grenada 85, 93, 94
New Zealand 21, 42, 72, 114, 117, 120, 122, 208, 214, 216, 222
Nicaragua 46

Niger 33
Nigeria 30, 66
Norfolk Island 5
North Atlantic Treaty Organization (NATO) 76, 170–4, 175, 177, 179–80, 181, 184–5, 186, 192, 199
North Korea 66, 182, 208
Norton, G. 73

Olivier, Borg 171–9, 181, 182
Oman 13, 210
Organization of African Unity (OAU) 66, 77, 135, 149
Organization of American States (OAS) 66, 77
Organization of Eastern Caribbean States (OECS) 66, 215
Orkney 45

Pacific Ocean xv, 5, 9, 11, 20–2, 30, 56, 113, 114, 120–2, 123, 207, 209, 214, 216, 222, 224
Pakistan 154
Palme, Olaf 221
Palmer, Sir Richard 188
Papandreou, Andreas 198
Papua New Guinea 120
Parti Mauricien Social et Democrate (PMSD) 133–4
Parti Socialiste Mauricien (PSM) 134
People's Progressive Party (PPP) of The Gambia 149–51
People's Revolutionary Government (PRG) of Grenada 85, 87–94
Philippines, The 208
Pitcairn Island 22
Pitt, D. 31, 35
Plischke, E. 19, 22
Polynesia xvii, 7
Portugal 30, 208
Progressive Labour Movement (PLM) of Antigua 102, 105–9, 110
Progressive Party of the Working People (AKEL) of Cyprus 188, 191, 192, 196, 198
Puerto Rico 89, 208

Quester, G. H. 63–4, 72–3

Ramgoolam, Sir Seewoosagar 133–4, 135–6
Ramphal, Shridath xiv, 51

Index

Reagan, Ronald 110, 121
Reid, G. L. 19
Republican Turkish Party (CTP) 192, 197
Réunion 7, 138, 205
Roberts, Douglas 104
Robinson, E. A. G. 50

St Helena xxi, 75, 205
St Kitts-Nevis 9–10, 12, 21–2, 101
St Luce, John 99
St Lucia 9, 11–13, 14, 20–1, 101
St Vincent 9, 11, 20–2, 67, 73, 101
Sampson, Nikos 74, 193
San Marino 32
Sandys, Duncan 172
Sanyang, Kukoi Samba 154
São Tomé 42–3, 72
Sark 44
Schaffer, Bernard xix
Schumacher, E. 28, 35
Selwyn, Percy xviii–xxi, 7, 31, 35
Senegal 72, 141, 147–8, 151–5
Seychelles, The xxi, 10–12, 20–1, 65, 210
Shetland Isles 45
Sierra Leone 210
Singapore xx, 117
Singham, Archie xvii
Smith, M. G. 86
Sobhuza, King 156, 158, 164–5, 166
Socialist Party (EDEK) of Cyprus 192, 197
Solomon Islands 9, 12, 14, 20–1
South Africa 29, 32, 108, 156–7, 160–4, 165–7, 209, 211
South Korea 66, 208
Southern African Customs Union (SACU) 161–2
Southern African Development Co-ordination Conference (SADCC) 160
Soviet Union (USSR) 20, 66, 74, 75, 88–9, 91, 94, 146, 175, 180, 182, 208–9, 212, 214, 222
Spain 72, 204, 208
Spence, J. E. 157
Sri Lanka 29, 40
Stevens, Reginald 104
Sudan 33
Surinam 43

Swaziland xvii, 9–13, 20–1, 32, 156–69 (Chapter 10), 209, 226
Sweden 76
Switzerland 51, 76, 217

Taiwan 66, 167
Tanzania 58
Taylor, L. 50
Thomas, C. Y. 57
Tonga 9, 11–12, 20–1, 22
Tory Island xvii
Transkei 163, 166
Transvaal 157, 158, 160
Trinidad & Tobago 16, 22, 83–4, 87
Tufte, E. R. 7, 8, 13
Turkey 66, 68, 72, 184–9, 191–5, 197, 198–9, 219
Turkish National Party 191
Turkish Resistance Organization (TMT) 191–2
Turks & Caicos Islands 205
Turner, William 189
Tuvalu 9–12, 20–2

Uganda 30, 33
United Arab Emirates 210
United Front of the Democratic Party of Cyprus 198
United Nations xiii, xv, 3–5, 22, 28, 33, 70, 76–7, 84, 86, 146, 149, 152, 167, 172, 198, 206, 213, 219, 221, 225
United Nations Conference on Trade and Development (UNCTAD) 21, 22
United Nations Institute for Training and Research (UNITAR) xxiii, 4–5
United People's Movement (UPM) of Antigua 107–9
United States (US) xiii–xiv, 6, 20–1, 66, 68, 70, 72, 74, 75–7, 86–9, 91–4, 97–100, 107–10, 113–14, 117, 120–1, 122, 130, 136, 146, 154, 159, 162, 173, 176, 177, 180, 185, 188, 192, 199, 206, 208–9, 212, 214, 216, 219, 222–3

Vanuatu 9–10, 12, 14, 20–1, 214
Vatican City 32
Venezuela 66, 72, 219
Vietnam 65, 205–6, 207, 208
Viner, J. 58–9

Walter, George 102, 105–8
Ward, M. 52–3
Warren, Bill 137
Warsaw Pact 185
West Indies Federation 83–4, 100
Western Sahara 5, 31
Western Samoa 9–10, 11, 20–1, 72
Whittington, G. W. 158

Wilson, Harold 173, 175–6
Wolfers, A. 63
Wood, Donald xvi
World Bank 22, 33, 99, 132, 149

Yugoslavia 76

Zimbabwe 165